ADVANCED PRAISE FOR
EATING DISORDERS IN SPORT

"Once again, Ron and Roberta team up to share their wonderful expertise, insights, and knowledge to give a clear view into the confusing and often frustrating world of eating disorders in sport. As an elite athlete who battled through this dark abyss and emerged out into the glorious light of freedom, I recommend this book as a wonderful resource for anyone whose life is touched by an eating disorder in any way."

Kimiko Soldati
Olympic Diver, 2004 Olympic Games in Athens, Greece

"This is a rich, comprehensive book. The authors demonstrate tremendous depth, perception, and insight into all issues related to eating disorders in sport. This book is deeply needed and I strongly recommend this book for all health professionals dealing with athletes, coaches, administrators, and sport and physical education students."

Jorunn Sundgot-Borgen, PhD
Professor in Physical Activity and Health, The Norwegian School of Sport Sciences

"Thompson and Sherman have crafted the definitive opus on eating disorders and sport. This book is the new dialogue bridge between sports personnel and health care providers. Their review of the field is comprehensive, scholarly, and accessible. The wisdom they have earned through decades of clinical experience is reflected in their deep respect for professionals in both the sports and health arenas. Above all else, their compassion and passion are evident in their paramount focus on the health and well-being of sportswomen and sportsmen around the world."

Cynthia M. Bulik, PhD
FAED, Jordan Distinguished Professor of Eating Disorders, University of North Carolina at Chapel Hill; Director, University of North Carolina Eating Disorders Program

"This book is a timely and up-to-date integrative presentation of eating disorders in athletes, including less discussed issues such as eating disorders in sportsmen and unique sport activities. The organization of the chapters, each with an excellent introduction and helpful endnotes, enhances the value of the volume and also provides practical recommendations for the identification, management, and treatment of the delicate and complex relation of eating disorders and sport."

Naama Constantini, MD, DFM, FACSM
Chair of the Medical Commission, Olympic Committee of Israel; Director of the Sport Medicine Center at the Hadassah-Hebrew University Medical Center in Jerusalem

"From ski jumping to beach volleyball, not a base is missed in this text! Roberta and Ron have done an incredibly inclusive job of presenting the latest disordered-eating research, including new findings in genetics, for the most expansive grouping of sports ever reviewed. New issues are also covered, such as BMI guidelines for sports, the latest ACSM position statement, muscle dysmorphia, male athlete eating disorders, and the effects of clothing trends on the athlete's body image. Excellent diagnostic lists, screening tools, and current medical issues are outlined along with information on how to refer athletes to treatment and what treatment should encompass. As a sports dietitian working with therapists to help elite athletes heal their bodies and get back to peak performance, I can attest that this book is a must for any professional on the sports medicine team!"

Page Love, MS, RD, LD, CSSD
Registered and Licensed Dietitian, Nutrifit, Sport, Therapy, Inc.

"Authors Ron Thompson and Roberta Sherman, established experts in the field of eating disorders in sport, have done an excellent job in creating a text that summarizes current eating disorders research and provides comprehensive treatment avenues attuned to the unique world of sport. This book should be on the bookshelves of any researcher or practitioner interested in understanding and treating athletes with eating disorders."

Kirsten Peterson, PhD
U.S. Olympic Committee Senior Sport Psychologist

"Ron Thompson and Roberta Sherman have drawn on their decades of professional work with athletes and eating disorders to create a book that is based in theory and research but speaks to the practitioner who works daily with athletes, coaches, and sport teams. Their coverage of current topics within the eating disorder field is thorough and their suggestions for practice and future research are excellent. This book should be on the shelf of any healthcare professional who works with athletes."

Trent Petrie, PhD
Director, Center for Sport Psychology and Professor, Department of Psychology, University of North Texas

Eating Disorders in Sport

Eating Disorders in Sport

Ron A. Thompson
Roberta Trattner Sherman

Routledge
Taylor & Francis Group
New York   London

Routledge
Taylor & Francis Group
270 Madison Avenue
New York, NY 10016

Routledge
Taylor & Francis Group
27 Church Road
Hove, East Sussex BN3 2FA

© 2010 by Taylor and Francis Group, LLC
Routledge is an imprint of Taylor & Francis Group, an Informa business

Printed in the United States of America on acid-free paper
10 9 8 7 6 5 4 3 2 1

International Standard Book Number: 978-0-415-99836-9 (Hardback)

Library of Congress Cataloging-in-Publication Data

Thompson, Ron A.
    Eating disorders in sport / Ron A. Thompson and Roberta Trattner Sherman.
       p. ; cm.
    Includes bibliographical references and index.
    ISBN 978-0-415-99836-9 (hardcover : alk. paper)
    1. Eating disorders. 2. Athletes--Nutrition. 3. Sports medicine. I. Sherman, Roberta Trattner, 1949- II. Title.
    [DNLM: 1. Eating Disorders. 2. Sports--psychology. WM 175 T475e 2010]

RC552.E18T458 2010
616.85'26--dc22
                                                                            2009030084

Visit the Taylor & Francis Web site at
http://www.taylorandfrancis.com

and the Routledge Web site at
http://www.routledgementalhealth.com

CONTENTS

CONTENTS

ACKNOWLEDGMENTS

We first thank our editor, Dana Bliss. In truth, we had been putting off writing this book for many years because we just didn't want to deal with what we had anticipated would be a long and difficult process, but, primarily thanks to Dana, it wasn't at all such a process. His support, positive attitude, and expert guidance have not only served us well in producing this book, but have made this experience a most rewarding one. Most importantly, thank you, Dana, for allowing us to write the book we wanted to write, and thanks to all of the production staff at Routledge for making this such a positive process.

We thank our friends and colleagues for their time, patience, and helpful comments regarding their readings of earlier drafts of the manuscript. In this regard, special thanks go to Mary Wilfert and Dave Klossner of the NCAA; these two special people work at what we believe to be the sport governing body at the forefront of eating disorder education. A special thank you goes to Dr. Pauline Powers, whose friendship, guidance, and expertise are always valued and appreciated, not only for reading and commenting on the manuscript, but also for her thoughtful and scholarly contribution of Chapter 8. A final special thank you goes to Jim Sherman, who tirelessly read and provided helpful comments on the entire manuscript numerous times, a process that was exceeded in time spent only by his devoted following of his beloved Boston Red Sox. His experience and expertise as a "sports nut" were most helpful and appreciated.

We thank several members of the International Olympic Committee (IOC). Special thanks go to Dr. Patrick Schamasch, medical and scientific director of the IOC Medical Commission, and Susan Greinig, medical programs manager of the IOC Medical and Scientific Department, for their continued support of sportswomen's health and for their cooperation regarding the reproduction and use of IOC materials. We also owe a thank you to Anouk Ruffieux, documentalist at IOC headquarters, for her assistance and cooperation in providing such excellent choices of photographs for us. In this case, your pictures truly are worth a thousand words.

We also thank our colleagues, and especially the leadership in the Academy for Eating Disorders, who have not only significantly contributed to our knowledge of eating disorders, but have always graciously encouraged and supported our work with sport participants.

We especially thank Dr. Barbara Drinkwater, whose seminal research 25 years ago on the relationship between menstrual dysfunction and loss of bone mineral density in physically active women started the ball rolling. We applaud and support her continued efforts to bring these important issues to the attention of those in the sport and healthcare worlds who most need to be aware of and responsive to them. We have very much appreciated the opportunity to work with Barbara during the past several years.

Finally, we thank the many sport-participant patients who have taught us most of what we know and wrote about in this book. You have taught us enough to know that we do not know nearly enough. Keep teaching us, and we promise to continue learning.

AUTHORS AND CONTRIBUTOR

Ron A. Thompson, PhD, FAED, is a psychologist in private practice in Bloomington, Indiana, who specializes in the treatment of eating disorders. He has been a consulting psychologist to the athletic department at Indiana University–Bloomington for the past 20 years. Additionally, he provides education and training on eating disorders to athletes, coaches, and other sport personnel and healthcare professionals at National Collegiate Athletic Association (NCAA) member institutions. He coauthored the "Disordered Eating" section of the International Olympic Committee Medical Commission Position Stand on the Female Athlete Triad, the *NCAA Coaches Handbook: Managing the Female Athlete Triad,* and *Managing Student-Athletes' Mental Health Issues* for the NCAA. Included in his publications are the books *Bulimia: A Guide for Family and Friends; Helping Athletes With Eating Disorders* with Roberta Sherman, PhD; and *The Exercise Balance* with Pauline Powers, MD. Dr. Thompson is a fellow in the Academy for Eating Disorders, where he served as cochair of the Special Interest Group on Athletes from 2001 to 2009. Dr. Thompson and Dr. Sherman jointly received the Academy for Eating Disorder's 2008 Leadership Award for Clinical, Administrative, or Educational Service.

Roberta Trattner Sherman, PhD, FAED, is a psychologist who specializes in the treatment of eating disorders in private practice in Bloomington, Indiana, where she is also a consulting psychologist to the Department of Intercollegiate Athletics at Indiana University. Additionally, she provides education and training on eating disorders to athletes, coaches, and other sport personnel and healthcare professionals at NCAA member institutions. She coauthored the "Disordered Eating" section of the Position Stand on the Female Athlete Triad for the Medical Commission of the International Olympic Committee, the *NCAA Coaches Handbook: Managing the Female Athlete Triad,* and *Managing Student-Athletes' Mental Health Issues* for the NCAA. Included in her publications are the books *Bulimia: A Guide for Family and Friends* and *Helping Athletes With Eating Disorders* with Ron Thompson, PhD. Dr. Sherman is a fellow in the Academy for Eating Disorders and cofounded the Athlete Special Interest Group within the academy. She has worked on several committees and projects of the IOC

Medical Commission, focusing on issues related to the Female Athlete Triad and improving the health of sportswomen. Dr. Thompson and Dr. Sherman jointly received the Academy for Eating Disorder's 2008 Leadership Award for Clinical, Administrative, or Educational Service. Additionally, she serves on the editorial board of *Eating Disorders: The Journal of Treatment and Prevention.*

Pauline Powers, MD, FAED, authored Chapter 8 on medical considerations. Dr. Powers is professor of psychiatry and behavioral health in the Clinical and Translational Science Institute at the Health Sciences Center, University of South Florida (USF). She has been treating patients with eating disorders for over 30 years and is currently director of the USF Center for Eating and Weight Disorders, the medical director of the Eating Disorder Program at Fairwinds Residential Treatment Center, and the director of the USF Hope House for Eating Disorders. Dr. Powers was the founding president of the Academy for Eating Disorders and is a past president of the National Eating Disorders Association. She was a member of the American Psychiatry Association Work Group on Eating Disorders that prepared the 2006 *Practice Guidelines for the Treatment of Patients With Eating Disorders.* Dr. Powers also recently coauthored *The Exercise Balance* with Ron Thompson, PhD, and coedited the *Clinical Manual of Eating Disorders* with Joel Yager, MD.

DISCLAIMERS

The photos used in Chapter 4 are generic and are used solely for the purpose of illustration. They are not intended to indicate, suggest, or imply that any of the sport participants in those photos have a problem with eating, weight, or body image.

The case studies used throughout this book were created for purposes of illustration. Although in large part based on actual cases, information provided in each case represents an amalgamation of material from several cases, combined with specific diagnostic criteria to illustrate a specific point or issue. Such cases are not intended to describe or depict any particular sport participant. Any similarity to any particular sport participant that may have occurred is purely coincidental.

This book and the information contained in it are not intended to be used as a substitute for treatment of eating-related problems. There is no substitute for timely, appropriate, and effective evaluation and treatment by qualified and experienced healthcare professionals.

1

Introduction

When our book *Helping Athletes With Eating Disorders* was published in 1993, little was known about eating problems in sport. Much of the book contained a review of the available literature, as well as anecdotal information we provided based on our clinical experience. In the succeeding 15 years, much has changed. Most important, the general literature on eating disorders has burgeoned, and the literature specific to sport in this area has grown significantly. Our clinical and consulting experience has broadened and deepened, and we have been involved with educational and preventive endeavors with the National Collegiate Athletic Association (NCAA) and the Medical Commission of the International Olympic Committee (IOCMC). As a consequence, we believe that *Eating Disorders in Sport* is a better documented, more in-depth, and more scholarly edition, while hopefully still serving as a practically useful resource for healthcare professionals and sport personnel.

One aspect of eating disorders in sport that has not changed in recent years is the seriousness and extent of the problem. Most recent prevalence data (Torstveit, Rosenvinge, & Sundgot-Borgen, 2008) indicate that clinical eating disorders continue to be significant problems for more than 46% of elite females in lean sports and almost 20% in nonlean sports. Because sport participants face the same general risk factors as the general population, as well as risks unique to the sport environment, we contend that they are more at risk. As a consequence, we believe that those in sport comprise a very special subpopulation of eating disorder patients in need of specialized approaches to identification, management, treatment, and prevention.

Our primary objectives for this book include providing the reader with practical recommendations regarding the following:

- Special issues that complicate identification
- Techniques to facilitate managing the competitor–patient
- Components of effective treatment
- Educational strategies for enhancing primary and secondary prevention

TWO WORLDS

How to identify, manage, treat, and prevent eating disorders in sport requires an understanding of, and appreciation for, two worlds—the world of sport and the world of eating disorder treatment. Although we are psychologists who specialize in the treatment of eating disorders (with more than 50 years of combined experience), we have also spent a considerable amount of time in the sport world. We are not, however, typical sport psychologists in that we do not usually work with sport participants regarding enhancement of sport performance. Rather, we are psychologists who typically work clinically with those in sport.

Specifically, we have worked as consulting psychologists to the Department of Intercollegiate Athletics at Indiana University–Bloomington for the past 20 years. In that capacity, we have worked clinically with sport participants and as consultants to the medical, coaching, and training staffs. Additionally, in recent years we have been fortunate to have worked with the National Collegiate Athletic Association (NCAA), as well as with the Medical Commission of the International Olympic Committee (IOCMC). Our work with the NCAA has included conducting research related to eating disorders in sport, providing education and training on eating disorders at NCAA member institutions, and the development and writing of two NCAA manuals—*Managing the Female Athlete Triad* (NCAA, 2005) and *Managing Student-Athletes' Mental Health Issues* (NCAA, 2007). Our work with the IOCMC primarily involved coauthoring (with Jorunn Sundgot-Borgen, PhD) the "Disordered Eating" section of the IOCMC Position Stand on the Female Athlete Triad (IOCMC, 2005). We feel that our work in both worlds provides us with the knowledge, experience, and objectivity to provide the information and practical guidance necessary to work effectively with this very special subpopulation of patients with eating problems.

Despite being concerned with the welfare of those in sport, the two worlds of sport and eating disorder treatment are quite different in their focus, their concern, and their management of eating problems. Even from a research or scientific standpoint, the two worlds often are reading different professional literature. We hope to help bridge the gap between the two with this book and an integration of the literature, such that it could be more helpful to both worlds.

Unfortunately, there has sometimes been a misunderstanding or lack of trust of one world by the other. In our work, we have often heard healthcare professionals and colleagues attribute eating problems to sport or to coaches, or even suggesting that they *are* the problem and that the participant should leave the sport. On the other hand, individuals in the sport world have suggested that many healthcare professionals do not appreciate the importance of sport in the life of serious competitors and may tell them to leave their sport without appreciating the consequences. Additionally, many coaches have told us that they cannot get any information from mental health practitioners about their sport participants when they go into treatment, making them feel as if the practitioner does not trust them. Thus, they may become reticent about making referrals. We feel that this problem can be alleviated with relationship building and improved communication.

Because we view relationship building and communication as being more under the purview of mental health and psychology than sport, we believe the onus for bridging the gap between the two worlds falls on practitioners such as ourselves. Therefore, when and where appropriate, we will try to provide practical recommendations for avoiding or resolving these issues, as well as others that can sometimes interfere with the identification and treatment of eating disorders in this special population.

This focus on worlds should also remind us that eating disorders in sport are not simply a problem in the United States. Eating disorders are nondiscriminatory; they can, and do, occur virtually anywhere and everywhere. Thus, our focus will be an international one. When taking an international approach, one must try not to be too ethnocentric, and remember to use a common language. A prime example is the term *athlete*, which in the United States could refer to a competitor in any sport, whereas in the UK and other parts of Europe, it refers to a competitor in track and field. Conversely, sport participants other than those in track and field are referred to as *sportsmen* in the UK and other parts of Europe, whereas the term *sportsmen* in the United States could be taken to mean hunters and fishermen. In this book, we will try to use ethnicity-neutral terms such as *competitors* or *sport participants* when appropriate, or refer to the specific individual(s) in a particular sport, such as *gymnasts, runners,* or *wrestlers.*

Related to the issue of communication is how different sports are grouped or labeled throughout this book. Unfortunately, it is some-times difficult to evaluate some studies in the literature because of a lack of consistency of labeling between studies. In an effort to facili-tate communication in this regard, we have chosen to use two sets of labels. The first involves the general terms *lean* and *nonlean* sports. Lean sports include those for which there is a weight-class requirement, or in which a low body weight or lean body is believed to confer a competi-tive advantage either from a biomechanical standpoint (i.e., moving the body through space) or from a judging standpoint based on appearance. In essence, all other sports that do not have such an emphasis or focus on a small or lean body shape or have a weight-class requirement will be considered nonlean. At the same time, this should not be construed to mean that leanness is unimportant in nonlean sports. In fact, dur-ing the past 15 to 20 years, most sports—even most power sports—have been emphasizing body leanness as performance enhancing. For classi-fying specific sports within these two major categories, we have chosen to use a classification system suggested by Sundgot-Borgen and Larsen (1993) that includes the following sport or event categories: technical (e.g., fencing, golf), endurance (e.g., cycling, distance running), aesthetic (e.g., gymnastics, figure skating), weight class (e.g., judo, wrestling), ball game (e.g., volleyball, basketball), power (e.g., shot put, speed skating), and antigravitation (e.g., high jump, pole vault). Endurance, aesthetic, and weight-class sports will comprise the lean sports, and technical, ball game, power, and antigravitation sports will comprise the nonlean sports. For a variety of reasons, however, not all entities fit neatly into specified categories, whether these are individuals into diagnostic cat-egories, or sports into what appear to be logical sport categories. We will explain our rationale on the few occasions when we feel a need to depart from this classification system, from either a logical or illustra-tive standpoint. The classification of sports will be discussed in more depth in Chapter 3.

HOW THIS BOOK IS ORGANIZED

In Chapter 2, we discuss the clinical conditions related to eating problems. This discussion, of course, includes the eating disorders—anorexia nervosa, bulimia nervosa, and eating disorder not otherwise specified. Additionally, we discuss what have been termed partial or subthreshold syndromes that do not meet diagnostic criteria for an eating disorder but compromise physical or psychological health or interfere with work, school, sport, or relationships. Specifically, we discuss disordered eating, low energy availability, anorexia athletica, and the female athlete triad. In Chapter 3, we review the literature related to sport and eating problems, as well the factors such as gender and type of sport that may moderate the risk. We continue with risk factors in Chapter 4 by discussing general and sport-specific factors that increase the risk of eating problems.

Chapters 5 to 8 are clinical chapters. In Chapter 5 we discuss identification of participants with disordered eating. Although there are many challenges in identification because it is easier for them to hide their disorder than for those in the general population, we discuss specific symptoms and how they manifest themselves in sport. Chapter 6 focuses on management issues for sport personnel, coaches, athletic trainers, and healthcare professionals. Additionally, advice on how to approach the individual believed to be at risk is included. Chapter 7 focuses on treatment. The types of treatment and treatment professionals that comprise the treatment team are explained. Issues of confidentiality and decisions regarding training and competing while in treatment are addressed. Finally, issues regarding motivation in treatment as well as handling patient resistance are addressed. In Chapter 8, Pauline Powers, MD, discusses specific medical issues, including the use of psychotropic medications. We conclude with a discussion of prevention in Chapter 9. Finally, we have an appendix with useful resources. Additionally, there is a glossary to assist the reader with terms that may be unfamiliar.

A FINAL THOUGHT

A final thought regarding *Eating Disorders in Sport* involves the issue of the risk factors for eating disturbances associated with specific sports or sport participation. Some have suggested that sports are a big part of the problem, and thus sport participation should not be encouraged, especially for girls and young women. We would heartily disagree with this conclusion. We view sport participation as providing a variety of opportunities for physical and psychological growth and development. From a physical standpoint, sport participation can increase strength, speed, coordination, endurance, and overall health. Psychologically, sports can increase self-esteem and self-efficacy, promote identity development, and foster a sense of teamwork, not to mention providing opportunities for healthy competition. As we will discuss in this book, sport participation per se is not the problem, and thus does not need to be avoided. Rather, it is the risks to sport participants that need to be eliminated or avoided—a topic that will be thoroughly discussed in this volume.

Other individuals have sometimes suggested that even writing about the issues and problems contained in this book can discourage young people from participating in sport. Obviously, our goal is not to discourage sport participation. Rather, our goal is to make others more aware of the potential risks associated with sport, as well as how to decrease, eliminate, or avoid them in an effort to provide a healthier and an even more satisfying sport experience.

2

Eating Disorders
Clinical and Subclinical Conditions

In this chapter, we discuss clinical eating disorders, but we have also included descriptions and discussions of other eating-related attitudes and behaviors that can affect an athlete's health and performance. These have sometimes been described as subclinical, subthreshold, and subsyndromal, and have been given names such as anorexia athletica, disordered eating, muscle dysmorphia, and the female athlete triad. These conditions are of importance not only because of their deleterious effects on health and performance in their own right, but also because they can progress to clinical eating disorders if left untreated. The conditions discussed in this chapter are described in large part as if they were discrete and separate conditions primarily for purposes of illustration. In actuality, they tend to occur on a continuum or spectrum of eating-related difficulties, and individuals who experience them cross over from one condition to another (Tozzi et al., 2005).

EATING DISORDERS

Eating disorders are not simply disorders of eating. Also, they are not simply a misguided attempt to be thin; nor are they simply a sport participant's means to reduce body weight or body fat in an effort to enhance sport performance. They are mental disorders that manifest themselves in a variety

7

of eating and weight-related signs and symptoms. They are not caused by sports or coaches, although sports and coaches can increase the risk of developing such a disorder or exacerbate an existing disorder. Rather, they are potentially life-threatening disorders with multiple determinants and risk factors, including sociocultural, familial, and personality factors, as well as genetics. They can serve multiple functions and purposes for the patient and his or her family. The diagnosis of an eating disorder requires that the individual meet criteria as currently listed in the *Diagnostic and Statistical Manual of Mental Disorders,* Fourth Edition, Text Revision (DSM-IV-TR, American Psychiatric Association [APA], 2000) for anorexia nervosa, bulimia nervosa, or eating disorder not otherwise specified.

Anorexia Nervosa

Anorexia nervosa has been called simply anorexia, and is often described as the self-starvation syndrome.

> Paula is a 17-year-old distance runner. She is 5'5" (165 cm) tall and weighs 98 pounds (44.45 kg). Despite being quite thin, she often refers to herself as being fat. She has not had a menstrual period in 15 months. Paula is running 80 to 90 kilometers (50 to 56 miles) per week as recommended by her coach. However, she feels that this is not enough, in part because her performance has decreased in recent weeks, but also because she fears gaining weight. Paula reports being a "healthy" eater. She limits her carbs because they are "fattening" and avoids foods with too much dietary fat.

Diagnostic Criteria

Diagnostic criteria include the cardinal symptom of refusing to maintain a weight above 85% of expected body weight, a fear of gaining weight or becoming fat despite being thin or underweight, body image disturbance in which the body is perceived to be larger than its actual size, and amenorrhea in females (APA, 2000). Anorexia nervosa can be of two types—restricting or bingeing/purging, depending on how the patient primarily attempts to maintain a suboptimal weight.

Although these criteria appear straightforward, they may not be as straightforward as they appear. For example, "85% of expected body weight," seems straightforward, but what is expected body weight? How is it computed? In analyzing 99 studies involving the diagnosis of anorexia nervosa, Thomas, Roberto, and Brownell (2009) found that 10 different methods were used to calculate weight cutoffs for the diagnosis, and each produced different weight cutoffs. The diagnostic criterion regarding amenorrhea is also potentially problematic because some clearly anorexic patients never lose their menstrual cycle. Some lose it before they meet the weight criterion. It is difficult to determine menstrual status in some patients because they are taking hormone replacement, such as oral contraceptives. Also, there is not a corresponding criterion for male patients.

Another possible diagnostic problem with anorexia nervosa is that there appears to be considerable diagnostic crossover for many anorexic patients to bulimia nervosa (Tozzi et al., 2005). That is, their diagnosis may change over time. Eddy et al. (2008) followed anorexia nervosa and bulimia nervosa patients over a 7-year period. Over half crossed between the restricting and binge/purge subtypes during this period, and one-third crossed over to bulimia nervosa, although they were apt to cross back into anorexia nervosa. Interestingly, bulimic patients were not likely to cross over to anorexia nervosa.

Prevalence and Incidence

Recent U.S. population-based data indicated a lifetime prevalence estimate of 0.9% for women and 0.3% for men (Hudson, Hiripi, Pope, & Kessler, 2007). A Finnish study (Raevuori et al., 2009) reported a similar lifetime prevalence in males of 0.24%. Studies investigating the incidence of anorexia nervosa have found that the incidence increased through the 1970s (Hoek & van Hoeken, 2003) but has not been increasing in recent years (Milos et al., 2004; Currin, Schmidt, Treasure, & Jick, 2005; van Son, van Hoeken, Bartelds, van Furth, & Hoek, 2006) except in adolescent females (van Son et al.). Regarding adolescent females, Isomaa, Isomaa, Marttunen, Kaltiala-Heino, and Bjorkqvist (2009) reported a lifetime prevalence rate for Finnish females age 18 of 2.6%.

Physical/Medical Presentation

Anorexic patients are characterized by their very thin, often gaunt, even emaciated appearance. Their skin tends to be dry and may be pale or yellow due to carotinemia with light, fine hair (lanugo) growth on the face, arms, legs, and back. Their heads sometimes appear out of proportion (too big) for their bodies, especially in severe or chronic cases, and their hair tends to be thin with little body or shine. Younger patients often appear to be younger than their actual age, whereas older patients often look older than their age. Patients frequently wear either several layers of clothing or heavy clothing, such as sweat suits, perhaps to make it more difficult to see the body, but sometimes in an attempt to be warm because the anorexic patient is usually cold due to hypothermia. Despite being very thin, these patients may make comments related to being fat or needing to lose weight. In the case of a sport participant (especially one in a sport that emphasizes leanness), she may express a need to lose body fat in order to perform better or to train harder in order to improve her fitness level.

Medical signs and symptoms can occur in every major organ system and can range from essentially benign symptoms to complications that can be life threatening. Most symptoms result from complications related to starvation or purging techniques (i.e., self-induced vomiting, laxative/diuretic abuse, etc.) designed to remove or "undo" the effects of eating. Anorexia nervosa has the highest mortality rate of all psychiatric disorders, with death occurring primarily due to organ failure and suicide. The standard mortality ratio (SMR; the ratio of observed to expected deaths) for women with anorexia nervosa as compared to women in the general population has been found to range from 0.71 to 17.8, with a recent Canadian study reporting an SMR of 10.5 (Birmingham, Su, Hlynsky, Goldner, & Gao, 2005).

Cardiovascular problems (i.e., bradycardia, arrhythmias, prolonged QT interval, etc.) occur frequently in these patients, often in response to malnutrition or electrolyte abnormalities such as hypokalemia (low potassium). Estimates suggest that half of the deaths among anorexic patients are due to cardiac complications (Powers, 1999), with sudden death due to ventricular arrhythmias as one possibility (Pomeroy & Mitchell, 2002). Many patients experience orthostatic hypotension (dizziness on standing), but do not report it on evaluation unless asked specifically if they feel dizzy or lightheaded when standing up quickly.

Common gastrointestinal (GI) complications include abnormal motility, delayed gastric emptying, and constipation. Such difficulties can increase the likelihood of laxative abuse. Complications related to the mouth, teeth, throat, and esophagus are often associated with induced vomiting.

Abnormalities in the endocrine system often involve the hypothalamic-pituitary axes—gonadotropin, adrenal, and thyroid. Amenorrhea is a cardinal symptom in anorexia nervosa, although some patients lose menses before reaching weight criterion for anorexia nervosa, and sometimes menstrual irregularities persist after weight restoration. The roles of body weight, body composition, nutrition, and exercise in menstrual irregularities are still being debated. In the sport world, however, the role of "low energy availability" (Loucks, 2003), rather than body weight, body fat, or exercise stress, has been postulated as the explanation for exercise-induced menstrual dysfunction (American College of Sports Medicine [ACSM], 2007). (This will be discussed in a later section of this chapter on the female athlete triad.) These patients often have low serum levels of testosterone, estradiol, luteinizing hormone, and follicle-stimulating hormone. Other common lab values for these patients include elevated cortisol and decreased triiodothyronine (T_3; thyroid function test).

Metabolic abnormalities in these patients involve bone health and can be related to menstrual dysfunction. Without adequate estrogen in females or testosterone in males, increased bone resorption occurs without bone accrual, resulting in bone demineralization. Thus, many patients show decreased bone mineral density (osteopenia). Bone loss may be exacerbated by poor nutrition (inadequate intake of calcium and vitamin D) and hypercortisolism. Another interesting metabolic abnormality sometimes found in anorexia patients is hypercholesterolemia (elevated serum cholesterol), an abnormality that is not fully understood but one that remits with refeeding (Ohwada, Hotta, Oikawa, & Takano, 2006) and should not be treated with cholesterol-lowering drugs (Ohwada et al.; Schlechte, 1999).

As mentioned previously, medical complications of anorexia nervosa can involve all major organ systems. An exhaustive review of such complications is well beyond the scope of this book. Some of these complications will be discussed further in Chapter 8, but for more information regarding medical signs and symptoms, the reader is directed to Herzog and Eddy (2007) and Mehler and Andersen (1999).

Psychological/Behavioral Presentation
Keep in mind that the psychological and behavioral characteristics of patients with anorexia nervosa can be as individual as the patients themselves. Nonetheless, there are characteristics that are typically found. These patients' need for control is a hallmark of their disorder. Unfortunately, this need for control is manifested in considerable restraint in not only eating. Anorexia nervosa can be viewed as "control that is out of control." Anorexic patients often resist treatment because many do not believe that they have a problem and may come to treatment as a result of a referral from family members, physicians, or coaches. Their body image disturbance prevents them from seeing themselves accurately, which facilitates their denial. For a variety of reasons, these individuals may not give an accurate report of their symptoms. Many of the characteristics

11

seen in anorexic patients, such as depressed mood, decreased concentration, and insomnia, may be effects of (semi)starvation, which tend to remit with refeeding and weight restoration. Emotion is typically restricted, but these patients experience considerable fear and anxiety regarding weight gain, despite being quite thin. Obsessionality and perfectionism are characteristic of many anorexic patients, and the pairing of perfectionism with obsessive-compulsive personality disorder may be a core feature underlying an individual's vulnerability to an eating disorder (Halmi et al., 2005). Perfectionism may persist even after successful treatment of the eating disorder (Kaye et al., 1998; Sutandar-Pinnock, Blake, Carter, Olmsted, & Kaplan, 2003). Thinking is almost always obsessive with respect to eating, food, and weight and tends to be concrete, absolute, and "all or nothing." That is, they are either fat or skinny, and because they are never thin enough, they must be fat. Despite being malnourished, many patients are hyperactive, have difficulty sitting still or relaxing, and most are apt to exercise too much, given their health status and negative energy balance. Relationships are often negatively affected or sacrificed, in part due to the demands of the disorder, but this may also occur due to avoidance of social situations in which they might feel uncomfortable or in which eating might be expected. Common comorbid conditions include depressive, anxiety, and personality disorders, as well as substance use disorders in some cases. (Comorbid conditions will be discussed in more detail in Chapter 7.)

Special Considerations for Sport Participation
Although anorexia nervosa can begin at any stage of the life cycle, most cases have their onset around ages 13–14 or 17–18 (APA, 2000). These ages may be significant for young people because eating disorders usually have their onset during adolescence (Striegel-Moore & Bulik, 2007). A point we will make numerous times is that those who participate in sport are more at risk for eating disorders because they have the same risks as the general population, but also additional risks unique to sport participation. Thus, the typical transition difficulties encountered by adolescents may be exacerbated for those in sport as they move to a higher competition level and perhaps to greater pressures and expectations to perform well in their sport.

Obviously, competitors in sports that emphasize a thin body, size, shape, or low weight—what we will refer to as lean sports—would be at increased risk for the development of anorexia nervosa. Lean sports include those for which there is a weight-class requirement, or sports in which leanness is thought to confer a competitive advantage either from a biomechanical standpoint (i.e., moving the body through space) or from a judging standpoint based on appearance. Such sports could include distance running, diving, equestrian, figure skating, gymnastics, rowing, synchronized swimming, weightlifting, and martial arts. For men, these sports could include distance running, diving, horseracing, wrestling, martial arts, rowing, weightlifting, and ski jumping. This is not to suggest that the sport is the problem or that individuals in the "nonlean" sports are not at risk. Rather, the individual who may be predisposed to develop anorexia nervosa may be drawn to lean sports. Instead of being a cause of the disorder, participation in a lean sport would be another risk factor that could precipitate anorexic symptoms. In essence, sport participation could become another rationale for losing weight.

Many, if not most, anorexic patients engage in excessive or unhealthy exercise (Katz, 1996). Excessive exercise can be difficult to identify in the general population, but especially so in the sport world. We will discuss this issue in Chapter 5.

Bulimia Nervosa

Bulimia nervosa is often referred to as bulimia, and has been characterized as the binge-purge syndrome.

Karen is a 19-year-old gymnast. She is 5'1" (155 cm) tall and weighs 94 pounds (42.62 kg). Her only current medical problem is irregular menstruation. Karen is inducing vomiting two to three times per week because she says that she eats too much, especially when she is hungry. She worries that she will look fat in her uniform if she doesn't get rid of the food. Karen sometimes will use laxatives if she feels she "didn't throw up all of the food." She says she needs to be thin in order to perform well. Additionally, even though her coach has not said anything directly about her weight, she knows she wants her to be thinner. Karen is not particularly concerned about her vomiting or her menstrual cycle and does not believe that she has a problem other than the fact that she sometimes looks fat in her uniform.

Diagnostic Criteria
The cardinal symptoms for bulimia nervosa include binge eating and compensatory methods to avoid or prevent weight gain, and these occur at least twice per week for a period of at least three months. DSM-IV-TR

13

(APA, 2000) defines a *binge* as eating an amount of food that is larger than most people would eat during a specified period of time or circumstance and feeling a lack of control over eating during that period or circumstance. Many patients define it more subjectively (Keel, Mayer, & Harnden-Fischer, 2001). Often it is related to the emotional discomfort (associated with a loss of control) a patient feels during or after eating rather than the amount of food consumed. Or, as one patient said, "Bingeing is any eating that is followed by purging." As a result, some of these patients would be more appropriately diagnosed as eating disorder not otherwise specified rather than bulimia nervosa because they do not meet full criteria for bulimia nervosa (i.e., consuming a large amount of food) but have sufficient eating difficulties or general psychopathology to warrant an eating disorder diagnosis. It has been suggested that some of these patients have a purging disorder (Keel, Haedt, & Edler, 2005) with symptoms that are both similar to and distinct from those of other eating disorder patients (Fink, Smith, Gordon, Holm-Denoma, & Joiner, 2009).

Purging involves removing the effects of food through a compensatory process, such as self-induced vomiting, or the misuse of laxatives, diuretics, or enemas. A distinction is made between bulimic patients who use these methods and patients DSM-IV-TR (APA, 2000) refers to as "nonpurging type," who typically use fasting or excessive exercise as the primary means to weight control. Although these two sets of compensatory behaviors are listed separately, many bulimic patients employ methods from both. In the sport literature, both the purging and nonpurging forms of compensation are often referred to as pathogenic weight control methods. Regarding the prevalence of using such methods, 80 to 90% of bulimic patients engage in self-induced vomiting, whereas approximately one-third misuse laxatives (APA, 2000). One form of purgation that may be used more inside sport than outside is a sauna. Johnson, Powers, and Dick (1999) found that 6.59% of collegiate sportswomen and 24.26% of sportsmen in their study had used a sauna or steam bath to lose weight. The prevalence of excessive exercise, another compensatory method that may be used more in sport, is unknown, in part because defining and determining *excess* can be difficult in nonsport participants, but especially so in the sport environment. We will discuss this issue further in Chapter 5.

An additional diagnostic criterion for bulimia nervosa involves the undue importance that these patients place on their body size, shape, and weight regarding how they evaluate and feel about themselves. Finally, the diagnosis of bulimia nervosa is not given if the aforementioned symptoms occur as part of anorexic episodes. If criteria for both anorexia and bulimia nervosa are met, the patient is given the diagnosis of anorexia nervosa.

Crossover was discussed previously regarding patients with anorexia nervosa who cross over to bulimia nervosa. Although bulimia nervosa patients do not frequently cross over to anorexia nervosa, they do sometimes cross over from bulimia nervosa to binge eating disorder (Fichter, Quadflieg, & Hedlund, 2006).

Prevalence and Incidence

Hudson et al. (2007) reported a lifetime prevalence estimate for bulimia nervosa of 1.5% among women and 0.5% among men in a population-based survey. Although incidence studies indicated increases in bulimia nervosa in the 1980s (Keel & Klump, 2003), a recent Dutch study did not find an increase in the 1990s, with an incidence rate of 6.1 per 100,000, but did find that the highest risk group had decreased in age from 25- to 29-year-old females to 15- to 24-year-old females (van Son et al., 2006). Other studies have suggested that the point prevalence of bulimia nervosa has remained relatively constant from 1990 to 2004 (Crowther, Armey, Luce, Dalton, & Leahey, 2008; Keel, Heatherton, Dorer, Joiner, & Zalta, 2006).

Physical/Medical Presentation

Unlike patients with anorexia nervosa, bulimic patients are difficult to identify by their appearance. Their weight can fluctuate quickly and range from underweight to overweight. Through their disorder, these patients' weight can decrease, not change, and even increase. Other than bloating or edema secondary to purging, perhaps the only appearance-related symptoms occur in a subset of patients, and these include swollen salivary glands and a callous or mark on their fingers or the back of their hands due to digital stimulation of the gag reflex. In severe or chronic cases, dental or gum erosion may be apparent due to frequent and persistent vomiting. These patients may not be reliable in their reporting due to possible shame or embarrassment related to their symptoms and their need to present themselves in a positive light.

Medical complications from bulimia nervosa can be numerous and can run the gamut from benign to severe. Most are secondary to purging. Death resulting from bulimia nervosa is rare, but it usually involves cardiac abnormalities related to hypokalemia due to purging or to suicide (De Zwaan & Mitchell, 1999). As might be expected, gastrointestinal (GI) problems due primarily to purging (vomiting and laxatives) are common and can involve every aspect of the GI tract from dental and gum erosion, to esophageal problems (i.e., esophagitis, gastric reflux), to stomach dilatation or (rare) gastric rupture in severe cases, to lower GI tract abnormalities, including constipation, diarrhea, cathartic colon, and irritable bowel syndrome. Menstrual irregularity is common among bulimic patients, but its etiology is not clearly understood. Again, an exhaustive review of the medical complications of bulimia nervosa is beyond the scope of this book. Medical issues will be discussed further in Chapter 8, but for more information regarding medical signs and symptoms, the reader is directed to Herzog and Eddy (2007) and Mehler and Andersen (1999).

Psychological/Behavioral Presentation

As with patients with anorexia nervosa, patients with bulimia nervosa are also somewhat difficult to characterize because they can also be individual in their presentation. In comparison to anorexic patients, these individuals are typically more willing to accept that they have a problem in need of treatment; are more emotionally available, that is, more willing to talk about their emotions; and may experience affective instability (faster, wider, and greater change of emotion) and a lack of self-control (more impulsive). Typically, these patients are focused on weight and eating with respect to body shape and appearance. Part of this focus is driven by body dissatisfaction. Even when at a weight at or below their ideal weight, these patients (mis)perceive themselves to be fat. Their evaluation of self is intimately tied to this preoccupation or obsession with weight and shape. Common comorbid conditions for bulimic patients include mood and substance use disorders (APA, 2000). Anxiety and personality disorders are also apt to exist with bulimia nervosa. Comorbidity will be discussed in more detail in Chapter 7.

Special Considerations for Sport Participation

We view the sport environment to be a microcosm of society at large. Bulimia nervosa occurs more frequently than anorexia nervosa in the general population. The available research in the area suggests that it occurs more frequently than anorexia in sport as well (e.g., Torstveit, Rosenvinge, & Sundgot-Borgen, 2008). As with anorexia nervosa, bulimia nervosa is more apt to occur in sports that emphasize weight or leanness, but can occur in all sports with both genders. It should be remembered that sport participation can play many roles in an eating disorder, but it may also play an insignificant role. That is, the individual would likely have developed an eating disorder even without sport participation. Sport is simply another risk factor, and participation in a lean sport is a bigger risk factor.

Bulimia nervosa is most apt to develop in late adolescence and early adulthood (APA, 2000), which corresponds to transition periods that can increase the risk of an eating disorder. It is also a time when many young athletes become more serious about their sport and may be looking for an "edge" (i.e., decreased body weight/fat) to enhance performance.

Intuitively, participants in weight-class sports would appear to be more at risk for practicing at least bulimic behaviors if not developing bulimia nervosa. Many in these sports (i.e., boxing, judo, wrestling, etc.) believe that "cutting weight" to compete at a weight class below their natural weight will result in a competitive advantage of being heavier and stronger than others in the weight class. Of course, this reasoning is based on being able to cut weight during a period prior to weigh-in and then nourishing and rehydrating their bodies between weigh-in and competition. Such "weight loss" typically involves fluid loss and is often accomplished through dehydration techniques, some of which are referred to as pathogenic weight control methods. These methods often include induced vomiting, misuse of laxatives or diuretics, fasting, and excessive exercise—in essence, compensatory behaviors used by bulimic patients. The eating that is done between weigh-in and competition may in some cases qualify as binge eating. Thus, the sportsman may be practicing binge/purge behaviors each week during a season of competition. Is this bulimia nervosa? Research with weight-class sports suggests that the risk of disordered eating is higher than in non-weight-class sports (Fogelholm & Hiilloskorpi, 1999; Sundgot-Borgen & Torstveit, 2004), but does this translate into more eating disorders in sport participants? The data are equivocal (e.g., Dale & Landers, 1999; Dick, 1991). These issues will be discussed in greater detail in Chapter 3.

Eating Disorder Not Otherwise Specified

The diagnosis of eating disorder not otherwise specified (EDNOS) is reserved for cases of eating disorder that do not meet all criteria for either anorexia nervosa or bulimia nervosa (APA, 2000). Given this, it is important that clinicians not think of EDNOS patients as having less serious difficulties or being less in need of treatment (Devlin, Allison, Goldfein, & Spanos, 2007). Although most cases of eating disorder are diagnosed EDNOS, little research has been conducted on this large and heterogeneous subpopulation of eating disorder patients (Machado, Machado, Goncalves, & Hoek, 2007). We briefly described purging disorder earlier and will discuss two other examples here: binge eating disorder and night eating syndrome.

Binge Eating Disorder

Binge eating disorder (BED) is currently listed in the DSM-IV-TR (APA, 2000) under "Criteria Sets and Axes Provided for Further Study," which means that at present there is insufficient information for BED to be included as an official category. That status could change for DSM-V, however, due to research suggesting that BED warrants its own diagnostic entity based on epidemiology, symptoms, and treatment response (Pull, 2004), as well as the fact that it has established clinical utility and validity and is distinguishable from bulimia nervosa and obesity (Striegel-Moore & Franko, 2008). The cardinal symptom for BED is recurrent episodes of binge eating that occur at least two days per week for six months. Eating is characterized by a sense of a lack of control and marked distress, as well as the speed with which food is eaten, the amount eaten, and the negative affect associated with the binge (APA, 2000). BED is distinguished from bulimia nervosa by the lack of regular use of compensatory behaviors and the fact that more BED patients are overweight.

Night Eating Syndrome

Night eating syndrome (NES), which was first described by Stunkard and associates (1955), has gained renewed interest in recent years, most likely due to a recent emphasis on binge eating and obesity. NES is not listed in the DSM-IV-TR (APA, 2000), although it has been suggested that it should be included in DSM-V (Stunkard, Allison, & Lundgren, 2008). The predominant symptom involves the ingestion of a significant portion of the individual's daily food intake (i.e., at least 25%) after a specified time late in the day (i.e., 7 p.m.). Other symptoms have included morning anorexia (lack of eating/appetite) and insomnia or awakenings during the night (Devlin et al., 2007). It is distinguished from BED by the timing (night vs. day) of the eating, but in at least one study BED patients had greater eating pathology than NES patients (Allison, Grilo, Masheb, & Stunkard, 2005). Regarding prevalence, one study found that about 25% of young adults

18

met criteria for NES, and interestingly, (higher) body mass index (BMI) did not appear to be relevant to the definition of NES (Striegel-Moore, Franko, Thompson, Affenito, May, & Kraemer, 2008). Other prevalence estimates suggest that these patients include 1.1 to 1.5% of the general population, 6 to 16% of individuals in weight loss programs, and 8 to 42% of bariatric surgery candidates (Stunkard et al., 2008). These patients are usually diagnosed as EDNOS. For more information regarding the diagnosis and treatment of NES, see Allison, Stunkard, and Thier (2004). Nighttime eating that is sometimes confused with NES is sleep-related eating disorder, which involves eating episodes following arousal from nighttime sleep, and it is often associated with other sleep disorders (Howell, Schenck, & Crow, 2009).

Implications of EDNOS

Partial syndrome conditions will be discussed in the following section. Although many of these conditions found in the sport environment would likely be diagnosed as EDNOS, their names and descriptions originated in the sport environment and have often been used to describe eating, weight, body image, and health-related problems in sport. The rationale for their use was that these conditions put sport participants at significant health risks without meeting stringent DSM-IV criteria for an eating disorder. Thus, by identifying and treating them early in the process, perhaps before they reached the severity of a clinical eating disorder, the medical and psychological consequences of such disorders could be prevented or at least attenuated.

Finally, the category of EDNOS has sometimes been referred to as a "residual" or catchall category. For this and other reasons, changes in the EDNOS category and its utility may be forthcoming in DSM-V.

PARTIAL SYNDROME/SUBCLINICAL CONDITIONS

Anorexia Athletica

The term *anorexia athletica* (AA) was first used by Pugliese, Lifshitz, Grad, Fort, and Marks-Katz (1983) and refined by Sundgot-Borgen (1993). Sundgot-Borgen described AA as involving an intense fear of gaining weight or becoming fat despite being underweight, and a weight loss of at least 5% of expected body weight, usually accomplished by reducing total energy intake, often with "extensive or compulsive exercising." These individuals also frequently engage in binge eating as well as the use of pathogenic weight control methods (i.e., self-induced vomiting or use of laxatives or diuretics). Sundgot-Borgen believed that such cases should be considered as subclinical cases of anorexia nervosa or bulimia nervosa.

Disordered Eating and the Female Athlete Triad

The term *disordered eating* was adopted by the American College of Sports Medicine (ACSM) as part of its Position Stand on the Female Athlete Triad (ACSM, 1997). In large part, the female athlete triad was derived from the pioneering work by Drinkwater and associates (Drinkwater, Bruemner, & Chestnut, 1990; Drinkwater et al., 1984; Drinkwater, Nilson, Ott, & Chestnut, 1986), investigating the relationship between amenorrhea and loss of bone mineral density in exercising women. As first conceived, the triad involved the constellation of the interrelated problems of disordered eating, amenorrhea, and osteoporosis (Yeager, Agostini, Nattiv, & Drinkwater, 1993). Disordered eating reportedly played a role in the development of menstrual dysfunction in active females by supplying insufficient energy to fuel the individual's physical activity, as well as the energy necessary to fuel normal bodily processes of health, growth, and development, including reproduction. Disordered eating's role in bone health/loss involved providing insufficient nutrients (i.e., calcium, vitamin D, etc.) for bone formation. In the original position stand (ACSM, 1997), disordered eating was defined as

> a wide spectrum of harmful and often ineffective eating behaviors used in attempts to lose weight or achieve a lean appearance. The spectrum of behaviors ranges in severity from restricting food intake, to binging and purging, to the DSM-IV defined disorders of anorexia nervosa and bulimia nervosa. (p. i)

There are both positives and negatives with the term *disordered eating*. It was chosen by ACSM rather than *eating disorders* in part because the menstrual and bone complications associated with the triad can occur when eating is disturbed or disordered at levels not severe enough to meet diagnostic criteria for an eating disorder. Thus, intervention was recommended to take place before more disturbed eating (disorders) occurred. The term also implied less severity and less stigma than *eating disorder*, perhaps making it less difficult to accept by the affected individual. From a negative standpoint, the definition of the term was so broad that its use could be subjective on the less severe end of the spectrum. At the same time, *eating disorders* and *disordered eating* were perhaps not broad enough, as they did not cover "inadvertent" eating patterns that could reportedly result in triad symptoms. Recent prevalence studies of disordered eating suggest that its prevalence tends to increase with the level of competition with a rate of 18.2% with high school sport participants (Nichols, Rauh, Lawson, Ji, & Barkai, 2006), 26.1% in collegiate sportswomen (Reel, SooHoo, Doetsch, Carter, & Petrie, 2007), and 46.2% in elite sportswomen (Torstveit, Rosenvinge, & Sundgot-Borgen, 2008). In the recent update of the ACSM Position Stand on the Female Athlete Triad (ACSM, 2007), the term *disordered eating* was replaced with *energy availability*.

Energy Availability and the Female Athlete Triad

Energy availability (EA) is defined as "dietary energy intake minus exercise energy expenditure," or the energy that is left (available) after the energy cost of exercise has been spent (Loucks, 2003). Like disordered eating in the initial ACSM position stand on the triad (ACSM, 1997), energy availability is viewed as a spectrum from "optimal energy availability to low energy availability with or without an eating disorder" (ACSM, 2007, p. 1868). Low energy availability (LEA) occurs when the physically active female ingests insufficient calories to fuel her physical activity and support normal bodily processes of growth and development. If this condition persists or is severe, the hypothalamus in concert with the pituitary will "turn off" the reproductive system in order to conserve energy, resulting in inadequate estrogen. Specifically, LEA disrupts luteinizing hormone pulsatility that results from "a disturbance in the gonadotropin releasing hormone pulse generator in the hypothalamus" (Loucks, 2003, p. 144).

Reportedly, LEA can be inadvertent (involving a lack of information regarding amount of calories necessary), intentional (involving a desire to lose weight and may involve disordered eating), or psychopathological (involving eating disorders) (ACSM, 2007). The prevalence of low energy availability is unknown, although one study (Hinton, Sanford, Davidson, Yakushko, & Beck, 2004) reported that only 15% of collegiate female athletes (and 26% of male athletes) ingested sufficient carbohydrate and protein to meet dietary recommendations for athletes. The incidence of the LEA being inadvertent is still open to question, as 62% of the females

21

wanted to lose at least 5 pounds, suggesting restrictive eating related to desired weight loss. Part of the difficulty in assessing LEA is that some athletes will not suspect they are undereating and thus not seek an evaluation, whereas others will deny or not report it due to willful disordered eating. Obviously part of what needs to be assessed once LEA is suspected is the individual's explanation or rationale. That is, is she eating inadequately because she is unaware of her nutritional needs? If so, these sport participants should be amenable to increasing their caloric intake or decreasing their exercise when given appropriate information explaining their condition and the need for change. If an individual's eating is due to a lack of nutritional knowledge regarding what is necessary, then she should not have difficulty with eating more. If she is unable or unwilling to increase her caloric intake or unwilling or unable to decrease her activity, one would assume at least disordered eating if not an eating disorder. Usually, resistance to eating increases with the extent of eating disturbance. It is important for those in the sport world to remember that eating disturbances are not simply due to the competitor's desire to lose weight in order to perform better.

In the 2007 position stand, *amenorrhea* was replaced with *menstrual function*, the "spectrum of menstrual function ranging from eumenorrhea to amenorrhea," including oligomenorrhea, luteal deficiency, and anovulation (ACSM, 2007, p. 1869). Low energy availability has been proposed as the explanation for exercise-induced menstrual dysfunction in female athletes rather than exercise stress, low body weight, or low body fat (Loucks, 2003). Although this explanation is currently accepted in the sport world, it is viewed as being somewhat controversial by some in the traditional eating disorder healthcare world. Nonetheless, Louck's research can explain instances with eating disorder patients and menstrual dysfunction in some women that have been difficult to explain. For example, some eating disorder patients do not lose menses even at emaciated weights. Also, some eating disorder patients lose menses prior to reaching the weight criterion for anorexia nervosa (< 85% of expected body weight). And, some heavier sportswomen (i.e., throwers) lose menses despite being at a high weight. Low energy availability could be used as a possible explanation for any or all of the aforementioned examples. The recommended treatment for LEA is increased caloric intake, decreased energy expenditure, or both.

It should be noted that "functional hypothalamic" or "exercise-induced" menstrual dysfunction, as described in the triad position stand

(ACSM, 2007), is an exclusion diagnosis. That is, all medical conditions that could explain the dysfunction must be excluded in order for the diagnosis to be made. Such conditions include anabolic steroid use, pregnancy, pituitary tumors, thyroid disease, and polycystic ovary syndrome (PCOS). Because treatment is determined based on the diagnosis, the accuracy of that diagnosis is of paramount importance, regardless of the medical condition being included or excluded. That importance is illustrated by a recent study of Swedish Olympic sportswomen, for whom menstrual dysfunction was more often associated with PCOS than with hypothalamic inhibition due to low energy availability (Hagmar, Berglund, Brismar, & Hirschberg, 2009). Treatment based on an assumption of low energy availability (increased caloric intake or decreased training) in such cases could have exacerbated PCOS symptoms.

The third component of the female athlete triad, referred to previously as osteoporosis, is now called bone mineral density and involves a spectrum of bone mineral density "ranging from optimal bone health to osteoporosis" (ACSM, 2007, p. 1869). Bone growth requires adequate levels of estrogen. Due to estrogen deficiency, bone resorption exceeds bone formation, resulting in a loss of bone mineral density. In turn, bone loss is exacerbated by inadequate nutrition (i.e., calcium, vitamin D).

Male Athlete Triad?

Obviously, the female athlete triad refers to physically active females. Is there a male corollary? Are males who participate in sport at risk for compromised reproductive and bone health? Findings in this area are equivocal and incomplete. Most studies have involved males in endurance sports, primarily runners, and results have suggested that endurance training can decrease testosterone levels but may be clinically insignificant because they are usually still within normal limits (Arce & De Souza, 1993; Hackney, Sinning, & Bruot, 1990). Even though testosterone levels are often low in these individuals, a clear relationship has not been established between these levels and decreased bone mineral density. For example, studies have shown that significantly decreased testosterone levels can occur in endurance sportsmen without impacting bone mineral density (Maimoun et al., 2003). It has been suggested that training volume may play a role in decreased testosterone (De Souza & Miller, 1997), in that higher-mileage runners tend to have lower testosterone levels than lower-mileage runners (Wheeler, Wall, Belcastro, Conger, & Cumming, 1986). Findings in this area, however, have been equivocal as MacKelvie, Taunton, McKay, and Khan's (2000) higher-volume runners had greater bone mineral density despite the fact that training volume was inversely related to testosterone levels. Additionally, a negative relationship between training volume and bone mass has been reported in the absence of unchanged sex hormone levels (Bilanin, Blanchard, & Russek-Cohen, 1989; Hetland, Haarbo, & Christiansen, 1993). Bone mineral density varies by sport, with weight-bearing sports such as weightlifting (Sabo, Bernd, Pfeil, & Reiter, 1996) having greater bone mineral density, and non-weight-bearing sports such as cycling (Nichols, Palmer, & Levy, 2003) having lower bone mineral density.

The aforementioned studies have examined the hormonal/reproductive and bone density components of the triad, but the other component of the triad—disordered eating/energy availability—the energy or nutritional component, has not been adequately investigated. The reason for this is unclear, but one possible explanation relates to gender and eating disorders. Despite data from a recent national population-based survey suggesting that eating disorders among males are more common than previously thought (Hudson, Hiripi, Pope, & Kessler, 2007), eating disorders and disordered eating are much more prevalent in females. As a consequence, eating disorders have sometimes been viewed as a woman's disorder, and discussion, investigation, and treatment of such issues with males may not be viewed in the same way as when they occur in females.

Although problems with eating, weight, and body image are more often associated with females, this should not be misconstrued to mean that eating disorders and their sequelae do not occur in males. In the next chapter, we will present data to indicate that disordered eating and eating disorders are significant problems for many males in the sport environment—problems that could lead to health consequences similar to those of the female athlete triad. As we reported earlier, excessive exercise is often a characteristic of female and male patients with eating disorders, especially anorexia nervosa. It should be noted that, although osteoporosis is most often diagnosed in older women, it is not exclusively an older woman's disease. Twenty percent of those diagnosed with osteoporosis are male (National Osteoporosis Foundation [NOF], 2003), and this is probably an underestimate of the actual prevalence. The NOF lists undiagnosed low testosterone as a risk factor for males. Low testosterone is often a medical consequence of anorexia nervosa in males (Andersen, 1999b; APA, 2000), and at least one study (Andersen, Watson, & Schlechte, 2000) found that male anorexic patients often suffer osteoporosis, and it may be more severe than in their female counterparts. We will discuss risk factors in Chapter 4, and issues related to identification of eating disorders in the sport environment will be discussed further in Chapter 5. Suffice it to say at this point, however, that we think of identification problems as a significant risk factor (Sherman & Thompson, 2001).

Muscle Dysmorphia/Reverse Anorexia

Reverse anorexia was first described and investigated by Pope and colleagues (Pope, Katz, & Hudson, 1993), who later changed the term to muscle dysmorphia (Pope, Gruber, Choi, Olivardia, & Phillips, 1997). Muscle dysmorphia involves a preoccupation with not being muscular enough despite having very highly developed muscularity. In typical anorexia nervosa, the patient has a body image disturbance (or distortion) in which the body is (mis)perceived as being larger than it actually is. Many males with muscle dysmorphia experience reverse anorexia; that is, they (mis)-perceive their body as being much smaller than it actually is. As a consequence, they tend to be excessive and obsessive with their exercising and engage in anabolic steroid use. Reverse anorexia and muscle dysmorphia primarily affect males and are often more related to body image and exercise than eating, although many males with these particular difficulties are diagnosed with eating disorders. Although muscle dysmorphia has sometimes been found with weightlifters and bodybuilders, neither weightlifting nor bodybuilding per se appears to be the key risk factor. Olivardia, Pope, and Hudson (2000) found that men with muscle dysmorphia differed from normal comparison weightlifters on body dissatisfaction, eating attitudes, prevalence of anabolic steroid use, and lifetime prevalence of mood, anxiety, and eating disorders.

Orthorexia Nervosa

The term *orthorexia nervosa* (Bratman & Knight, 2000) has been used to describe a pattern of eating that begins with an attempt by the individual to make his or her eating "healthier." There is reportedly an obsessive need to make one's eating "pure" that can lead to a very restrictive diet that is much like that of anorexic patients with consequent medical complications. Preliminary research efforts regarding this eating pattern have focused on prevalence, assessment, and diagnosis (Donini, Marsili,

Gratziani, Imbriale, & Cannella, 2004, 2005). Orthorexia nervosa is not listed in the DSM-IV-TR (APA, 2000), and its inclusion seems unlikely, given that many of these individuals could be diagnosed as anorexia nervosa or EDNOS with obsessive compulsive disorder, depending on the specific dominant characteristics and symptoms. We have included it here because intuitively it seems to be a disordered eating pattern that might be chosen by someone in sport with the rationale (rationalization) of eating healthier in order to enhance athletic performance, either from a weight, leanness, appearance, or health perspective.

Obesity/Overweight

Obesity (BMI of 30 and higher) is not classified as an eating disorder. That is not to say that obesity is unrelated to eating or that it is not a serious medical problem with life-threatening complications. It will not be dealt with in this book in large part because it is unlikely to be a problem for many in sport other than in a few special instances (i.e., Sumo wrestlers and former college and professional linemen in American football).

Being overweight (BMI = 25.0 to 29.9) also is not an eating disorder. In some cases, it may be a consequence of EDNOS with binge eating as a prominent symptom (i.e., binge eating disorder, night eating syndrome). In any event, our use of the term *overweight* refers to a weight in a range established by the World Health Organization as overweight. A goal of enhancing sport performance is not an adequate rationale for asking an overweight sport participant to lose weight. For us, it is a medical issue, and as such should be assessed and treated for medical reasons by health-care professionals. This issue will be dealt with in Chapter 7.

Relationships Among Energy Availability, Disordered Eating, and Eating Disorders

We have described several clinical conditions in the previous pages of this chapter. It is important to remember that most are related in that they occur along a continuum or spectrum of eating behaviors. It is also helpful to understand the relationships between and among them. We have chosen (low) energy availability, disordered eating, and eating disorders because most of the conditions discussed previously could be contained in one, two, or all three of those categories.

Most cases of disordered eating (DE) involve low energy availability (LEA). Those not involving LEA would typically include those cases that have binge eating as a symptom. Eating problems involving LEA but not DE or eating disorders (EDs) would include those individuals who inadvertently undereat, usually because they are not aware of their nutritional needs. Many ED cases involve LEA. These include all cases of anorexia nervosa (AN), some cases of bulimia nervosa (BN), and some cases of eating disorder not otherwise specified (EDNOS). ED cases without LEA would include most of those with a binge eating component. All eating disorders involve disordered eating, but not all disordered eating would meet diagnostic criteria for AN or BN. Many cases of disordered eating meet criteria for EDNOS.

FINAL THOUGHTS

The diagnostic information presented in this chapter is in effect at the time of this writing. With DSM-V's anticipated arrival in 2012, discussions abound regarding necessary changes (Eddy et al., 2009; Walsh, 2007; Wonderlich, Joiner, Keel, Williamson, & Crosby, 2007). It has been suggested (Holm-Denoma, Gordon, & Joiner, 2007) that some of the issues and changes that may appear in DSM-V include movement toward a classification system that is more dimensional as opposed to the current categorical one, changes in EDNOS that might include binge eating disorder becoming a distinct entity, and changing the arbitrary 85% of ideal body weight criterion for anorexia nervosa, as well as two changes that are germane to our discussion in this chapter—possibly removing excessive exercise as a compensatory behavior in bulimia nervosa and amenorrhea as a diagnostic criterion for anorexia nervosa. Currently, the amenorrhea criterion for anorexia nervosa is helpful to those who want to emphasize the relationship between and among eating disorders, menstrual dysfunction, and bone loss. It is difficult to guess how its removal as a diagnostic criterion because it is "gender biased" (Berg & Andersen, 2007) would affect the acceptance of the female athlete triad. For additional information regarding the anticipated changes that will occur in DSM-V, as well as general issues related to diagnosis and classification of eating disorders, the reader is directed to a "Special Issue on Diagnosis and Classification," published in the *International Journal of Eating Disorders* (Striegel-Moore & Wonderlich, 2007).

Finally, rather than being overly concerned with what a particular set of symptoms is called (i.e., a diagnosis), focus should be on the effects of these symptoms on the individual with regard to whether the person needs treatment. We use a simple, practical rule in this regard. The individual could benefit from treatment if the symptoms: (1) compromise physical health, (2) compromise psychological health, or (3) interfere with everyday life (i.e., job, school, sport, or relationships). Typically, resistance to change or treatment increases as the individual's eating becomes more disordered.

3

Eating Disorders and Disordered Eating in Sport
A Review of the Literature

This chapter reviews the literature in the area of eating disorders in sport. It is a literature that is somewhat difficult to evaluate, in part because results are heterogeneous and somewhat equivocal. A bigger part of the difficulty, however, involves the different methodologies employed. Rather than investigating the presence of eating disorders per se, many studies look at attitudes and behaviors that are characteristic of individuals with eating disorders, or refer to sport participants as being "at risk." Additionally, different researchers employ different measures and use terms describing partial syndrome disorders (i.e., anorexia athletica, subclinical eating disorders, and female athlete triad) rather than *eating disorders* or *disordered eating* to describe eating-related problems in sportsmen and women. Even the term *disordered eating* is not always clearly defined and is used inconsistently. In addition, most of the data collected in this area are self-reported and come from studies with collegiate or elite athletes, raising questions about reliability of reporting and generalization of results, respectively. Some studies look specifically at one sport, whereas others compile aggregate data from several sports. There is also inconsistency of sport classification, with studies classifying their sports using a variety of terms (i.e., lean, nonlean, refereed, judged, weight class, weight dependent, aesthetic, strength, endurance, antigravitation, technical, ball, etc.).

In this chapter, we will first discuss how sportsmen and women compare to nonsport participants with regard to eating problems. Second, we will discuss how variables such as gender, type of sport, and competition level moderate the risk of eating problems in sport participants. Third, because body image issues and body dissatisfaction contribute to the development of eating disorders, we will review and discuss body image issues and problems that are common among sport participants. Last, given that much of the apparent risk to sport participants involves the belief that leanness is related to enhanced sport performance, we will review the literature relevant to the relationship between leanness/thinness and sport performance.

SPORT PARTICIPANTS VERSUS NONSPORT PARTICIPANTS

Sport participation can have a positive effect on attitudes and behaviors related to eating or body (e.g., Fulkerson, Keel, Leon, & Dorr, 1999), self-efficacy (Taub & Blinde, 1992), or self-perceptions of competence and ability (Biddle, 1993). In such cases, sport participation can act almost as a buffer against such problems. Despite the positive effects of sport participation, however, many sport participants still appear to be at increased risk due to facing the same risks as nonsport participants but also risks unique to the sport environment.

The preponderance of data in this area suggests that sport participants (especially sportswomen competing in lean, aesthetic, endurance, and weight-dependent sports) tend to have more eating problems than nonathletes (Byrne & McLean, 2001, 2002; Holm-Denoma, Scaringi, Gordon, Van Orden, & Joiner, 2009; Parks & Read, 1997; Resch & Haasz, 2009; Smolak, Murnen, & Ruble, 2000; Sundgot-Borgen, 1993; Sundgot-Borgen & Klungland, 1998; Toro et al., 2005; Torstveit, Rosenvinge, & Sundgot-Borgen, 2008; Torstveit & Sundgot-Borgen, 2005b). Nonetheless, several studies report findings that some sport participants not only do not have more eating problems (DiBartolo & Shaffer, 2002; Kirk, Singh, & Getz, 2001; Reinking & Alexander, 2005; Rosendahl, Bormann, Aschenbrenner, Aschenbrenner, & Strauss, 2008; Sanford-Martens et al.,

2005; Schwartz, Gairrett, Aruguete, & Gold, 2005; Torstveit & Sundgot-Borgen, 2005a), but may actually be healthier and less at risk (e.g., Wilkins, Boland, & Albinson, 1991). Results in this area are heterogeneous and can vary depending on several factors, as suggested by Smolak et al.'s (2000) meta-analysis of 64 studies related to sportswomen and eating disorders. Overall, they showed more eating problems than nonsport participants, but the differences were small. Findings were heterogeneous in that elite sportswomen and those in some lean sports were found to be at higher risk, but even within lean sports differences varied. Gymnasts, swimmers, and runners did not differ from their nonsport counterparts. High school girls participating in sports did not differ from nonsport participants. Additionally, nonelite and nonlean participants scored better than nonparticipants on measures of eating attitudes and behaviors, as well as body (dis)satisfaction.

In conclusion, do sport participants experience more eating and body image problems than their nonparticipant counterparts? Most likely they do, especially those in lean sports. We can say with more assurance that they are more at risk for such problems. However, the fact that some sportsmen/women are at increased risk of eating or body image problems should not be misconstrued to imply that sport participation is the problem and thus should be avoided. Smolak et al. (2000) suggested that the heterogeneity of findings of greater pathology implies that sport participation per se is not the problem. Eating and body image difficulties tend to result from a complex combination of risk factors. Sport participation is an additional risk factor for some individuals who compete in sport. However, it is not sport participation that needs to be avoided, but rather the factors that increase the risk. In the next three sections, we will look more closely at factors that may moderate the risk: gender of athlete, type of sport, and competition level.

GENDER: SPORTSMEN VERSUS SPORTSWOMEN

A recent population-based prevalence study reported that the lifetime prevalence of eating disorders was 1¾ to 3 times higher among females than males (Hudson, Hiripi, Pope, & Kessler, 2007). Throughout this book, we will work from the reasonable assumption that the sport environment is a microcosm of the society at large. As a result, we would expect to find a prevalence disparity between the genders in sport in much the same way as we do in society at large.

In one of the largest studies investigating eating problems in sportsmen and women, Johnson, Powers, and Dick (1999) found no female college sport participants who met criteria for anorexia nervosa, although 2% identified themselves as anorexic. Only 1.1% met criteria for bulimia nervosa, but 5.5% self-identified as bulimic. An additional 13% reported "clinically significant symptoms," whereas 35% and 38% were assessed to be "at risk" for anorexia and bulimia, respectively. None of the males met criteria for an eating disorder, but 12% reported that they engaged in binge eating, and 9.5 and 38% were assessed to be at risk for anorexia and bulimia, respectively. In another study of collegiate sport participants, Hausenblas and McNally (2004) classified 13.93% of the female track and field athletes in their study in a category they called "eating disorder/symptomatic," as compared to 4% of the males. The women also reported a greater drive for thinness and body dissatisfaction than the men. Almost 7% of the collegiate sportswomen in a study by Reel, SooHoo, Doetsch, Carter, and Petrie (2007) were assessed to have a clinical eating disorder. Regarding collegiate males, Petrie, Greenleaf, Carter, and Reel (2007) found that only 1% of the collegiate sportsmen in their study had an eating disorder, and that they appeared to feel little pressure regarding weight, tended to be satisfied with size and shape, and had minimal fear about becoming fat. Petrie et al. suggested that males may not experience the same psychosocial risk factors as their female counterparts.

Research with elite sportsmen and women has not reported results significantly different from research with college sport participants. In one of the most thorough and methodologically sound investigations with sport participants, Sundgot-Borgen and Torstveit (2004) found that 20% of elite Norwegian sportswomen had clinical or subclinical eating disorders, as compared to 8% of their male counterparts.

TYPE OF SPORT—LEAN

Lean sports include those for which a thin or lean body or a low weight is believed to provide an advantage in sport performance or in the judging of sport performance. For women, sports in this group typically include distance running, diving, equestrian, figure skating, gymnastics, rowing, and synchronized swimming. For men, sports usually included in this group are bodybuilding, distance running, diving, horseracing, martial arts, rowing, ski jumping, wrestling, and weightlifting. As we discuss these sports individually in later sections, we will explain why each is considered a lean sport, as well as the suspected risks associated with each.

As reported earlier, participants in sports that emphasize a thin or lean body size and shape or a low weight appear to be at greater risk (Byrne & McLean, 2001, 2002; Davis & Cowles, 1989; Hagmar, Hirschberg, Berglund, & Berglund, 2008; Parks & Read, 1997; Petrie, 1996; Picard, 1999; Sundgot-Borgen, 1993, 1994a; Sundgot-Borgen & Larsen, 1993; Sundgot-Borgen & Torsteveit, 2004; Torstveit et al., 2008). Lean sports have often been classified as weight-class (or weight-dependent), aesthetic (judged), or endurance sports (Beals, 2004), and at least in one study (Sundgot-Borgen, 1993) such sports had the highest use of pathogenic weight loss methods.

Weight-Class Sports

Research with weight-class sports suggests that the risk of disordered eating in such sports is higher than in non-weight-class sports (Hagmar et al., 2008; Sundgot-Borgen & Torstveit, 2004).

Wrestling

Wrestlers probably represent the male sport group that, rightly or wrongly, is most often associated with disordered eating, in part due to the risks associated with weight-class sports (Fogelholm & Hiilloskorpi, 1999), but probably due more to the use of pathogenic methods to "cut weight" that are commonly practiced by wrestlers (Oppliger, Nelson-Steen, & Scott, 2003). Many wrestlers attempt to wrestle one or two weight classes below their natural weight. They believe that such a practice will provide them with the strength of a larger body when competing at a lower weight. This reasoning is contingent upon them successfully making the lower weight and then nourishing and rehydrating their bodies during the period between weigh-in and competition. The possible risk to wrestlers was indicated in an early study by Enns, Drewnowski, and Grinker (1987), who suggested that disturbances in eating might be "sports induced."

Not surprisingly, a study by Dick (1991) reported that 20 of the 67 reports by athletic directors at National Collegiate Athletic Association (NCAA) member institutions regarding the incidence of eating disorders involved wrestling. Research related to weight-cutting methods used by wrestlers found the frequent use of laxatives and diuretics, excessive exercise, and thermal methods, such as sauna use and wearing rub-ber suits (Steen & Brownell, 1990; Steen & McKinney, 1986), in addition to self-induced vomiting (Oppliger, Landry, Foster, & Lambrecht, 1993). Regarding the presence of eating disorders, Thiel, Gottfried, and Hesse (1993) reported that 16% of the low weight wrestlers in their study had a "subclinical eating disorder," whereas Oppliger et al. reported that 1.7% of wrestlers in their study met diagnostic criteria for bulimia nervosa.

In 1997, three college wrestlers died as a result of complications related to weight cutting (Thompson, 1998). As a result, the NCAA imple-mented several changes to safeguard wrestlers, including establishing new weight classes, new procedures for setting a weight class early in the season, the timing of weigh-ins, and banning pathogenic weight loss methods. Were these changes effective? Oppliger, Utter, Scott, Dick, and Klossner (2006) found that the incidence of rapid weight loss prior to weigh-ins and rapid weight gain following weigh-ins decreased signifi-cantly for wrestlers in the NCAA national championship tournaments for the period 1999–2004.

Bodybuilding

Bodybuilding is a sport that is somewhat difficult to categorize. In fact, some might question whether it is in fact a sport. Intuitively, a case could be made for it to be classified as a power sport. Also, an even stronger case could probably be made for its classification as an aesthetic sport with its empha-sis on appearance. However, because it is so different from the traditional aesthetic sports, we have chosen to include bodybuilding in this section because it has competitions for males and females, utilizes weight classes, and has some similarities to the weight-class sport of weightlifting.

Regardless of how bodybuilding is classified, it is a sport that appears to involve considerable risk for the development of eating disorders. It involves increasing muscle size, definition, and symmetry, but at the same time decreasing body fat through weight training and aerobic exercise. Nutritional and (de)hydration strategies are used to give the body a mus-cular but lean and cut look. Bodybuilders want to maximize muscularity while minimizing body fat to achieve an appearance that is purported to be pleasing to judges. Additionally, women bodybuilders have a somewhat more difficult task as they must meet femininity requirements, and in recent years they have been asked to decrease their muscularity. Another recent change in women's bodybuilding has been the addition of fitness and figure competitions, which emphasize even less muscularity. The need to simultaneously gain lean (muscle) weight and decrease body fat would appear to be a difficult task for both male and female bodybuilders.

With bodybuilding having the risk factors of appearance, judging, and weight classes, are bodybuilders predisposed to dieting, disordered eating attitudes and behaviors, and even eating disorders? From a nutritional standpoint, early studies suggested that bodybuilders used nutrition plans that were heavily loaded with protein (Spitler, Diaz, & Horvath, 1980) and training programs that emphasized leanness (Sandoval, Heyward, & Lyons, 1989). In a review of studies with bodybuilders, Goldfield, Harper, and Blouin (1998) concluded that eating disorders were common, along with their associated symptoms of severe dieting, weight/shape preoccupation, body image disturbance, and pathogenic weight control methods. Similarly, more recent studies have reported findings suggestive of disordered eating, such as body image disturbance (Ravaldi et al., 2003), the taking of supplements designed to increase body size, dietary restriction, and frequent body checking (Muller, Dennis, Schneider, & Joyner, 2004); higher levels of self-objectification and body dissatisfaction than other athletes and controls (Hallsworth, Wade, & Tiggemann, 2005); and personality characteristics similar to those of female anorexic patients (Davis & Scott-Robertson, 2000). At least one study (Pickett, Lewis, & Cash, 2005), however, reported more positive results in that bodybuilders had a more positive global appearance evaluation than controls and were more satisfied with their upper torso and muscle tone.

The limited literature with female bodybuilders suggests that the findings of eating disorders, weight preoccupation, restrictive dieting, and body dissatisfaction among male bodybuilders are also common among female bodybuilders. Fifty-six percent of Walberg and Johnston's (1991) sample of female competitive bodybuilders reported being terrified of becoming fat. Such a fear may in part explain the severe dieting reported by female competitive bodybuilders in a study by Lamar-Hildebrand, Saldanha, and Endres (1989). Similarly, Andersen, Brownell, Morgan, and Bartlett (1998) reported that 60% of the female competitive bodybuilders in their study were very unsatisfied with their weight on the day of a competition. Regarding eating disorders, 17% of Walberg and Johnston's (1991) sample of female competitive bodybuilders claimed to have been anorexic in the past, whereas Goldfield (2009) found a lifetime prevalence of 15% for bulimia nervosa in a sample of female bodybuilders.

Weightlifting

For competitive male and female weightlifters, the goal is to increase strength in order to increase the amount that can be lifted. Weightlifting involves weight classes, and if there is a body size advantage, short lifters may have advantages over taller ones. Pasman and Thompson (1988) reported that "obligatory" weightlifters were more accurate in body size estimation than were runners or controls, suggesting that individuals desiring a larger body would experience less overestimation than those wanting a smaller body. Nonetheless, weightlifters had higher levels of eating disturbance than controls. Very little work has been done in this area with females, but in one study (Walberg & Johnston, 1991) 15.5 and 23.3% of 103 female weightlifters had elevated Eating Disorder Inventory (EDI; Garner, 1991) drive for thinness and body dissatisfaction scores, respectively, and 42% reported having been anorexic.

Horseracing

Even though horseback riding was included as a technical sport in Sundgot-Borgen and Larsen's classification system (1993), logic suggests that horseracing or jockeying should be classified as a weight-class sport because of the weight requirement. There is a paucity of research regarding jockeys, and the available studies employed very small samples. King and Mezey (1987) found that the 10 jockeys in their study used pathogenic weight control methods (dehydration, strenuous exercise, fasting, laxatives, and diuretics), but none of them were assessed to have an eating disorder. Leydon and Wall (2002) reported that only one of six male jockeys in their study had elevated Eating Attitudes Test (EAT-26; Garner, Olmsted, Bohr, & Garfinkel, 1982) scores. Rather than looking at disordered eating per se, Caulfield and Karageorghis (2008) examined the psychological effects of dieting and rapid weight loss in jockeys. Jockeys reported significantly more negative moods and eating attitudes at a minimal weight achieved through rapid weight loss than when not excessively restricting their eating. Jockeys may be more at risk because they are more motivated than many athletes to lose weight, given that they must make weight in order to ride and earn a livelihood. The fact that many racetracks have special facilities that include oversized toilets ("heaving bowls") to facilitate vomiting, as well as a sauna ("hot box") for jockeys to use to maintain their weight in a suboptimal range, suggests a subculture that has "normalized" the use of pathogenic weight control methods.

Sprint (Lightweight) Football

Sprint football is an American college football program designed to make it possible for lighter weight males to participate in American football—a sport that has seen the weights of players increase significantly in recent years. This sport currently has a weight limit of 170 pounds. When the weight limit was 158 pounds, DePalma et al. (1993) found that 74% of these lightweight players engaged in binge eating and 17% had engaged in self-induced vomiting.

Rowing

Available research with rowing—another sport employing weight classes (lightweight and heavyweight)—suggests an increased risk. Findings include eating symptoms such as binge eating, fasting, weight fluctuations (Sykora, Grilo, Wilfley, & Brownell, 1993), weight reduction strategies such as dieting, fluid restriction, increased training loads (Slater et al., 2005), diuretic abuse (Karlson, Becker, & Merkur, 2001), and score elevations on measures of eating attitudes and problems (Stoutjesdyk & Jevne, 1993; Thiel et al., 1993; Terry, Lane, & Warren, 1999). In at least one study with rowers, age, weight class, and hunger appeared to have an effect on eating restraint and body dissatisfaction (Pietrowsky & Straub, 2008). When compared to heavyweight male rowers, adult lightweight rowers had very high restrained eating scores and more body dissatisfaction under hunger conditions as compared to satiety. Juvenile lightweight rowers also showed considerable restraint, but body dissatisfaction was unaffected by weight class or hunger. The difference in juvenile and adult rowers' body satisfaction suggests that body dissatisfaction increases with the time in sport.

Do such findings suggest the risk for disordered eating or eating disorders in rowers? Thiel et al. (1993) reported that 8% of their sample of male rowers had "pathologic EDI profiles," suggesting a "subclinical eating disorder." Karlson et al. (2001) found that collegiate female lightweight rowers had less concern about shape and did not show an increased prevalence of eating disorders compared to other sport participants or nonsport participant controls. However, when NCAA coaches of sportswomen were asked to recall sport participants with eating disorders or disordered eating, rowing coaches recalled having coached more symptomatic sportswomen than coaches from any other sport (Sherman, DeHass, Thompson, & Wilfert, 2005).

Judo

Rouveix and colleagues (Rouveix, Bouget, Pannafieux, Champely, & Filaire, 2007; Filaire, Rouveix, Pannafieux, & Ferrand, 2007) investigated weight pressures and eating disorder risk in the weight-class sport of judo. Regarding weight pressures, 25% of male judoists reported not being satisfied with their weight and feeling pressure to lose weight, and more judoists than controls reported using drastic methods to lose weight, including fasting and laxatives. With respect to eating disorder risk, Rouveix et al. (2007) assessed 25% of female judo athletes to be at risk for an eating disorder, whereas no male judoist was judged to be at risk. Additionally, 58.3% of the females reported menstrual dysfunction.

Aesthetic Sports

Not only are aesthetic sports considered to be lean sports, but they also tend to focus on the appearance of the participants as well as their performance. Aesthetic sports are also judged. Do appearance and judging further increase the risk for sportswomen who are already competing in a lean sport? Another possible risk for participants in these sports involves wearing revealing attire—revealing in terms of either shape perception or the amount of skin exposed. It has been suggested that such uniforms or attire may increase weight and appearance concerns (Reel, SooHoo, & Estes, 2005) and facilitate competitive thinness and unhealthy body comparisons (Sherman, 2007; Thompson & Sherman, 1999a).

Schwarz, Gairrett, Aruguete, and Gold (2005) found sportswomen in judged sports to have a higher incidence of dieting than those in refereed sports. Additionally, at least one study (Zucker, Womble, Williamson, & Perrin, 1999) found participants in judged sports (diving, gymnastics, and cheerleading) to show a greater drive for thinness and a higher trend for eating disorder diagnoses than participants in refereed sports (tennis, basketball, volleyball, and track) or controls. A study by Bachner-Melman, Zohar, Ebstein, Elizur, and Constantini (2006) reported a lifetime prevalence of 4.5% for anorexia nervosa, 1.8% for bulimia nervosa, and 11.7% for EDNOS among Israeli aesthetic sportswomen (gymnasts, synchronized swimmers, dancers, and acrobats) as compared to 1.4, 1.4, and 5.8%, respectively, for nonaesthetic sportswomen (runners, swimmers, ball players, technical sportswomen, and martial artists), and 3.2, 2.8, and 4.4%, respectively, for a control group.

(Artistic) Gymnastics

Gymnastics is viewed as a sport in which performance is facilitated by a thin or small body size and shape. Thus, we would expect to see the frequent use of dieting and other weight control methods by female gymnasts. Several early studies investigating the eating/dieting habits of female gymnasts confirmed that they were dieting and eating less than recommended daily allowances for nutrients (Coleman, 1988; Costar, 1983; Moffatt, 1984).

Do appearance pressures and consequent restricted eating result in eating problems for gymnasts? Research by Rosen, Hough, and colleagues (Rosen & Hough, 1988; Rosen, McKeag, Hough, & Curley, 1986) found that most gymnasts were dieting—for both performance and appearance. They also noted the frequent use of pathogenic weight control methods (self-induced vomiting, laxatives, diuretics, fluid restriction, or diet pills). Petrie and Stoever (1993) also found the use of pathogenic weight control methods (excessive exercise, vomiting, and use of laxatives or diuretics) in their female college gymnasts. Similarly, O'Connor, Lewis, and Kirchner (1995) found that 22% of 23 female college gymnasts had elevated EDI-2 drive for thinness scores, and more than half had used at least one pathogenic weight loss method.

Rhythmic Gymnastics

Whereas artistic gymnastics has been investigated frequently with regard to eating disorders, little work has been reported with rhythmic gymnasts. In two investigations, Klinkowski and colleagues (Klinkowski, Korte, Pfeiffer, Lehmkuhl, & Salbach-Andrae, 2008; Salbach, Klinkowski, Pfeiffer, Lehmkuhl, & Korte, 2007) compared elite female rhythmic gymnasts with anorexic patients and normal controls. The experimenters concluded that, despite the fact that these gymnasts may show a "lean, almost anorexic-like physique," they showed no psychological distress comparable to anorexics (Klinkowski et al., 2008), nor did they show problems related to attitudinal aspects of eating disorders (Salbach et al., 2007). Do these findings indicate a high prevalence of DE or ED in female gymnasts? Sundgot-Borgen (1996) found that 6 of 12 female rhythmic gymnasts engaged in disordered eating. Two met DSM-III criteria for anorexia nervosa, two met criteria for anorexia athletica, and the other two were regularly using pathogenic weight loss methods.

Diving

One would assume that participants in an aesthetic, lean, judged sport that employs revealing attire like diving would show considerable body concerns. In one study, however, Hausenblas and Mack (1999) found that divers had lower "social physique anxiety" than athlete controls and non-athlete controls. This suggests that perhaps athletes seek out sports that emphasize the physique because they are confident about making a good impression (Haase & Prapavessis, 2001). We will revisit this topic in a later discussion of swimming.

Figure Skating

In assessing body image and dietary intake in male and female skaters, Rucinski (1989) found that 48% of the females had EAT scores in what the author called the anorexic range, compared to none of the males. Average daily caloric intake was 1,174 for females and 2,897 for males. Ziegler et al. (1998) found that only 2 of 21 female competitive skaters scored above the EAT cutoff suggesting disordered eating. Conversely, Barkley (2001) found that 20.5% of competitive skaters reported previous eating disorders, and 50% of these reported still having an eating disorder. Most (62.5%) reported symptoms of anorexia nervosa. Ninety-four percent of those with previous eating disorders and 100% of those with current eating disorders said their symptoms were related to the pressures associated with skating (feeling that weight loss was required for the sport, needing to conform to aesthetic ideals of the sport, or to obtain better scores). Similarly, Taylor and Ste-Marie (2001) found that more than 90% of figure skaters felt pressure to lose weight.

If figure skating is a sport with pressures regarding thinness, those pressures might be even greater for synchronized figure skating that involves teams of 12 to 20 skaters attempting to maintain uniformity. In a study designed to assess the nutritional intake of female synchronized figure skaters (Ziegler et al., 2005), caloric intake was lower than would be recommended for their level of activity. This restrained eating was probably related to the fact that 89% of the skaters wanted to weigh less than their current weight despite the majority being within a normal weight range, as they perceived themselves to be more overweight than they actually were.

Synchronized Swimming

Intuitively, synchronized swimming would seem to be a sport that holds considerable potential for eating disorder risk. As will be discussed in

Chapter 4, it is not only an appearance/judged sport in which participants wear revealing swimsuits; uniformity of participants' bodies could perhaps enhance scoring. Such factors would likely increase the emphasis on body size and shape. In a study by Ferrand, Magnan, and Philippe (2005), elite synchronized swimmers reported greater negative feelings regarding their appearance than did sportswomen in nonlean sports or nonsportswomen but did not show more eating problems.

Endurance Sports

The risk to endurance athletes has been noted by Sundgot-Borgen and colleagues, who found eating disorders in 9% of elite sportsmen in endurance sports (Sundgot-Borgen & Torstveit, 2004) and 25.7% of elite Norwegian endurance sportswomen (Torstveit et al., 2008).

Triathlon
Considerable work has been done by DeBate and colleagues (DeBate, Wethington, & Sargent, 2002a, 2002b; Wethington, Flowers, Turner, & DeBate, 2002) with triathletes, an athlete group the investigators suggested could be at risk for disordered eating, in part because the triathlon sports—cycling, swimming, and running—probably have differing body ideals. Findings by Wethington et al. (2002) suggested that food restriction, body size distortion, and disordered eating attitudes were common among the female triathletes. Do the risks associated with the three endurance sports of a triathlon result in more female athlete triad symptoms? Hoch, Stavrakos, and Schimke (2007) found that 60% of club triathletes were in calorie deficit, that 40% had a history of amenorrhea, but that bone mineral density was normal. Do the risks associated with the sport of triathlon translate into more eating disorders? Beals (2002) reported that 20 and 12.5% of female triathletes indicated a history of anorexia nervosa and bulimia nervosa, respectively, compared to 1.5% for anorexia and bulimia in male triathletes.

Cycling
Ferrand and Brunet (2004) found that more than half of male cyclists had EAT-26 scores above 20. Of the female cyclists in a study by Bartok-Olson and Keith (1996), 84% reported that low body fat or low body weight would enhance performance, but they did not show a greater probability of eating disorders than a control group. Filaire et al. (2007) reported that

41

46% of elite male cyclists felt pressure to lose weight and 41% used fasting for weight loss. Sportsmen differed from controls on EAT scores, but even those without high EAT scores reported using pathogenic weight loss methods (vomiting, laxatives, and diet pills) several times per year, especially during competition periods.

Distance Running

Rosen et al. (1986) reported that more than half of the distance runners in their study indicated the use of at least one pathogenic weight control method (self-induced vomiting, laxatives, diuretics, diet pills, etc.). Similarly, Bonogofski, Beerman, Massey, and Houghton (1999) found that 12% of female collegiate cross-country runners had EAT-26 scores indicating a high risk for anorexia nervosa. More specific to the presence of an eating disorder, Clark, Nelson, and Evans (1988) found that 13% of the elite female runners in their study had a history of anorexia nervosa, 27% reported having had a body mass index (BMI) of less than 17, and 9% reported bingeing and purging. Hulley and Hill (2001) reported that 16% of elite distance runners in their sample indicated a present diagnosis of an eating disorder, in addition to another 3% who had received previous treatment for an eating disorder. Similarly, 19.4% of Thompson's (2007) sample of female collegiate cross-country runners reported a previous or current eating disorder.

Regarding female athlete triad symptoms in 99 collegiate athletes in eight sports, runners had the highest percentage of menstrual dysfunction (44%) and the lowest total body, lumbar spine, and pelvis bone mineral density (Mudd, Fornetti, & Pivarnik, 2007). Barrack and colleagues have investigated triad symptoms in younger (13 to 18 years) runners. Barrack, Rauh, Barkai, and Nichols (2008) reported that those with elevated dietary restraint had a greater incidence of low bone mineral density (lumbar spine and total body bone mineral density [BMD]) than did runners with elevated weight and shape concerns. In a related study, Barrack, Rauh, and Nichols (2008) reported that total hip and lumbar spine BMD were lower in the 25.8% of adolescent runners who experienced menstrual irregularity.

Most of the work in this area has involved female runners. In one study that included male runners, Kiernan, Rodin, Brownell, Wilmore, and Crandall (1992) found that 8% of males and 24% of female runners had symptomatic scores on the EAT. Exercise level expressed in weekly mileage was positively associated with excessive concerns about weight and eating in males but not females. A history of weight cycling was predictive for symptomatic EAT scores in both males and females.

The aforementioned studies investigating distance runners suggest that these individuals are at increased risk for eating disorders, or at least for disordered eating. Some studies, however, suggest that they are not at increased risk or are not similar to individuals with eating disorders. Although 14% of the female distance runners in their study scored above an EAT cutoff score indicative of disordered eating, Weight and Noakes (1987) found only 1 of 125 female distance runners with a past diagnosis of anorexia nervosa. Gleaves, Williamson, and Fuller (1992) compared runners who used exercise predominantly as a way to lose weight and who had lost at least 4.5 kg with a control group and a group of bulimic patients regarding symptoms of bulimia and body image disturbance. Runners and controls did not differ and were assessed to be less disturbed than bulimic patients. Powers, Schocken, and Boyd (1998) compared habitual (obligatory) male and female distance runners with female anorexia nervosa patients on several physiological and psychological measures. Patients had significantly more psychopathology than the runners and greatly overestimated their body size compared to the relatively accurate body perceptions of the runners. Additionally, body composition measures were within the normal range for both male and female runners, and the runners were more satisfied with their body image. Interestingly, 9 of the 20 female runners were amenorrheic, but 8 of them were at a normal weight. Similarly, in a review of 17 studies related to distance running and disordered eating in female distance runners, Morse (2008) concluded that distance runners were not similar to individuals with eating disorders, other than with respect to perfectionism and menstrual dysfunction. Further, she suggested that distance running possibly deters the development of eating disorders by providing the runner with the activity of running as a healthier means to channel her perfectionism. We concur that distance running is not in and of itself the problem, but we contend that it may be another risk factor, or at least another rationale for a need to be thin.

Ultra-Endurance Sports

In recent years, we have seen a burgeoning of ultra-endurance competitions in sports such as cycling and swimming, but especially in running. More and more competitors—men and women—are participating in ultra-marathons, some of which are in excess of 100 miles and are run in extreme conditions. Does a discussion of such sport participation belong in a book devoted to eating disorders in sport? Such competitions involve what many would describe as excessive exercise, more recently described as unbalanced exercise (Powers & Thompson, 2008). And, as discussed in Chapter 2, such exercise plays a critical role in many eating disorders. Additionally, sports in which such unhealthy exercise is an accepted part of the sport would provide an environment in which exercise problems, whether a part of an eating disorder or not, would be difficult to identify. In the only study of such sport participants, Knechtle and Schulze (2008) investigated the nutritional habits of the runners in the 2006 Deutschlandlauf, which consisted of 1,200 kilometers and 17 stages. Interestingly, 70% of the runners followed no specific eating regimen before such a grueling competition, but during a stage, they preferred carbohydrate-rich foods and water.

Other Lean Sports

Most lean sports are categorized as weight-class, aesthetic, or endurance. But as we suggested in Chapter 1, some sports are difficult to categorize. That is, even though they are not technically weight-class, aesthetic, or endurance sports, they emphasize leanness as facilitating sport performance or positively affecting judging that is based, at least in part, on appearance. Unfortunately, like many other lean sports, their participants may be at increased risk for eating and body image problems.

Ski Jumping

Although the "antigravitation" sport of ski jumping is not technically a weight-class sport, recent changes in the sport have resulted in the establishment of a weight standard that creates a situation similar to "making weight" in traditional weight-class sports. Specifically, a minimum BMI was established to dissuade jumpers from losing too much weight. Because such a weight standard was established, jumpers knew the minimum weight they could attain without penalty. As a result, we would expect to see many jumpers at the minimum weight for their height, not unlike participants in traditional weight-class sports.

Investigations regarding the relationship between a low weight and ski jumping performance have indicated that a lighter jumper flies further with an easier touch down; such advantages did not go unnoticed by male ski jumpers as the mean BMI for competitors in World Cup and Olympic events decreased 4 kg/m^2 from 1970 to 1995 (Müller, 2009). To remedy the problem, a self-regulating approach was suggested in 1995 (Müller, Platzer, & Schmolzer, 1995) in which the length of skis was to be shortened for underweight jumpers. Ski length affects flight, and shorter skis result in shorter flight. Based on this work, the Federation Internationale de Ski (FIS; international governing body for ski jumping) adopted the model but established a lower BMI than the one suggested by Müller et al. (1995). Prior to the 2006 Olympics, the FIS invoked what was termed by some as the "anorexic rule" for male ski jumpers. In the FIS (2006) procedure, skis would be shortened to compensate for the performance advantage of low weight. Skis can be as long as 146% of the skier's height. A weight minimum was established as a nude BMI of 18.5 and a BMI of 20 with ski gear. If the skier was below that standard, his skis were shortened 2% for each kilogram of weight he was below the standard. Was this rule effective? In the 2006 Olympics, only 4 of the top 50 jumpers in the Individual K90 were under a BMI of 18.5 (Sherman, 2007).

Sport Climbing

Sport climbing has rapidly become a very popular sport around the world. More than 70 federations representing five continents make up the International Federation of Sport Climbing (IFSC, 2009). In 2007, the International Olympic Committee (IOC) granted provisional recognition to the IFSC. Like ski jumping, sport climbing is difficult to categorize. Although indoor rock climbing was listed as an antigravitation sport in the classification system proposed by Sundgot-Borgen and Larsen (1993), it is very similar to a lean endurance sport in that low body fat and low body weight are purported to enhance competitive rock climbing performance (Zapf, Fichtl, Wielgoss, & Schmidt, 2001).

In a situation similar to that previously discussed regarding ski jumping, climbers were losing too much weight in an effort to enhance their climbing performance. Although there are no weight measurements and thus no consequences for a low BMI for international competitions, the Austrian federation established a BMI minimum standard of 17 for female climbers and 18 for male climbers. Climbers below those marks are prevented from competing, and those women with a BMI between 17.0 and 18.8 and men between 18.0 and 20.0 can participate, but must consult a sports physician (W. Groschi & W. Müller, personal communication, May 15, 2009). One study examining the nutrient intake and eating habits of elite rock climbers (Zapf et al., 2001) was suggestive of potential eating-related problems. Zapf et al. found that the climbers with better performances

45

had lower BMIs and lower energy and fat intakes. Additionally, nearly 50% of the climbers failed to meet nutritional recommendations for top-level sport activities.

Equestrian

Equestrian is another sport that is somewhat difficult to categorize. In the classification system proposed by Sundgot-Borgen and Larsen (1993), horseback riding was classified as a technical sport. At the time of this writing, there were no studies involving equestrians and eating problems. Nonetheless, we have chosen to include equestrian in this discussion of lean sports because of its apparent risk factors of appearance, revealing (tight, form-fitting) attire, and the fact that it is a judged sport, all of which are characteristics of aesthetic sports. An anecdotal account of our first experience in talking with a collegiate female equestrian team suggests that it is an appearance sport and perhaps has the risks associated with appearance (aesthetic) sports. One young rider in the group said, "Equestrian is the quintessential appearance sport. The horse is the athlete; we just have to look good and try not to fall off." Interestingly, however, the equitation (rider's position when mounted) manual used by USA Equestrian (2002), instructed judges to focus primarily on the rider, compare one rider to another, and try not to be too influenced by the rider's body shape or attractiveness. The fact that the individuals writing the rules for judging thought it was necessary to caution judges not to be too influenced by shape or attractiveness suggests that such appearance factors can and probably do affect judges' scoring.

Other Lean Demand Activities

Other activities that might not be sports in the traditional sense but that appear to carry the same risks as the lean/appearance sports include cheerleading and dance. Although both genders are involved in these activities, the risk for females appears to be much greater.

Cheerleading

It has been suggested that cheerleaders may be at risk for body image and eating problems due to weight issues related to performance—tumbling as well as stunting (being tossed and lifted), appearance, and revealing uniforms (Thompson, 2003). The fact that cheerleading competitions are now occurring at all ages is only apt to increase the risk. Research with female cheerleaders has confirmed the risk factors of weight pressures/ concerns (Gottlieb, Smith, Cleveland, Flick, & Capps, 1994; Reel & Gill, 1996, 1998) and revealing uniforms (Reel & Gill, 1996), as well as the use of disordered eating behaviors as a means to weight control (Gottlieb et al., 1994; Lundholm & Littrell, 1986) and self-deprecatory attitudes regarding their bodies (Freischlag, 1989).

Dance
Dance is similar to cheerleading in terms of its risks in that it is an aesthetic/appearance activity that often employs revealing costumes, and in some forms of dance (i.e., ballet), dancers are lifted by part- ners. Early investigations of nutrient intake indicated that weight and diet were chief concerns and that intake was often inadequate (Druss & Silverman, 1979), sometimes to less than 70% of the RDA (Benson, Geiger, Eiserman, & Wardlaw, 1989). Subsequent studies have con- firmed an increased risk of eating problems (Brooks-Gunn, Warren, & Hamilton, 1987) and associated pathogenic weight loss methods (Hamilton, Brooks-Gunn, Warren, & Hamilton, 1988; Robson, 2001). These problems tend to increase with length of time in ballet (Dotti et al., 2002). Thomas, Keel, and Heatherton (2005) found that ballet stu- dents in more competitive ballet schools were more likely to exhibit disordered eating than those in less competitive schools, and that per- fectionism in these students likely contributed to such eating. What does this mean in terms of eating disorders? Ringham et al. (2006) reported that 83% of the ballet dancers in their study met lifetime cri- teria for an eating disorder, with 6.9% meeting criteria for anorexia nervosa (AN), 10.3% for bulimia nervosa (BN), 10.3% for AN+BN, and 55.0% for eating disorder not otherwise specified. In marked contrast, however, Toro, Guerrero, Sentis, Castro, and Puertolas (2009) did not find ballet students to be more at risk for eating disorders than female adolescents in the general population.

Most of the work in this area has been done with ballet dancers, but at least one investigation regarding modern dancers (Schnitt, Schnitt, & Del A'Une (1986) found many to be underweight but at less risk for eating disor- ders than ballet dancers. A retrospective study investigating a wide range of dance experiences (Annus & Smith, 2009) found that learning experi- ences concerning thinness during dance class rather than the amount of time in dance class predicted adult disordered eating. Nonetheless, three- fourths of the modern dancers in a study by Reel (1998) indicated body image and weight pressures that related to costumes and comparisons with other dancers.

TYPE OF SPORT—NONLEAN

As we reported previously, the preponderance of research indicates that sport participants in the lean sports tend to be more at risk. This is not to suggest that eating problems do not occur in nonlean sports, however. Rosen et al. (1986) reported that one-fourth to one-half of the participants in some nonlean sports (i.e., field hockey, softball, etc.) had used pathogenic weight loss methods. Torstveit and Sundgot-Borgen (2005a) found that 55.3% of elite sportswomen in nonlean sports were at risk for the female athlete triad. Most important, however, is the recent finding of clinical eating disorders in 19.8% of elite sportswomen in nonlean sports by Torstveit et al. (2008). Additionally, body size and body image also appear to be important in nonlean sports, at least for males, as evidenced by studies that found sportsmen in strength sports (i.e., football) desired larger chests, thighs, arms, and legs (Stewart, Benson, Michanikou, Tsiota, & Narli, 2003), as well as a desire by sportsmen in other nonlean sports (i.e., soccer, basketball, swimming, lacrosse, etc.) to be more muscular than their actual physique (Raudenbush & Meyer, 2003).

Swimming

A study by Dummer, Rosen, Heusner, Roberts, and Counsilman (1987) with young competitive swimmers found that 15.4% of the girls and 3.6% of the boys were using pathogenic weight loss methods. Additionally, many of the swimmers were likely to misperceive their body weights, and particularly the girls were likely to perceive themselves as being overweight and larger than their actual weights. The experimenters suggested that the swimmers' weight concerns were more related to societal influences than to the demands of the sport. Regarding the female athlete triad, a study of elite Brazilian swimmers reported that although only 1.3% were assessed to have the triad, 44.9% met criteria for disordered eating (Schtscherbyna, Soares, Oliveira, & Ruberio, 2009).

Even though swimming is often grouped with nonlean sports, as with most sports in recent years, an emphasis has been placed on lowered body fat. Reel and Gill's (2001) investigation of swimmers found that 45% of the female swimmers in their study reported a revealing swimsuit as a stressor. A Spanish study with sportswomen representing 18 sports or events (Toro et al., 2005) found the highest percentage of induced vomiting (10%) in swimmers, who also had concerns related to public body exposure (wearing a swimsuit). Concerns were strongly associated with the presence of eating disorder symptoms and attitudes, such as considering oneself to be fat, fearing weight gain, and dieting to lose weight. These concerns were also found with other sportswomen wearing revealing uniforms or costumes—gymnasts and skaters. However, Krane, Stiles-Shipley, Waldron, and Michalenok (2001) found that sport participants (some of whom were swimmers, gymnasts, and skaters) in different types of uniforms did not differ on body dissatisfaction, drive for thinness, or social physique anxiety (SPA). Similarly, research investigating SPA in sportswomen via sport apparel did not find greater SPA in those who wear more revealing attire (Hausenblas & Mack, 1999; Haase & Prapavessis, 2001).

Ball Game Sports

Marshall and Harber (1996) found that 17.1% of elite female field hockey players demonstrated increased body dissatisfaction compared to 3.6% with an elevated drive for thinness, suggesting that body shape and size were more of a concern than weight. The players assessed to be at risk were "significantly heavier, fatter, and had higher BMIs" (p. 543). But does such body dissatisfaction contribute to disordered eating or eating disorders? Most of the work with ball players has been done by Sundgot-Borgen and Torstveit, who found eating disorders in 5% of elite male ball game players (Sundgot-Borgen & Torstveit, 2004). They also reported that 52.5% of elite female ball game players were at risk for the female athlete triad (Torstveit & Sundgot-Borgen, 2005a). More important, Sundgot-Borgen and Torstveit (2007) reported that 24% of 17 elite female football (soccer) players and 29% of 14 elite handball players met DSM-IV criteria for an eating disorder.

COMPETITION LEVEL AND EATING PROBLEMS

Performance at higher levels of competition is often associated with increased importance and pressure. Additionally, at higher levels the slightest edge may make the difference between medaling and not placing in a national or international competition. As a result, one might assume that risk increases as competition level increases. Certainly, the high percentage of elite sportswomen reported by Torstveit et al. (2008) suggests that many sportswomen at this highest competition level have eating disorders. Are those at higher levels more at risk, and if so, does that increased risk translate to a greater prevalence than those at lower levels?

Again, results have been mixed but suggest that lower competition levels may not be predictive of less risk of eating disturbance. Oliosi, Dalle Grave, and Burlini (1999) reported a high frequency of dieting, weight fluctuation, alcohol abuse, and steroid use in *noncompetitive* bodybuilders. Ravaldi et al. (2003) investigated eating and body image disturbance among *nonelite* female ballet dancers, female gymnasium users, and male *noncompetitive* bodybuilders. Eating disorders were found in 26.6, 20.6, and 14.7% of the dancers, gymnasium users, and controls, respectively, but none of the bodybuilders. Body image disturbance was found in all eating disorder subjects but also in 14.1% of non-ED dancers and in 43.2% of the bodybuilders, suggesting that low competition levels did not serve as a protective factor. Similarly, Toro et al. (2005) found that Spanish sportswomen at higher competition levels scored lower on a measure of disordered eating than those at lower competitive levels. In a study designed to assess the degree to which participation in sports activities among college students was related to eating disordered attitudes and behaviors, Levitt (2008) found that participants in recreational sports appeared to be more at risk than those in organized sports.

Even sport participants at the highest or elite levels of competition were not always found to be more at risk. Ferrand and Brunet (2004) did not find elite cyclists to be at greater risk than those at lower competitive levels, nor did Blaydon and Lindner (2002) when comparing elite versus subelite triathletes. Even more interesting, Harris and Greco (1990) found that elite gymnasts scored *lower* on measures related to disordered eating.

Regarding a direct relationship between eating disorder risk with competition level, recreational runners had a lower percentage of high EAT scores than did elite or collegiate runners (Weight & Noakes, 1987). Similarly, Okano et al. (2005) found a higher prevalence of disordered eating in Japanese gymnasts and runners who competed at higher levels of competition, and Picard (1999) reported more signs of pathological eating and an increased risk for developing an eating disorder in collegiate sportswomen competing at higher levels. Also with collegiate sportswomen, cross country runners from NCAA Division I programs scored significantly higher than did Division III runners on an exercise measure related to risk for developing subclinical and clinical eating disorders (Thompson, Smith, & DeBate, 2004). De Bruin, Oudejans, and Bakker (2007) found that elite female gymnasts dieted and used pathogenic weight loss methods more often than nonelite gymnasts. In comparing varsity athletes, club athletes, and independent exercisers, Holm-Denoma et al. (2009) reported a trend for women who participated in higher levels of competition to have higher levels of eating disorders. Thomas et al. (2005) found ballet students at more competitive schools to be more at risk for disordered eating than those at less competitive schools.

In summary, the exact nature of the relationship between competition level and eating disturbance is unclear. It appears that lower competition levels may not be protective and that higher levels are not always predictive of more eating problems.

BODY IMAGE ISSUES AND PROBLEMS
FOR SPORT PARTICIPANTS

Body image refers to a person's perceptions, attitudes, and experiences about his or her body, and in particular, its appearance (Cash, 2002). Disturbances in body image and body dissatisfaction have been associated with the development of eating disorders (American Psychiatric Association, 1994). For individuals with eating disorders, mood and self-esteem can be related to their perceptions of their body shape and weight (Yager, 2007b). Males are more often satisfied with their bodies than females (Spillane, Boerner, Anderson, & Smith, 2004). When they are dissatisfied with their bodies, many males want to be larger (Raudenbush & Zellner, 1997) or more muscular (Lynch & Zellner, 1999; Pope, Phillips, & Olivardia, 2000), compared to females, who typically want to be smaller or thinner (Silberstein, Striegel-Moore, Timko, & Rodin, 1988). Pope et al. (2000) found that men preferred an ideal body size that was significantly more muscular than their actual size.

Do sportswomen prefer a smaller, thinner body, whereas sportsmen prefer a larger, more muscular body, as did many nonathletes? Selby, Weinstein, and Bird (1990) reported that 14% of male sport participants viewed themselves as being overweight, compared to 63% of female sport

51

participants. In actuality, however, 84% of these women were at a healthy weight. Interestingly, one-third of these sportswomen believed that their coaches thought they were overweight. Wilkins et al. (1991) found that 22% of sportsmen perceived themselves to be underweight compared to 8% of sportswomen, whereas 25% of the women viewed themselves as overweight compared to 7% of the men.

As expected, this trend toward sportswomen desiring a smaller, thinner body and sportsmen a larger, more muscular body was found for sports that have traditionally been associated with a small body, such as women's gymnastics and bodybuilding for men. Harris and Greco (1990) reported that female gymnasts were dissatisfied with their bodies, considered themselves to be fat, and believed their coaches thought they were fat, despite the fact that their weight, BMI, and body fat percent were low. They felt that even a small increase in weight would negatively affect performance. O'Conner, Lewis, Kirchner, and Cook (1996) found that collegiate gymnasts were preoccupied with thinness, but that their body dissatisfaction was more strongly related to a discrepancy between ideal and actual body weight than to percent body fat. De Bruin et al. (2007) found that elite female gymnasts' dieting was more a result of weight-related causal attributions or perceived weight pressures from their coaches than negative body image. Research findings related to bodybuilders include body dissatisfaction and steroid use (Blouin & Goldfield, 1995; Oliosi et al., 1999), body image disturbance (Ravaldi et al., 2003), the taking of supplements designed to increase body size, and frequent body checking (Muller et al., 2004), as well as higher levels of self-objectification and body dissatisfaction than other athletes and controls (Hallsworth et al., 2005).

In a study by Raudenbush and Meyer (2003), college sportsmen in different sports (track/cross country, soccer, basketball, swimming, and lacrosse) preferred a physique that was more muscular than their actual physique. Although most sportsmen appear to desire a larger and sometimes more muscular body, at least one study with cyclists suggested otherwise. Filaire et al. (2007) reported that 46% of elite male cyclists felt pressure to lose weight. They also reported greater negative feelings about their appearance and body weight satisfaction than controls.

Some studies have investigated body image issues in both genders in the same sports. Stewart et al. (2003) assessed male and female athletes for somatotype and body image. Body satisfaction differed regionally by gender, with males desiring a larger chest, thighs, arms, and legs than did female sport participants. As expected, Hausenblas and McNally (2004) found that female track and field athletes reported a greater drive for thinness and body dissatisfaction than the males. Triathlon is an interesting sport in terms of body image in that the three sports involved—cycling, swimming, and running—probably have differing body ideals. The work by DeBate and colleagues (DeBate et al., 2002a, 2002b; Wethington et al., 2002) found that male triathletes tended to perceive themselves to be larger than their BMI and desired to be larger, whereas female triathletes tended to see themselves as smaller than their BMI and wanted to be much smaller. Of the sportswomen whose BMI was in a healthy range, 61%, compared to 19% of the males, wanted to be smaller.

Body dissatisfaction plays a role in eating disorders in nonsport participants. Does it play a similar role in sport participants? In the excellent study by Torstveit et al. (2008), even though nonlean elite sportswomen were found to have fewer eating disorders than their lean sport counterparts, they experienced more body dissatisfaction. In essence, the leaner sportswomen were more satisfied with their bodies, despite more often having an eating disorder. Interestingly, the nonlean sportswomen more often engaged in the use of pathogenic weight loss methods, ostensibly to deal with their greater body dissatisfaction.

Pope and colleagues (Pope & Katz, 1994; Pope, Katz, & Hudson, 1993; Pope et al., 2000) have investigated body-related symptoms or problems in addition to eating disorders—muscle dysmorphia (preoccupation with not being muscular enough), reverse anorexia (misperception of the body as being smaller than it actually is), and steroid use—that have often been associated with male bodybuilders and weightlifters. (For a recent review of the relationship between steroid use and muscle dysmorphia, see Rohman [2009]). Although muscle dysmorphia has sometimes been found with weightlifters and bodybuilders, participation in weightlifting or bodybuilding per se does not appear to be the key risk factor. Olivardia, Pope, and Hudson (2000) found that men with muscle dysmorphia differed from normal comparison weightlifters on body dissatisfaction, eating attitudes, prevalence of anabolic steroid use, and lifetime prevalence of mood, anxiety, and eating disorders. Again, on the positive side, Pickett et al. (2005) did not find competitive bodybuilders to be more muscle dysmorphi han other athletes in their study.

A f note on body image of sport participants involves the fact that body satisfaction and even body image perception and disturbance are more complex than they appear. In support of this notion, we offer the contention by Russell (2004), supported by De Bruin et al. (2007), that a sport participant's body satisfaction may be transient; that is, body satisfaction is different while performing as a sport participant than it is for her outside of the sport arena. This idea may relate to the contention by Powers and Thompson (2008) that body image is not just how an individual sees her body, but that an important aspect of body image may be tactile or kinesthetic. That is, how a person experiences her bodily movements in space and time is also important. Intuitively, it would seem that this type of experience would be particularly important for a sport participant because it relates to how she is performing athletically. Body image among sport participants warrants more empirical investigation, but we recommend that body satisfaction measures be employed that are more complex and sensitive than a single measure taken from an eating disorder screening inventory.

CONCLUDING REMARKS

Research in the area of eating disorders in sport has burgeoned in the past 15 years. At the same time, the apparent incidence and prevalence of eating problems among sport participants continues to be too high. Thus, much of the discussion that follows relates to questions that are more clinical in nature.

Most of the research on sport participants has focused on elite or collegiate levels of competition. These sportsmen and women probably have the most experienced and informed coaches and medical personnel caring for them, and for those reasons, they may be at less risk than younger athletes with fewer and less sophisticated personnel watching out for them. In order to implement prevention efforts, it is critical to focus on younger athletes who are participating in sports at a life stage when body concerns are most critical and at a time when the risk of developing eating disorders is highest.

We agree with Petrie et al. (2007), who recently called for research focusing on risk factors, rather than more athlete (sport-participant) versus nonathlete (nonsport-participant) and sport-type comparisons. Two such factors might include excessive (unhealthy) exercise and revealing sport attire. Excessive or unhealthy exercise plays a role in most eating disorders (Katz, 1996), but may be difficult to identify in athletes because it is apt to be misperceived as a desired behavior rather than as an eating-related symptom (Thompson & Sherman, 1999a, 1999b). Except for a few notable exceptions (e.g., Torstveit & Sundgot-Borgen, 2005a), excessive or unhealthy exercise has not been included in most studies as a variable and possible risk factor for sport participants. Given its role in eating disorders, the belief that increased training is the means to enhanced sport performance, and the difficulty of its identification in the sport environment, such exercise as a risk factor warrants more investigation.

The possible risk factor of revealing sport attire on issues related to social physique anxiety and competitive thinness needs thorough investigation. Preliminary research in this area is at best equivocal. Several relevant questions exist. Does a sportswoman's sport attire affect her attitudes and behaviors related to body satisfaction, eating, and weight? Do some younger sport participants avoid certain sports because of the uniform they are required to wear? Do some sport participants (e.g., divers) become desensitized over time due to repeated exposure? Do some in part choose a sport with revealing attire because they are confident and comfortable with their bodies? Are some sportswomen's feelings and behaviors regarding their comfort with what they are wearing different within and outside of their sport? The issue of revealing sport attire will be discussed further in Chapter 4.

Finally, there is a dearth of studies in this area that are longitudinal in nature. Do factors and effects stand the test of time? Some effects can be adequately judged only over a period of time, such as the effects of rule changes and other preventive efforts that are designed to decrease the risk or prevalence of eating and body image problems in athletes. Oppliger et al.'s (2006) five-year study evaluating the NCAA rule changes regarding weight loss practices in collegiate wrestlers is an illustrative example of the type of research that is needed.

4

Risk Factors for the Development of Problem Eating

Identification of risk factors for eating disorders is important for determining high-risk groups, for designing prevention programs, and for public policy (Striegel-Moore & Bulik, 2007). In this chapter, we will first discuss general (non-sport-related) factors that put individuals at risk for developing an eating disorder—factors that may predispose people to such disorders without regard to sport participation. A full discussion of the risk factors for eating disorders is well beyond the scope of this book. Thus, we will confine our general discussion to two areas of particular interest to researchers and practitioners: genetic and sociocultural factors.

We will then discuss the sport-related risk factors, that is, risk factors that are unique and specific to the sport environment and sport participation. Because sport participants encounter both general and sport-specific risk factors, they are more at risk than those who do not participate in sport. Based on the literature reviewed in Chapter 3, this may or may not result in more eating disorders. Eating disorders are multiply determined; that is, they result from a combination of factors. Whether such a disorder occurs in an individual in sport will be dependent on an interaction cf factors, with sport participation being one of them.

Although sport participants are at increased risk, we do not believe that sport participation should be avoided. On the contrary, sport participation can have a positive effect on general psychological factors, such as psychological well-being (DiBartolo & Shaffer, 2002) and feeling worthwhile (Petrie, 1996), as well as more specific psychological factors, such as self-efficacy (Taub & Blinde, 1992) and self-perceptions of competence and ability (Biddle, 1993). Regarding eating disorders, it has been suggested that sport participation in some cases might act as a buffer against eating-related problems (Fulkerson, Keel, Leon, & Dorr, 1999; Morse, 2008; Wilkins, Boland, & Albinson, 1991). Thus, it is not sport participation that should be avoided, but rather the risks associated with sport. Evidence of this is provided in a study by Hulley, Currie, Njenga, and Hill (2007) in which they compared Kenyan runners, runners from the UK, Kenyan non-sport–participant controls, and a control group of non-sport participants from the UK. Although 19.5% of the UK runners had a present or past eating disorder, the Kenyan runners had the lowest prevalence of such disorders of all four groups and had the least eating disorder pathology. Hulley et al. concluded that distance running in and of itself does not predispose a runner to an eating disorder, but rather eating disorder risk is a combination of risk factors that include culture, sport, and the person—factors that will be discussed in the sections that follow.

GENERAL RISK FACTORS

Genetics

Eating disorders were believed to result primarily from environmental factors prior to recent genetic epidemiological and molecular genetics studies suggesting that such disorders aggregate in families in part due to genetic factors (Mazzeo, Slof-Op't Landt, van Furth, & Bulik, 2006). Family and twin studies have suggested a strong heritable component for eating disorders with heritability estimates as high as 76% for anorexia nervosa (Klump, Miller, Keel, McGue, & Iacono, 2001) and 83% for bulimia nervosa (Bulik, Sullivan, & Kendler, 1998). Association studies indicate that many traits of eating disorders (i.e., obsessionality, perfectionism, etc.) are heritable, while linkage studies have identified genomic regions that could contain genes that predispose an individual to an eating disorder (Kaye et al., 1998).

What does all of this mean to the individual genetically at risk, or to a patient, a patient's family, or a healthcare practitioner? A genetic predisposition does not mean the person will have an eating disorder. Two points we will make numerous times in this book are that eating disorders are determined by multiple factors and that they involve individual differences. Genetic factors may be numerous and vary in their intensity. Manifesting the disorder will require other factors to interact with the genetic predisposition, perhaps at a particular time or developmental stage, to precipitate the disorder in a particular individual. It means that the patient and the patient's family are not to blame. Healthcare practitioners will need to assist the individual in avoiding possible precipitating factors. What does this mean for the relationship between sport and eating disorders? It means that sport participation does not cause eating disorders. Rather, it is another possible risk factor that could precipitate such a disorder. Because genetic factors are out of the individual's control, it indicates the importance of reducing or eliminating risk factors in the sport environment that might interact with the individual's genetic predisposition.

Sociocultural Factors

Striegel-Moore and Bulik (2007) suggest that the evidence supporting a cultural model for the development of eating disorders includes the preponderance of female cases, the increasing incidence coinciding with the decreasing ideal body size for females, higher incidence and prevalence in cultures valuing extreme female thinness, and the relationship between internalization of the thin ideal and disordered eating. They view this thin ideal internalization as increasing body image concerns, which in turn are related to the eating disorder symptoms of body dissatisfaction and dieting.

Media, Family, Peers, and Social Comparison

Stice (2002) has suggested that the idealization of thinness (as well as the disparagement of being overweight) is amplified by the media and promoted by family and peers. Several studies have found the media's amplification of the thin ideal to have an adverse effect on body image, eating attitudes, and eating behaviors (e.g., Becker & Fay, 2006). Likewise, research regarding risks associated with the family suggests the important role played by the family in eating difficulties (Annus, Smith, Fischer, Hendricks, & Williams, 2007; Young, Clopton, & Bleckley, 2004). Regarding the relationship between pressure from peers and eating-related problems, pressure from peers to be thin increased body dissatisfaction in college women (Stice, Maxfield, & Wells, 2003). Related to peer pressure, social (body) comparisons with "fit" (thin) peers not only decrease body satisfaction (Krones, Stice, Batres, & Orjada, 2005; Lin & Kulik, 2002), but they can also affect exercise duration (Wasilenko, Kulik, & Wanic, 2007). Regarding eating disorders and social comparisons, at least one study found that eating disorder patients made less positive comparisons than controls (Troop, Allan, Treasure, & Katzman, 2003). We will discuss the related concept of body comparisons in a later section devoted to competitive thinness.

Genetic and Sociocultural Factors

Rather than thinking in terms of genetic factors *versus* sociocultural factors, it is probably more helpful to think in terms of genetics *and* culture. We know that some individuals are genetically predisposed to an eating disorder, but not all will develop the disorder. We know that a culture that overvalues the thin ideal generates pressures to conform, but not all who live in this culture develop an eating disorder. Most who do develop the disorder will be female, and most of these disorders will have their onset during adolescence. Perhaps it is more helpful to think that genetic factors can set the stage for an eating disorder, but sociocultural factors interact with genetics at just the right (wrong) time to make it happen. In such a scenario, the sociocultural risks in the sport environment may provide the impetus for the onset or exacerbation of disordered eating attitudes and behaviors for some sport participants.

SPORT-RELATED RISKS

Enrique is a 24-year-old middle-distance runner who competes for his national team. He is described by his coach as a leader, whose work ethic is an example for his teammates. In terms of training, he does everything that is required by his coach and more. In fact, he is training significantly more than his teammates. He has been known to train despite illness and even injuries that have included stress fractures. He indicated that he trains under such adverse conditions because he must maintain his ideal competitive weight, body composition, and fitness level in order to perform as he feels he should. Enrique has only partially complied with his trainer's recommendation that he increase his carbohydrate intake in order to adequately fuel his intensive training.

Longitudinal studies are considered to be the gold standard for identifying the risk factors for eating disorders, and such research has not yet been conducted regarding sport competition or participation (Jacobi, 2005). Therefore, it is not possible to conclude with assurance that the following circumstances or issues found in the sport environment constitute risk factors as described by the conceptual framework for a typology of such factors provided by Kazdin and colleagues (Kazdin, Kraemer, Kessler, Kupfur, & Offord, 1997). At the same time, relevant studies regarding risk factors in the nonsport environment, as well as clinical experience, suggest the potential risks to those who participate in sport. Given the possible serious consequences of these potential risk factors to sport participants, we invoke the precautionary principle that says, "When an activity raises threats of harm to human health or the environment, precautionary measures should be taken even if some cause and effect relationships are not fully established scientifically" (Science and Environmental Health Network, 1998).

Weight/Body Fat Reduction and Enhanced Performance

Many, if not most, coaches (and sport participants) believe that "extra" weight can have a detrimental effect on sport performance. As a consequence, pressure from coaches (Berry & Howe, 2000; de Bruin, Oudejans, & Bakker, 2007; Harris & Greco, 1990; Jones, Glintmeyer, & McKenzie, 2005; Kerr, Berman, & De Souza, 2006; Rosen & Hough, 1988; Ryan, 2000; Sundgot-Borgen, 1994a) has been placed on many sport participants in most sports, but certainly in sports that emphasize a small size, a thin shape, or a low weight, in order to lose weight or body fat to enhance performance or to positively affect scores in judged sports. This is controversial because such pressure can precipitate disordered eating or exacerbate an existing disorder. Does the literature indicate that this approach to sport enhancement has merit? Do thinner or leaner sport participants perform better?

Wilmore (1992a) attempted to clarify the issue by suggesting that a high body weight could be an advantage in contact sports only if weight is fat-free, and that a lower body weight can be an advantage in endurance sports if the fat-free mass is not compromised. He maintained that body fat rather than body weight is the critical factor, and within a given sport, the leaner athlete will perform better (Wilmore, 1992b). Research in this area is at best equivocal, as is evidenced by findings in three sports that have often been associated with thinness and eating problems—gymnastics, distance running, and ski jumping.

Gymnastics

Falls and Humphrey (1978) found that the gymnasts who medaled (finished first, second, and third) in a national competition had lower body fat than those who did not place. However, Sherman, Thompson, and Rose (1996) found a curvilinear relationship between gymnast body mass index (BMI) and performance in a world championship; that is, better performance was generally associated with a lower BMI, but performance was negatively affected when BMI became very low.

Distance Runners

Early studies with distance runners (Boileau & Lohman, 1977; Cureton & Sparling, 1980; Pate, Barnes, & Miller, 1985) reported that leaner runners performed better. However, a study by Clark, Nelson, and Evans (1988) with elite female distance runners indicated there was no relationship between fastest racing times and BMI or body weight. Likewise, in a study by Bonogofski, Beerman, Massey, and Houghton (1999), there was no relationship between body size and performance, but interestingly, the faster runners (as judged by 5K PR) were judged to be at greater risk for disordered eating based on scores on a measure of attitudes related to anorexia nervosa (EAT-26). Runners who believed that they would run faster if they lost weight also tended to score higher on the EAT-26. Perhaps this suggests that the belief regarding leanness and better performance is more of a risk factor than low weight.

Ski Jumping

Investigations regarding the relationship between a low weight and ski jumping performance have indicated that a lighter ski jumper flies farther with an easier touch down (Müller, 2009). As was discussed in Chapter 3, a BMI standard was imposed to prevent male skiers from competing at a BMI of less than 18.5 (Federation Internationale de Ski, 2006). With this standard, only 4 of the top 50 ski jumpers in the Individual K90 at the 2006 Olympics were under the standard BMI of 18.5. Did the lightest ski jumpers perform better? The average BMI for all ski jumpers was 19.3, whereas the average for the medalists was 19.5 (Sherman, 2007). However, Müller (2009) has reported that lighter skiers (BMI < 18 kg/m^2) with shortened skis (to 142% of height) have performed well in competitions from 2006 to 2008, which suggests that some skiers may be willing to lose the length of their skis if their lower weight produces the results they seek.

Does Risk Translate Into Disordered Eating Symptoms?

Internalization of the thin ideal, body dissatisfaction, and dieting have been shown to predict the onset of disordered eating (McKnight Investigators, 2003). To establish risk in sport, sport participants must feel pressure regarding weight related to sport and respond with attitudes and behaviors associated with disordered eating. In Chapter 3, we established that participants in lean sports versus those in nonlean sports are at greater risk for body image and eating disturbance (Byrne & McLean, 2001; Davis & Cowles, 1989; Petrie, 1996; Sundgot-Borgen, 1993, 1994a; Sundgot-Borgen & Larsen, 1993; Sundgot-Borgen & Torsteveit, 2004; Torstveit, Rosenvinge, & Sundgot-Borgen, 2008). Additionally, in at least one study (Sundgot-Borgen, 1993), participants in lean sports had the highest use of pathogenic weight control methods, and more importantly in a recent Norwegian study, 46.7% of the participants had eating disorders (Torstveit et al., 2008).

The importance of being female as a risk factor in the sport environment was also established in Chapter 3 with body and eating disturbances in sport occurring significantly more often in females than males. This does not mean that males are exempt from dieting or the risk of an eating disorder, but the primary risk continues to be for women. A study of Swedish sportsmen and women, who competed in the 2002 Winter Olympics and the 2004 Summer Olympics (Hagmar, Hirschberg, Berglund, & Berglund, 2008) found that 47.9% of the men had attempted to lose weight during the 12-month period prior to their Olympic competition. Their dieting, however, did not appear to be related to the development of eating disorders, as none of the sportsmen reported a current eating disorder and only 1.7% (compared to 8.9% for sportswomen) had previously had an eating disorder. Similarly, a recent study with college male sport participants (Petrie, Greenleaf, Carter, & Reel, 2007) found that 1% of the male participants had eating disorders and 16.6% were symptomatic. Petrie et al. indicated that the psychosocial factors usually found with females were generally unrelated to the level of eating pathology in their male sample. Perhaps because females are more at risk, the preponderance of research in this area involves females. Findings in the lean sports of gymnastics, distance running, and figure skating are illustrative of a need or drive for thinness/leanness and related disordered eating attitudes and behaviors.

In gymnastics, preoccupation with thinness has been a common finding with female collegiate gymnasts (O'Connor, Lewis, & Kirchner, 1995; O'Connor, Lewis, Kirchner, & Cook, 1996; Rosen & Hough, 1988). Is this preoccupation with thinness simply a part of a need to be thin for either the appearance or performance of the sport? If not, what other factors could play a role? Studies by Rosen and colleagues (Rosen & Hough, 1988; Rosen, McKeag, Hough, & Curley, 1986) found most female gymnasts were dieting for performance and appearance, and frequently using pathogenic weight control methods, which were often associated with their coaches telling them that they were too heavy. Such weight pressures from coaches were also found in a study by Harris and Greco (1990) in which female gymnasts believed that their coaches thought they were fat, although their weight, BMI, and body fat percent were low. Nonetheless, part of their reason for dieting also appeared to be related to performance, as they believed that even a small increase in weight would negatively affect performance. It could be argued that the aforementioned findings are from early studies and that things have changed in gymnastics in recent years. However, a study by Kerr et al. (2006) comparing perspectives of former and current female gymnasts reported that, although retired versus current gymnasts reported more eating disorders, one issue that has not changed is that gymnasts who receive negative comments regarding their bodies or instructions to lose weight tend to have more disordered eating patterns. Similarly, de Bruin et al. (2007) found that elite female gymnasts' dieting was more a result of weight-related causal attributions or perceived weight pressures from their coaches than negative body image. This focus on coaches is not to blame them but to simply point out their power and influence with their sportswomen, which may be related to dieting and the development of an eating disorder. Sundgot-Borgen (1994b) reported that eating disorders were apt to occur in sportswomen who began an unsupervised diet following being told to lose weight by their coach. Thus, eliminating negative comments from coaches regarding the weight or appearance of their sportswomen would appear to be a logical step in prevention. The best way to accomplish this is not to have coaches involved with sportswomen's weight, a position we will discuss in Chapter 6.

A preoccupation with thinness is also apparent from the literature involving distance runners. Brownell, Rodin, and Wilmore's (1988) survey of male and female runners found that 48% of the women and 24% of the men were preoccupied with being thinner, 48% of the women and 21% of the men feared gaining weight, and 57% of the women and 37% of the men reported being dissatisfied with their size and shape. This preoccupation appears to result in attitudes and behaviors characteristic of disorder eating or eating disorders. For example, Kiernan, Rodin, Brownell, Wilmore, and Crandall (1992) found exercise level (weekly mileage) was positively associated with concerns about excessive weight and eating in male runners. Additionally, more than half of the female distance runners in the study by Rosen et al. (1986) reported the use of pathogenic weight loss methods, but what about the presence of an eating disorder? Clark et al. (1988) reported that 13% of the elite female runners in their study had a history of anorexia nervosa. Additionally, 27% indicated having had a BMI of less than 17, and 9% reported bingeing and purging. Similarly, 16% of elite female distance runners in a study by Hulley and Hill (2001) reported a present diagnosis of an eating disorder, whereas another 3% had received treatment previously for an eating disorder.

A preoccupation with weight and thinness also appears to be a part of figure skating, another sport often associated with eating disorders. More than 90% of female skaters in a study by Taylor and Ste-Marie (2001) reported feeling pressure to lose weight. Also, as reported earlier, 20.5% of the skaters in a study by Barkley (2001) indicated having a history of an eating disorder. Of those with a history of an eating disorder, half reported still having an eating disorder. Most of those with past and current eating disorders indicated that their eating symptoms were related to pressures associated with skating. These pressures were reported to be related to the belief that weight loss was required by the sport in order to conform to aesthetic ideals of figure skating or to obtain better scores.

Findings from the aforementioned studies imply that many coaches pressure their athletes to lose weight or be leaner. Also, many athletes believe that leanness will enhance performance, and that even a small increase in weight will negatively affect it, and are willing to participate in potentially risky behavior (i.e., restrictive dieting, use of pathogenic weight control methods, etc.). That these pressures and beliefs occur despite the fact that the research with respect to leanness enhancing performance is equivocal suggests that educational and preventive attempts are apt to be difficult. We do not have a problem with coaches encouraging their charges to improve their performance, as long as what they are being asked to do does not put them at risk medically or psychologically. The risks associated with dieting are well documented and will not be recounted here. We will discuss this more in Chapter 9, but suffice it to say that asking an individual (sport participant) to engage in a process that could lead to poor physical and psychological health for the sake of possibly enhancing sport performance is more a question of ethics than (sport) science.

Similarity of Good Athlete Traits and Eating Disorder Characteristics

We have suggested that traits of good athletes and eating disorder characteristics (see Table 4.1) are similar (Thompson & Sherman, 1999b), but we are not saying that "good athletes" are pathologically related or similar to eating disorder patients. In fact, when we refer to a good athlete, we are referring to a sport participant who not only performs well athletically but also possesses attributes a coach values. The sport participant who works harder and longer than others, denies (and plays with) pain and injury, is selflessly committed to the team, complies with all coaching instructions, is satisfied with nothing less than perfection, and is willing to lose weight to perform better is a coach's dream. Again, this is not to say that coaches want them to be anorexic, or that anorexia is responsible for their sport success. These traits may constitute a risk in two ways. First, simply possessing these traits may put them at risk. Second, we regard anything that complicates or interferes with identification of an eating disorder as a risk to the individual. An anorexic characteristic could be misperceived as a good athlete trait rather than a possible concern, especially in an individual in a lean sport who is performing well. This issue will be discussed more in this chapter, as well as in Chapter 5.

Of the anorexic characteristics that were included in Table 4.1, the one most researched with respect to sport participants is perfectionism. Interestingly, perfectionism has been associated with feeling fat in women

Table 4.1 Similarities Between Good Athlete Traits and Anorexic Characteristics

Good Athlete	Anorexic Individual
Mental toughness	Asceticism
Commitment to training	Excessive exercise
Pursuit of excellence	Perfectionism
Coachability	Overcompliance
Unselfishness	Selflessness
Performance despite pain	Denial of discomfort

Source: Thompson, R. A., & Sherman, R. T., *Eating Disorders: The Journal of Treatment and Prevention, 17*, 97–102. With permission.

who engage in body comparisons (Striegel-Moore, McAvay, & Rodin, 1986), a topic to be discussed in a later section. Research regarding perfectionism in sport participants suggests that they have higher levels of perfectionism than their nonsport counterparts (Hopkinson, & Lock, 2004; Krane, Stiles-Shipley, Waldron, & Michalenok, 2001; Schwarz, Gairrett, Aruguete, & Gold, 2005). Additionally, perfectionism has often been associated with an increased risk of disordered eating in sportswomen (Duffy, 2008; Hopkinson & Lock, 2004; Schwarz et al., 2005). But perfectionism in sportsmen and women has not always been viewed as problematic. In fact, Forsberg and Lock (2006) suggested that perfection may play a role in sport participation serving as either a protective or risk factor. Regarding perfectionism as protective in sport, Morse (2008) suggested that perfectionism in distance runners may be channeled more healthfully through exercise rather than through disordered eating.

Eating Symptoms May Be Encouraged and Rewarded

In the previous section, we discussed the issues related to the similarity of desired traits regarding sport performance and eating disorder characteristics. Related to that issue is the possibility that eating disorder symptoms may not only be overlooked as symptoms in the sport environment, but may be desired (Thompson & Sherman, 1999a, 1999b). Of particular concern in this regard are dieting and weight loss, amenorrhea or menstrual dysfunction, and excessive exercise.

Dieting and Weight Loss
Dieting for the purpose of weight loss and unhealthy weight loss are symptoms of an eating disorder (American Psychiatric Association [APA], 2000), and such disorders are most common in people most involved in dieting and weight loss (Wilson, 2002). This does not mean that all who diet will develop an eating disorder, as was discussed earlier, but for some (i.e., those genetically predisposed) it may trigger disordered eating or exacerbate an existing disorder. We established that many athletes, especially those in lean sports, are preoccupied with thinness (Brownell et al., 1988; O'Connor et al., 1995, 1996; Rosen & Hough, 1988); feel pressure to lose weight (Taylor & Ste-Marie, 2001); and are dieting for the purpose of performance or appearance (Rosen & Hough, 1988; Rosen et al., 1986), to meet the aesthetic ideal of a sport (Barkley, 2001), or in response to the urging or criticism of a coach (Kerr et al., 2006; Rosen & Hough, 1988;

Rosen et al., 1986). These same sports have been associated with a high prevalence of pathogenic weight control methods (Sundgot-Borgen, 1993) and eating disorders (Torstveit et al., 2008).

Amenorrhea
Although amenorrhea is a diagnostic criterion for anorexia nervosa and menstrual dysfunction is one of the components of the female athlete triad (ACSM, 2007) and a common complication of bulimia nervosa (APA, 2000), it may go unnoticed in the sport environment. Many sportswomen do not report menstrual irregularities for several reasons. They may be reticent about reporting the problem to a male coach or fear that their playing status might be affected. Some report that they do not want their menstrual period because it makes them feel fat, or it interferes with training. Given that the prevalence of amenorrhea has been reported to be as high as 66% in some athletes (Yeager, Agostini, Nattiv, & Drinkwater, 1993), some view it as normal. The most disturbing reports regarding menstrual functioning come from those sport participants who claim that amenorrhea signals that they are training at the appropriate level of intensity. The problem is complicated by the fact that many coaches still view menstrual dysfunction as being normal (Sherman, DeHass, Thompson, & Wilfert, 2005).

Excessive Exercise
Excessive exercise has been listed as a compensatory behavior in bulimia nervosa (APA, 2000) and is a common characteristic of anorexia nervosa (Katz, 1996) and muscle dysmorphia (Pope, Phillips, & Olivardia, 2000). Nonetheless, excessive exercise can be difficult to identify, in both non-sport and sport populations (Powers & Thompson, 2007, 2008), an issue that will be discussed in more depth in Chapter 5. As we suggested earlier, excessive exercise may be viewed as a good athlete trait in that the excessive exerciser may look like a committed individual who is working harder than his or her teammates. Rather than a symptom, it may look more like desirable behavior and a trait that is encouraged and rewarded by a coach.

Competitive Thinness

Women sometimes compete with other women in the context of physical attractiveness, specifically regarding thinness (Cashdan, 1998). They often compare themselves to other women to determine their weight status, and such comparisons may result in a woman feeling fat, which can in turn increase the tendency to engage in body comparisons (Striegel-Moore et al., 1986). This is a process we have referred to as competitive thinness (NCAA, 2005), which involves such body comparisons. When women compare themselves to a thin or fit peer, body dissatisfaction tends to increase (Krones et al., 2005; Lin & Kulik, 2002; Stice, 2002), and in one study these comparisons affected exercise duration (Wasilenko et al., 2007). Also regarding exercise, there appears to be a rivalry or competition among some women in exercise classes regarding body size, shape, and fitness level (Maguire & Mansfield, 1998). Reel (1998) investigated weight pressures among dancers and found sources of pressure that included comparisons with other dancers and peers noticing weight gain.

As we have suggested, women who compete in sport live in the same sociocultural environment with the same risks as those who are not involved in sport—in this case the risk is competitive thinness unrelated to sport. Based on reports from our patients, however, competitive thinness also operates within the sport environment. Sport participants are competitive—that is in part why they are in sports and in part why they perform well athletically. Competitive thinness within sport could involve physical attractiveness, but also athletic performance. Striegel-Moore et al. (1986) suggested that evaluation of one's body can be activated under feedback circumstances related to performance, even if the performance in question is unrelated to body size.

De Bruin, Bakker, and Oudejans (2009) suggested that highly ego-involved performers want to outperform everyone and will compare themselves with opponents and teammates, including a comparison of thinness. If a sportswoman is in a performance circumstance such as a competition, especially one that is being judged, body comparisons are likely. As we established earlier, many coaches and sport participants believe that the leaner, thinner sportswomen will perform better. If a sport participant in an aesthetic sport is defeated in a competition by a teammate or competitor, a body comparison with the winner could occur by a sportswoman who believes that the other individual performed better because she was thinner. This could provide a rationale for attempted weight loss, putting the person at risk. De Bruin et al. found that female gymnasts and dancers who are strongly ego oriented tend to exhibit more disordered eating correlates than those with a task (skill mastery) orientation.

For examples of body comparison and competitive thinness in the words of sportswomen who have experienced them, see Table 4.2. In many

Table 4.2 Sportswomen's Comments on Body Comparisons (BCs), Competitive Thinness (CT), and Revealing Sport Attire (RSA): In Their Own Words

1. "If she is competing against me, I definitely cannot win. I don't have such a thin body."[a] (CT, BC)
2. "Due to body comparisons with other athletes, I did not feel good enough … everyone was thinner, stronger, and more beautiful than me. I was always occupied with the others, watching how thin they were."[a] (BC)
3. "If I did not eat then my teammate did not eat either. That was an unspoken rule: 'I eat what you eat and preferably less.' It was also a kind of rivalry."[a] (CT)
4. "Everyone walks around in their swimsuits and everyone's wearing next to nothing—you can't hide … I felt like everyone was comparing me to the next person—like everyone thinks I'm the fattest, grossest person here."[b] (RSA, BC)
5. "I saw people comparing others and I knew that people were looking at my body and that made me more conscious of it."[b] (BC)
6. "I was really conscious going out onto the court having to wear those [bun huggers], especially because the yellow ones make your butt look bigger."[b] (RSA)
7. "Everybody was comparing each other. People were always making comments about other people's bodies—I remember really wondering what I was going to wear to practice because I didn't want to look big."[b] (BC, RSA)

[a] De Bruin, A. P. et al., *"Tell Me About Your Eating Disorder": Elite Women Athletes' Narratives and the Meaning of Their Eating Disorder.* Manuscript submitted for publication.
[b] From Greenleaf, C., *Women in Sport and Physical Activity Journal, 11,* 63–88, 2002.

sports, especially the aesthetic sports, body comparisons and competitive thinness can be facilitated by revealing sport attire.

Revealing Sport Attire

Objectification theory suggests that culture socializes females to adopt observers' perspectives on their physical selves (Fredrickson & Roberts, 1997); that is, they are socialized to treat themselves as objects to be evaluated on their appearance. Self-objectification has been found not only to increase body shame and restrained eating, but also to affect mental (math) performance for young women (Fredrickson, Roberts, Noll, Quinn, & Twenge, 1998). But, does self-objectification play a role in the sport environment? The work of Reel and colleagues would suggest that it does, as dancers reported costumes as a source of pressure related to body image and weight (Reel, 1998; Reel, SooHoo, Jamieson, & Gill, 2005). In a survey of cheerleaders, 58% indicated that revealing uniforms constituted the greatest pressure related to weight (Reel & Gill, 1996). Similarly, 45% of swimmers reported a revealing swimsuit as a stressor (Reel & Gill, 2001). Interviews with sport participants have also indicated that uniforms affected how they felt about their bodies, and in particular made them more conscious of, and mostly unhappy with, the shape of their bodies (Greenleaf, 2002). Does this relate to disordered eating? In a study of elite Spanish sportswomen (Toro et al., 2005), the highest prevalence of induced vomiting was found in swimmers who had the greatest concerns regarding "public body exposure" (revealing swimsuit). A qualitative study with elite female sport participants suggested that such uniforms can play a role in disordered eating (De Bruin, Oudejans, Bakker, & Woertman, 2009).

We have several concerns regarding revealing attire for sportswomen. First, from a purely functional point of view, if the individual is physically or psychologically uncomfortable in her uniform, she may be distracted from her sport performance. If she feels too exposed, it may foster more body consciousness, body image concerns, and a desire to lose weight in order to improve her appearance (and psychological comfort). We are also concerned that revealing uniforms make unhealthy body comparisons too easy.

It is interesting to note that women's sports with the most revealing uniforms or attire are usually lean sports that are judged, such as aesthetic sports. As we discussed in Chapter 3, females in the aesthetic sports (diving, equestrian, figure skating, gymnastics, and synchronized swimming) wear revealing attire and have a higher prevalence of eating difficulties than women in other sports, most of which (volleyball being an exception) do not have revealing attire. We do not regard this as a coincidence but rather as a complex issue possibly involving sexism, which should become more apparent in the discussion that follows.

As we have reported previously, females are more at risk for body image and eating-related disturbances. Are males affected by self-objectification? A study by Hallsworth, Wade, and Tiggeman (2005) found that bodybuilders experienced significantly higher levels of self-objectification than weightlifters or controls and more body dissatisfaction than controls, which suggested greater emphasis on appearance for the bodybuilders. However, this does not deal directly with the issue of revealing uniforms. At the present time, it is difficult to know whether uniforms are an issue or stressor for males. It is interesting to note that, when uniforms or sport attire are

71

FIGURE 4.1   Male high jumper. (Courtesy IOC/John Huet.)

revealing for males, their revealing nature can be explained at least partially in terms of functionality, such as a (Speedo) brief for male divers and swimmers. That is, the uniform serves a specific function (i.e., reduced drag in the water, unrestricted movement, etc.). In such cases, females in the same sport will also wear revealing attire, ostensibly because of function. However, the same explanation involving functionality cannot be made regarding other sports, such as beach volleyball, indoor volleyball, gymnastics, figure skating, and track and field. Why are women's uniforms in such sports more revealing than those of males? If their uniforms were really selected for functionality (facilitate sport performance), wouldn't males be wearing the same uniform? The photos that follow are illustrative.

In Figure 4.1, an elite-level male high jumper is wearing a jersey and shorts that are typical of not only high jumpers but most male track and field athletes at the elite level of competition. Most observers probably would not judge his uniform to be particularly revealing. Contrast the male high jumper's uniform with that of the elite female high jumper pictured in Figure 4.2. Why is her uniform different from that of the male? She is doing the same movements in the same sport, but yet her uniform

FIGURE 4.2 Female high jumper. (Courtesy IOC/Kishimoto.)

top is smaller and she is wearing a bikini bottom. Why is her midriff bare? Does her uniform provide a performance advantage over that of the male? It is unlikely; if it did, he would probably be dressed like her. Why is this type (style) of uniform worn by most sportswomen in most of the events in elite track and field?

The difference in sport uniforms is even more pronounced in the sport of beach volleyball. In Figure 4.3, two elite male beach volleyball players are dressed in loose-fitting jerseys and shorts. Again, most observers probably would not consider the uniforms as particularly revealing. Contrast their uniforms with those of the elite female beach volleyball players in Figure 4.4. The women are wearing tight bikinis with much of their bodies exposed. Again, they are playing the same sport as the men pictured in Figure 4.3. Why are their uniforms so different?

Our concern relates to girls and women who may feel uncomfortable wearing sport attire as revealing as those just pictured. Some young sport participants may not participate in a particular sport because of what they will be required to wear. Many sportswomen may not be affected by having to wear such attire, but what of those who are? Will they be

73

FIGURE 4.3   Male beach volleyball players. (Courtesy IOC/Kishimoto.)

"motivated" to engage in unhealthy weight loss strategies to try to lose weight in order to "look better?" Such uniforms also make unhealthy body comparisons much too easy. Will those comparisons lead to body consciousness, body dissatisfaction, and disordered eating? Why do sports use such attire? Who makes the decisions about uniforms? Why would women's uniforms be so much more revealing than those of men in the same sport? For examples of how sportswomen describe their experiences wearing revealing sport attire, see Table 4.2.

Contagion Effect

Crandall (1988) suggested that social pressures in groups (i.e., athletic teams) arising from social norms in the group regarding eating can lead group members to engage in behaviors consistent with those norms. This "social contagion" of Crandall's sounds as though the issue in question is contagious, that is, can spread among group members. We have seen this contagion effect in our clinical work with sport participants, but recent empirical studies suggest its existence as well. Engel et al. (2003) found

FIGURE 4.4   Female beach volleyball players. (Courtesy IOC/Kishimoto.)

that a sport participant's restrictive eating was associated with his or her perception that team members were excessively dieting to control their weight. Interestingly, the male's sport (e.g., wrestling) was more likely to affect his food restricting behavior than the female's sport. Related to this apparent contagion effect was Engel et al.'s contention that team-mates might not only model disordered eating, but also encourage it to new team members. Similarly, in a French study, elite male judoists and cyclists (Filaire, Rouveix, Pannafieux, & Ferrand, 2007) reported that one of the main sources of pressure regarding body image and weight came from fellow judoists and cyclists. The researchers suggested that a team environment might provide a subculture that stresses the importance of thinness through pressure to diet and be thin.

Subcultural Expectations/Pressures

Perhaps related to the contagion effects just discussed are aspects of a sport's subculture that emphasize a particular size, shape, or weight, and the methods used to attain such a sport body "ideal." Interestingly, male sports may have the dubious honor of leading the way in this regard. Wrestling is an obvious example. From the review of studies with wres-tlers and jockeys in Chapter 3, it is apparent that the use of pathogenic weight control methods has been a part of these sports for many years. Unfortunately, it has been an accepted part of this sport. When risky behaviors are accepted as a normal part of a sport, they become more of a risk because the sportsmen assume they are "okay" because "everybody does it" and apparently have been doing it for many years. Three colle-giate wrestlers who died as a result of weight cutting in 1997 were all with coaches when they were engaging in dehydration techniques (Thompson, 1998). How did this happen? Their attempts to cut large amounts of weight in a short period of time were an accepted part of the sport. The National Collegiate Athletic Association made several changes that appear to be changing the amount of weight lost and gained between wrestling com-petitions (Oppliger, Utter, Scott, Dick, & Klossner, 2006). Hopefully, wres-tlers will heed those safeguards, which will likely depend not only on performance but also on the support and enforcement of the new rules by their coaches. However, there were also safeguards in place prior to the deaths of the wrestlers. Also, sportsmen were hospitalized and unable to compete at the 2008 Summer Olympics because of serious medical compli-cations resulting from weight cutting (Thompson & Sherman, 2009).

We began this chapter by discussing the risk factors associated with eating disorders, and in addition to genetics, we emphasized the risks in the sociocultural environment. Regarding the sociocultural pressures related to the development of eating disorders, Stice (2002) suggested that such pressures are promoted by family and peers. In the subculture of a sport, we think of coaches and teammates as the sportsman's "other family." Subcultural risk factors have to be prevented rather than promoted at this level. We will discuss this more in Chapter 9.

Aesthetic/Lean/Judged Sports

As we established in Chapter 3 and reiterated in previous sections of this chapter, sportswomen in aesthetic sports appear to be at highest risk. With these sports' accumulated risk factors of being primarily female, being appearance focused, emphasizing thinness, being judged, wearing revealing uniforms, and stressing competitive thinness, we believe that these sports themselves should be considered risk factors.

Special Risks: Injury/Depression, Overtraining Syndrome, and Sexual Abuse

Injury/Depression

Injured sport participants may be at risk for eating-related problems, especially if the injury curtails or precludes training and competition. Without the rigors of training and competition, the individuals, especially those in lean sports, may become concerned about weight gain due to a significant reduction in physical activity. Depression may be a consequence of injury (Noakes, 2003), and depression is apt to affect the person's eating and weight (APA, 2000) in either direction. Some individuals are inclined to eat more when depressed, whereas others may have less of an appetite and eat less. Those who eat more may be concerned about weight gain due to eating changes but also because they are less physically active. Part of the individual's depression related to injury may be due to the fact that he or she cannot engage in the activity (sport) through which he or she finds self-esteem and an important sense of identity. Depression is a common comorbid condition with eating disorders and may precede or follow the onset of the eating disorder (Bulik & Allison, 2002); it is apt to worsen an existing eating problem and can complicate treatment and recovery.

Overtraining Syndrome
Symptoms of overtraining syndrome (staleness) include fatigue, amenorrhea, weight loss, sleep disturbance, and depression, in addition to a decrement in sport performance (Raglin & Wilson, 2000). Interestingly, this list of symptoms could also describe an individual with an eating disorder, not to mention that excessive exercise occurs frequently in anorexia nervosa (Katz, 1996) and is a common compensatory behavior in bulimic patients (APA, 2000). The issue regarding excessive exercise is relevant as the prevalence of staleness/overtraining syndrome has been reported to be as high as 64% among sportsmen and women in some endurance sports (Raglin & Wilson, 2000), and endurance sports have a high prevalence of eating disorders (Sundgot-Borgen & Torstveit, 2004; Torstveit, Rosenvinge, & Sundgot-Borgen, 2008). The recommended treatment for overtraining syndrome is complete rest (Raglin & Wilson, 2000). However, the good athlete we described earlier is apt to respond to poor sport performance by training even harder or attempting to decrease her weight or body fat through dietary restriction in an effort to improve performance. Because the onset of eating disorders is usually during adolescence (APA, 2000), it is important to realize that overtraining syndrome or staleness can occur in younger athletes as evidenced by a multicultural study that found the syndrome in 35% of adolescent swimmers (Raglin, Sawamura, Alexiou, Hassmen, & Kentta, 2000).

Sexual Abuse/Harassment
Canadian (Kirby, Greaves, & Hankivsky, 2000; McGregor, 1998), Danish (Toftegaard, 2001), Norwegian (Fasting, Brackenridge, & Sundgot-Borgen, 2003), and Australian (Leahy, 2001) studies have reported high rates of sexual harassment or abuse in sportswomen, often occurring within the sport environment. A study with Norwegian elite female sportswomen indicated that sexual harassment occurs in all sports (Fasting, Brackenridge, & Sundgot-Borgen, 2004). We are including this brief discussion of sexual harassment and abuse in sport because child sexual abuse is considered to be a nonspecific risk factor for eating disorders (Wonderlich, Brewerton, Jocic, Dansky, & Abbott, 1997).

Recently, the scope of abusive experiences has been broadened to include other experiences of childhood and adolescence, such as bullying, date violence/rape, physical neglect, and emotional abuse; eating disorder symptoms have been associated with these various forms of abuse (Brewerton, 2005). At least one study (Sherwood, Neumark-Stzainer, Story, Beuhring, & Resnick, 2002) with 7th, 9th, and 11th grade girls found that girls in weight-related sports were more likely to have eating disorders than girls in non-weight-related sports, as might be expected. Not expected, however, was the disturbing finding that the girls in weight-related sports with eating disorders had experienced more physical and sexual abuse than their counterparts without eating disorders. Sexual harassment and abuse have also been found in elite athletes with eating disorders. About 4% of Norwegian sportswomen reported that sexual harassment or sexual abuse was a reason for the development of their disorder (Sundgot-Borgen, 1994a), and a higher percentage of elite sportswomen with eating disorders than sportswomen without eating disorders reported experiencing sexual harassment or abuse (Sundgot-Borgen, Fasting, Brackenridge, Torstveit, & Berglund, 2003).

There are several potential problems with a sportsman or woman who has an eating disorder or has experienced sexual harassment or abuse, not the least of which is the difficulty in reporting. For many, the fear or shame associated with such issues may preclude reporting either an eating disorder or sexual harassment/abuse. Additionally, the individual may not remember sexual abuse experiences. It is important to ask an individual with an eating disorder about abuse experience or an abuse survivor about eating problems, but this must obviously be done by a very sensitive and experienced practitioner. For more information related to trauma, see a special issue on the subject entitled "Eating Disorders and Trauma" in *Eating Disorders: The Journal of Treatment and Prevention* (Levitt & Sansone, 2007).

Identification Difficulties

We regard any factor or issue that complicates or interferes with the identification of body image or eating-related problems as constituting a risk. Identification difficulties can cause a delay in referrals for appropriate treatment, thereby increasing the likelihood of serious medical and psychological consequences. There are several aspects of the sport environment that can complicate or interfere with identification, and these will be discussed in the next chapter.

FINAL THOUGHTS

As we indicated at the beginning of this chapter, very little research has been undertaken with sport participants to adequately test many of the potential risk factors and the variables that may moderate them that were discussed in this chapter. For a more in-depth discussion of these risk factors and moderator variables in the sport environment, as well as their inclusion as part of an innovative etiological model, the reader is directed to Petrie and Greenleaf (2007).

5

Identification of Eating Disorders and Related Conditions

Identification is the most important part of the process leading to recovery from an eating disorder because without it, treatment and recovery do not occur. Even delayed identification can lead to a longer duration of the disorder and thus greater medical and psychological consequences and complications to the sufferer. Although identification can sometimes be complicated and difficult in individuals outside of sport, it can be even more difficult within sport. In this chapter, we will first discuss issues that are specific to sport participation or the sport environment that can complicate or interfere with identification for the athlete, sport personnel, and healthcare professionals. We will also discuss practical recommendations for overcoming such identification problems, as well as more formal assessment measures and procedures.

ISSUES COMPLICATING IDENTIFICATION

Sport Body Stereotypes

In society and in the sport environment, those in sport are often expected to display a particular body size or shape that has become characteristic of a sport—what we have called "sport body stereotypes" (Sherman & Thompson, 2001). For example, jockeys are expected to be short, whereas basketball players are expected to be tall. We expect distance runners to be thin and Sumo wrestlers to be fat. Elite female gymnasts are tiny and (American) football players are expected to be huge. In this form of selective perception, expectations can affect perception and possibly identification of eating disorder signs and symptoms among certain sport groups. If, for example, the expectations are that elite female gymnasts are supposed to be tiny and distance runners are supposed to be thin, a gymnast who is too tiny or a distance runner who is too thin might be difficult to notice because her body is consistent with the stereotype. This could mean that sport personnel or sport participants would be less apt to perceive a size or shape as unhealthy if it is the expected one. Thus, an at-risk gymnast or runner might be overlooked. Contrast this with a bigger gymnast or a heavier runner. Because the bigger gymnast and the heavier runner do not fit the stereotype, they would be more noticeable. Thus, they might also be more likely to be perceived in the sport environment as having a problem (than those who fit the stereotype) if sport performance decreased or was less than expected.

Symptoms Versus "Normal" or Desired Characteristics in Sport

As we discussed in the previous chapter regarding risks for eating disorders, desired traits in sport participants can be characteristics of individuals with eating disorders or symptoms of an eating disorder (Thompson & Sherman, 1999a, 1999b). One of these symptoms is amenorrhea, but amenorrhea is often considered to be normal in the sport environment. In a study of collegiate coaches of female sports, less than half viewed amenorrhea to be "not normal and requiring medical referral" (Sherman, DeHass, Thompson, & Wilfert, 2005). In the same study, only 23% of coaches indicated that they would be aware if any of their team members missed three consecutive menstrual periods. Combine this with sport participants who either do not want a menstrual cycle, view amenorrhea as normal, or would be afraid or uncomfortable to talk about such issues, and identification of the possible eating disorder symptom of amenorrhea is made much more difficult and unlikely.

Another classic eating disorder symptom is weight loss. However, a sport participant who is losing weight may not be viewed as at risk. If she is losing weight, ostensibly for the purpose of performing better athletically, she is not apt to be identified as at risk, especially in a sport in which leanness is valued. But, is she simply losing weight to perform better? Is

82

she losing weight because she has an eating disorder? In a sport environment that values leanness and subscribes to the belief that performance is enhanced by losing weight, the at-risk individual may be viewed as engaging in a desired or valued behavior (dieting and losing weight).

If a sportsman is training harder and longer than his teammates, he is not apt to be identified as at risk. Training levels have increased significantly in recent years (Raglin & Wilson, 2000). Because of this, his "hard work" or "commitment to training" may not only be viewed as normal, but they are apt to be valued and even rewarded. But is he exercising excessively or in an unhealthy manner? Is his exercise in need of intervention? If so, is it part of an eating-related problem? We established that such behavior is characteristic of individuals with eating disorders, but this sportsman is not apt to be identified as at risk because his commitment to training is what coaches want to see. Most coaches (and athletes) view training as the single most important factor in improving athletic performance (Bompa, 1983). If it is what coaches want and expect to see in their team, it is not apt to be identified or even suspected as being problematic or symptomatic.

Gender Bias

A point we will continue to make is that the sport world is a microcosm of the society at large. Thus, what we find in the general population, we expect to find in the subpopulation of sport participants. In Chapter 3, we established that males are much less apt to have an eating disorder than their female counterparts. Additionally, males tend to have a different body focus than females. They tend to be more dissatisfied with their bodies from the waist up, while females tend to be more dissatisfied from the waist down (Andersen, 1999). When males in the general population are dissatisfied with their bodies, many want to be larger (Raudenbush & Zellner, 1997) or more muscular (Lynch & Zellner, 1999a; Pope, Phillips, & Olivardia, 2000), compared to females, who typically want to be smaller or thinner (Silberstein, Striegel-Moore, Timko, & Rodin, 1988). Berg and Andersen (2007) have suggested that eating disorders in males may be underidentified because males differ from females on certain nonessential characteristics, such as focusing more on the upper body than lower and desiring a shape change to a lean muscularity rather than weight loss, and that dieting is atypical with males. Research with males in sport confirms these same body preferences in that they want to be bigger in the arms, chest, and legs (Johnson, Powers, & Dick, 1999; Stewart, Benson, Michanikou, Tsiota, & Narli, 2003) and more muscular (Raudenbush & Meyer, 2003). Additionally, Berg and Andersen (2007) have reported that eating disorders are probably underidentified or underdiagnosed in males because males may feel too ashamed to report the disorder, because commonly used formal assessments may not be appropriate for males, and because current diagnostic criteria are gender biased.

Male sport participants with eating disorders are apt to be underidentified for the same reasons as males in the general population. Additionally, there may be another reason male sport participants are underidentified, and that relates to the nature of their disordered eating. In one of the largest studies with male sport participants Johnson et al. (1999) found no cases of anorexia nervosa or bulimia nervosa. However, 12% of the males in their collegiate sample were binge eating and 38% were assessed to be at risk for bulimia nervosa. Because many males in sport want to become larger and more muscular, they may be trying to gain weight through eating more, perhaps overeating or even binge eating, and increasing their time in the weight room. Because the increased eating and heavy lifting might be viewed as normal and desirable, respectively, for males, especially those in power sports, these behaviors are less likely to be identified as symptomatic or problematic.

Presumption of Health With Good Performance

When most people think of individuals who compete in sport, especially at higher levels of competition, they think of these individuals as being healthy. This presumption of health may in part be a result of what sport participants are able and willing to endure during training, conditioning, and competition. Because they display such toughness and physical prowess, we presume that they must be healthy. In our clinical practice, we have had numerous coaches and parents ask, "How can she perform so well, if she is sick with an eating disorder?" It is a very good question. Many with eating disorders do perform well despite their disorder, some longer than others. There are several possible answers to the question. Many individuals with an eating disorder, especially those who are anorexic, tend to display hyperactivity even when malnourished or because they are malnourished (Hebebrand et al., 2003). Some appear to be driven by their anxiety, fear, perfectionism, or compulsiveness, whereas some are driven by diet pills or excessive amounts of caffeine. Some are driven by their need to please (or fear of displeasing) coaches, teammates, parents, friends, and fans. And some may simply be mentally tougher and stronger than the rest of us in their "ability" to deny pain, discomfort, and fatigue. Regardless of the reason, the eating disorder will eventually compromise physical and psychological health to the point that sport performance has to decrease. When this occurs, these sport participants will be motivated (feel pressure) to try one or both ways they believe will enhance performance—lose weight and train harder. Obviously, we want to identify these individuals before they reach this point.

PREPARTICIPATION EXAMINATION

A recurring theme in this book is the need for early identification. Certainly, the preparticipation physical examination (PPE) that frequently occurs prior to the start of a sport season at many competitive levels provides an excellent opportunity to screen for eating-related difficulties. Various sport organizations (e.g., National Collegiate Athletic Association [NCAA]), health organizations (e.g., American Academy of Family Physicians), and sport medicine groups (e.g., American Medical Society of Sports Medicine) have recommended the content for PPEs, often based on a compendium developed through a joint venture involving the American Academy of Family Physicians, American Academy of Pediatrics, American Medical Society of Sports Medicine, American Orthopedic Society of Sports Medicine, and the American Osteopathic Academy of Sports Medicine (2004).

Consistent with the goal of early identification, the Position Stand on the Female Athlete Triad (American College of Sports Medicine [ACSM], 2007) recommends a screening for triad components at a preparticipation exam that includes a patient history, physical examination, and appropriate laboratory tests. The PPE is an ideal time to screen for eating-related difficulties (i.e., eating disorders, disordered eating, body image concerns, unhealthy exercise, menstrual functioning, bone health, etc.), but many existing PPEs vary with regard to the extent to which they screen for such difficulties. One that does address these issues, however, was developed by Mar Mountjoy, MD, for the Medical Commission of the International Olympic Committee (IOCMC). The contents of the PPE, as well as the triad screening questions and interview, are contained in Table 5.1. Additionally, more information on the PPE is available in Chapter 8.

Table 5.1 Female Athlete Triad Preparticipation Physical Exam and Screening

General History

(These items are part of the full PPE—not specific to triad alone.)

- Date:
- Age:
- Sport/discipline:
- Level of competition:
- Training regimen (weekly hours of training):
- Medications: Please list all of your medications (including oral contraceptives).

Physical Examination

- Height: Weight:
- Blood pressure: Pulse:
- Physical signs of eating disorder:
  (lanugo, parotid gland enlargement, carotonemia)
- Percent body fat (fat calipers):
- Tanner staging
- Skin: acne/male pattern hirsutism
- Musculoskeletal injury assessment
- **Laboratory examination** (as indicated)
- Hematology:
  CBC and differential, ferritin, vitamin B12, folate
- Biochemistry:
  Electrolytes, liver function tests, iron, TIBC, ferritin, MG phosphorus, Ca, cholesterol, total protein, albumin
- Hormone profile:
  TSH, T3, T4, LH/FSH, estradiol, testosterone, 17-OH-progesterone, sex hormone binding capacity, cortisol, DHEA-S and androstenadione, IGF-I
- Urinalysis
- Others: Electrocardiogram, bone mineral density

Triad Screening Questionnaire

• Are you satisfied with your eating pattern?	YES	NO
• Do you worry about your weight/body composition?	YES	NO
• Are you a vegetarian?	YES	NO
• Do you lose weight to meet weight requirements for your sport?	YES	NO

Table 5.1 Female Athlete Triad Preparticipation Physical Exam and Screening (Continued)

• Does your weight affect the way that you feel about yourself?	YES	NO
• Do you worry that you have lost control over how much you eat?	YES	NO
• Do you make yourself sick when you are uncomfortably full?	YES	NO
• Do you currently suffer or have you ever suffered in the past with an eating disorder?	YES	NO
• Do you ever eat in secret?	YES	NO
• What was your age at your first menstrual period? _____		
• Do you have regular menstrual cycles?	YES	NO
• How many menstrual cycles did you have in the last year? _____		
• When was your most recent menstrual period? _____		
• Have you had a stress fracture in the past?	YES	NO

Interview for Those Athletes Identified as High Risk for the Triad by Questionnaire
- Do you want to weigh more or less than you do?
- If you lose weight regularly to meet weight requirements for your sport, how do you do it?
- How much of an issue is weight/body composition for you?
- Do you think your performance is directly affected by your weight? If so, how?
- Do you have forbidden foods?
- Do you miss meals? If so how often?
- Do you have rapid increases or decreases in your body weight?
- What do you consider your ideal (competitive) weight?
- What do you do to control your weight?
- Does it worry you if you have missed a workout?
- What exercise do you do in addition to training for your sport?
- What are the stressors in your life outside of sport?
- What is your family structure?
- How do you cope with stress?
- Do you use laxatives, diuretics, self-induced vomiting, diet pills, or sitting in a sauna to lose weight?

Table 5.1 Female Athlete Triad Preparticipation Physical Exam and Screening
(Continued)

- Review of systems (headaches/visual problems, galactorrhea/acne/male pattern hair distribution)
- Complete history of injuries
- Nutritional analysis assessing energy balance and nutrient balance

Source: The International Olympic Committee Medical Commission. With
permission.

A final note on the PPE contained in Table 5.1: Obviously, because it
screens for the triad, it was developed for use with sportswomen. However,
a sign of a useful PPE is its adaptability. With only a few modifications
(i.e., elimination of questions related to menstrual function), it could also
be used with sportsmen.

SPECIAL IDENTIFICATION ISSUES AND RECOMMENDATIONS

In this section, we will give particular emphasis to excessive exercise
because of its complexity and prevalence in the sport environment, and
to the inevitable and controversial issue of the perceived or actual overweight sport participant. Other issues to be discussed include body-shaping drugs and vegetarianism versus pseudovegetarianism.

Excessive Exercise

Estimates of the prevalence of excessive exercise in eating disorder
patients range from 33% to more than 80% (Katz, 1996). The presence of
such exercise in patients is clinically significant in that it is associated particularly with anorexia nervosa (purging subtype) and with high levels
of trait anxiety, depression, obsessionality, and perfectionism (Shroff et
al., 2006). Excessive activity is also one of the last symptoms to improve
during treatment, and its presence tends to extend the recovery period
(Solenberger, 2001).

There are several issues with excessive exercise that make it difficult to identify in the general population and especially in the sport
subpopulation. Part of the difficulty is with the term itself. More than 30

terms have been used in the literature to describe or define such exercise (Adkins & Keel, 2005). *Excessive* implies too much in terms of frequency, duration, and intensity of the physical activity. Thus, it would appear to be a quantitative term. However, in the DSM-IV-TR (American Psychiatric Association [APA], 2000), exercise is defined more qualitatively as excessive if it "significantly interferes with important activities, when it occurs at inappropriate times or in inappropriate settings, or when the individual continues to exercise despite injury or other medical complications" (pp. 590–591). Considerable research has also suggested that such exercise is not unidimensional and that it involves more than just the quantity of such exercise (Ackard, Brehm, & Steffen, 2002). Thus, it should also be evaluated using qualitative variables such as attitudes (Seigel & Hetta, 2001), motivation (Beumont, Arthur, Russell, & Touyz, 1994), and emotions (Steffen & Brehm, 1999) such as anxiety (Beumont et al., 1994) or guilt (Mond & Calogero, 2009) when prevented from exercising. Additionally, Adkins and Keel (2005) found that exercise among bulimic patients was more compulsive than excessive.

We previously discussed the presumption of health associated with sport participants. That presumption of health would probably also be associated with exercise. That is, people who exercise frequently and intensely would be presumed to be healthy, and their presumed health would at least in part be attributed to exercise. Also, those who exercise more might be presumed to be very healthy. And, they may be. Certainly, elite sport participants would constitute a group that trains heavily and would be presumed to be healthy. However, even for such highly trained individuals, exercise needs to be balanced with a host of factors that determine whether it improves or compromises health. In Chapter 2, we discussed how low energy availability (inadequate energy available to the body after accounting for physical activity) can result in menstrual dysfunction and bone loss. Are other health conditions related to too much exercise?

Upper respiratory tract infections (URTIs) are experienced more often by elite sport participants than recreational sportsmen and women, they constitute the most common medical condition affecting elite competitors, and they tend to occur more frequently during the heaviest training periods (Spence et al., 2007). Although moderate, regular exercise tends to increase the body's immunity, too much intense exercise for an extended period can result in decreased immune function (Nieman, 2003), which may in part explain the high rate of colds and URTI among elite sport participants.

Given the health issues and the apparent qualitative factors associated with excessive exercise, it is probably more helpful from an identification standpoint to think of excessive exercise as physical activity that is unhealthy or unbalanced. This is not to deny that the quantity of exercise for some individuals is problematic. Many individuals do in fact exercise too much, too often, or for too long a period of time. But, these cases could be just as easily and accurately described as unhealthy or unbalanced.

We mentioned previously that several terms have been used to define or describe unhealthy or unbalanced exercise. *Exercise abuse* (Raglin & Moger, 1999) is one of the more useful ones, and it incorporates some of the characteristics discussed previously. Exercise abuse is characterized by three signs or symptoms. First, the individual relies on exercise as his or her primary means of coping with stress or difficulty. Second, the individual continues to exercise despite illness or injury. And third, he or she experiences withdrawal effects (i.e., insomnia, change in appetite, difficulty concentrating, moodiness, etc.) when exercise is decreased or stopped. Incorporating these signs with others related to health conditions (i.e., injuries, sex hormone deficiency, bone loss/fractures, decreased immunity, colds/infections, etc.), exercise inflexibility, and decreased sport performance (staleness), Powers and Thompson (2008) compiled a list of signs and symptoms of unhealthy/unbalanced exercise that can be used to identify sport participants who might be at risk. In using that list contained in Table 5.2, no one sign or symptom is definitively indicative of a problem. However, risk to the individual increases as the observed or documented number of signs and symptoms increases.

In addition to the list of signs and symptoms in Table 5.2, unhealthy exercise scales have been developed to assist in identification of unhealthy exercise. Two of the better scales based on psychometric properties are the Obligatory Exercise Questionnaire (Pasman & Thompson, 1988) and the Exercise Dependence Scale (Hausenblas & Symons Downs, 2002). Certainly, these are not to be used as the sole determinant of unhealthy exercise, but are simple assessments that can provide additional information in determining whether an individual's exercise is in need of modification.

A final thought on unhealthy/unbalanced exercise concerns "ultra-endurance" competitors. Although ultra-competitions are held in walking, swimming, and cycling, most of the interest in such competitions appears to be focused on ultra-marathons. At the time of this writing,

Table 5.2   Signs and Symptoms of Unhealthy or Unbalanced Exercise in Competitive Athletes

- Exercise is the individual's primary means of coping
- Exercise occurs despite injury
- Withdrawal effects (i.e., sleep and appetite disturbance, negative shift in mood, decreased concentration, etc.) occur when exercise is withheld
- Overuse injuries
- Stress fractures
- Menstrual irregularity in women or a decrease in testosterone levels in men
- Loss of bone density
- Decreased immunity
- Frequent colds or upper respiratory tract infections
- Inflexibility of exercise schedule (i.e., will not alter schedule, will not decrease exercise, will not *not* exercise)
- Decrease in sport performance
- Overtraining syndrome (staleness)

there are more than 30 such competitions of at least 100 miles in the United States. Some are made more extreme by the environmental conditions under which they occur. At the same time, the number of competitors—both men and women—is increasing each year. Are such competitors engaging in unhealthy/unbalanced exercise? The fact that many competitors are unable to finish these competitions may signal potential health issues. We can say with more certainty that they constitute unbalanced exercise because the time necessary for training for such competitions would most likely leave the competitor with inadequate time (and energy) for the normal aspects of life, such as work, relationships, social life, and sleep/rest.

Unhealthy/Unbalanced Exercise and Eating Disorders

Exercise Problem Without an Eating Disorder

To this point, we have discussed exercise problems extensively, almost without regard to eating problems. It is possible to have a problem with exercise in the absence of an eating problem, but the two often occur together. Treatment is warranted for an exercise problem when exercise compromises physical health, compromises psychological health, interferes with the maintenance of healthy interpersonal relationships, or interferes with the performance of everyday activities (i.e., work, school, or sport). Treatment for such problems will be discussed in Chapter 7.

Exercise as an Eating Disorder Symptom

As reported previously, unhealthy exercise is a part of an eating disorder for many, if not most, individuals with an eating disorder, as well as many individuals with subthreshold disorders. Exercise is a symptom of an eating disorder or disordered eating when it is used to compensate for eating. That is, the patient feels she must exercise more when she believes or feels she has eaten "too much." In essence, exercise is being used to "undo" the effects of eating. In actuality, "too much" may represent a large amount of food, or it could be a normal or even a small amount of food. It could refer to the ingestion of "forbidden" or "taboo" foods. The sense of too much may refer to calories or fat grams rather than the volume of food. Many individuals with eating disorders vastly overestimate how much they have eaten and how many calories or fat grams they have ingested, as well as the magnitude of expected weight gain. The actual amount of food may be less important than the feeling associated with eating. Because these individuals are usually restricting their caloric intake, any amount of food ingested may feel like too much. Many anorexic patients feel full after ingesting very small amounts of food. Some patients exercise excessively to punish themselves for having eaten "too much."

Exercise is a symptom of an eating disorder or disordered eating when it is used to legitimize eating. That is, exercise is used to make eating okay. The individual may feel that he must exercise in order to earn the right to eat. He may feel that if he exercises enough, he has earned the right to eat or to eat "more." Many times, however, even though he felt he earned the right to eat *before* eating, he may feel as though he has eaten too much *after* eating (and then must compensate). Typically, these individuals will significantly overestimate how much exercise they need to do in order to account (compensate) for the calories they believe/feel they have ingested.

Exercise is a symptom of an eating disorder or disordered eating when eating is used to reward exercise. This symptom is related to the previous one involving earning the right to eat. It is different in the sense that the individual uses the reward of being allowed to eat in order to motivate her to exercise enough. However, she may not ever feel that she has exercised enough to earn the reward (food). Or, after exercising, she may feel that she does not need the reward. Also, many of these patients will not take the reward because they do not want to ruin what they have accomplished with their exercise; that is, they do not want to put the calories back in that they just worked hard to burn. Their goal is always to be on the negative side of energy balance.

Exercise is a symptom of an eating disorder when it is used to maintain an unhealthy negative energy balance. Energy balance refers to the food that is eaten (energy in) minus the calories used (energy out). Theoretically, if an individual uses the amount of calories ingested, energy is balanced and weight is maintained. The individual with an eating disorder is attempting to lose weight by always using more calories than the amount ingested, creating a negative energy balance. Although a negative energy balance is a part of the previously discussed scenarios, this is a special case in which there are no pretenses about legitimizing or compensating for caloric intake, nor is food a reward. The goal is to burn more calories than are eaten solely for the purpose of losing weight. This goal is irrational and unhealthy for a variety of reasons. First, most individuals with eating disorders do not need to lose weight from a health standpoint or even an appearance point of view. Second, when weight is lost, this individual not only does not want to regain it but fears regaining it. Her fear is that if she goes back to normal exercise or eating, she will regain the weight (and she is probably correct). Thus, she is apt to feel that she needs to exercise more or eat less to ensure that she does not regain the weight. Third, the individual's assessment of how much exercise she needs to account for her calorie intake is based more on fear than fact, and thus is greatly exaggerated. When informed of the (f)actual amount of calories burned during exercise, she often responds, "I know that is how it is for most people, but I'm different." This is a classic rationalization of the eating disorder patient. We have sometimes referred to this rationalization (not to be confused with rational thinking) as, "Don't confuse me with the facts; I don't want to know." This individual ignores or discounts the fact that because exercise uses energy, it also requires energy. That is, it takes energy to exercise. Obviously, without the intake of food, the individual will be exercising on something other than energy (i.e., hyperactivity, fear/anxiety, stimulants, etc.).

Exercise is an eating disorder symptom when the individual uses dissatisfaction with size, shape, weight, or fitness level as a rationale (actually a rationalization) for unhealthy/unbalanced exercise when in fact size, shape, weight, and fitness level are within a normal, healthy range. Despite being in a normal, healthy range, these individuals often use the following statements to justify unhealthy or unbalanced exercise: "I'm too big." "I'm fat." "I need to lose weight." "I'm out of shape." The impetus for such statements primarily comes from the eating disorder. Being in a sport that emphasizes leanness or thinness simply gives the individual another rationale to make such statements to self or others.

A final note on exercise as an eating disorder symptom involves the relationship between eating and exercise. For individuals without eating or exercise problems, the relationship between the two is typically about balance. Exercise uses energy. When glycogen stores are low or depleted due to energy expenditure, the individual feels hungry and eats. Energy is restored and the individual now has energy to be active again. For eating disorder patients who engage in symptomatic exercise, the relationship between eating and exercise is not about balance but rather a negative balance. Obviously, in order for the patient to recover from an eating disorder, the nature of that relationship will need to be changed. This can be an important and sometimes difficult treatment issue for the sport participant who wishes to remain in his or her sport.

Overweight Sport Participants

Dealing with the issue of overweight is one of the more controversial ones we will discuss in this book. Part of the controversy involves dietary restriction as a "treatment" for being overweight. Many, if not most, healthcare providers who work with eating disorder patients see dietary restriction as part of the problem rather than a solution to, or treatment for, the problem. Dieting is a precursor for an eating disorder and often triggers the eating disorder. As we will discuss in a later chapter regarding treatment, the patient must give up dieting and the desire to lose weight in order to recover. Given that, we are opposed to dietary restriction in most cases. At the same time, sport participants are sometimes perceived to be overweight, and sometimes they are in fact overweight. Either scenario can cause a variety of potentially delicate situations in the sport environment that must be managed with considerable care and sensitivity. For this reason, appropriate identification is paramount.

First and foremost, being overweight should be considered a medical problem, and for that reason, a healthcare professional (i.e., physician, nurse, dietitian, etc.) should be the person to make the determination that a sport participant is overweight (IOCMC, 2005; NCAA 2005). We prefer the term *medical* rather than *health* for two reasons. First, even though being

94

overweight is often associated with many health problems, it is possible to be overweight and not have health problems. Second, we want to emphasize that being overweight is a medical problem and not a sport problem, and thus should be managed by healthcare professionals rather than sport personnel. The determination of a sport participant as overweight should not be based on the individual failing to meet the appearance standard of a particular sport or an ideal sport body stereotype. Also, it should not be based on a sport participant failing to meet a body composition standard purported to be characteristic of successful individuals in his or her sport. Rather, the status of being overweight corresponds to a medical standard for weight based on height. Also, if the individual is established to be overweight based on this standard, then possible medical conditions that could explain the weight or recent weight gain (e.g., polycystic ovary syndrome) should be ruled out.

Some may question the labeling of being overweight as a medical problem rather than a simple issue of will power. It is easy to assume that people are overweight because they eat too much. If weight management were a simple process, we would not see so many people struggling to lose or control their weight. Certainly, if will power were the key element in maintaining a weight within a prescribed range, "mentally tough" participants in sport should have no difficulty.

Weight is actually a complex process that is affected by several factors other than will power. Some are psychological (i.e., emotions, compulsions, obsessions, etc.), while others are environmental (i.e., living situation, availability of food, schedules, etc.). Some of these factors are to some degree under the individual's control. Other factors, more biological or neurobiological (i.e., neurotransmitters, hormones, peptides, etc.), also affect eating, weight, and energy balance but are not under the person's control, such as genetics (Bouchard, 2002; Leibel, 2002). Genetics has not only been found to be a major contributor to being overweight or obese, but "constitutional thinness" is also believed to be under genetic control (Bulik & Allison, 2002). Will power is not apt to have much effect on genetics.

The concepts of eating, weight, and energy balance seem quite simple when in fact they are quite complex. For example, the term *energy balance* appears to be a simple relationship of "calories in" versus "calories out," but it is more complex than it appears and is not totally under a person's conscious control. "Calories in" is not difficult to determine but "calories out" is more involved. In addition to calories burned due to one's basal metabolic rate (calories used while at rest) and physical activity, calories are also used by a process called "nonexercise adaptive thermogenesis" (Powers & Thompson, 2008). Thermogenesis refers to calories used to maintain fundamental body activities, such as keeping the body warm and processing food that is eaten. The various factors that influence energy balance are in large part regulated by the brain, specifically the hypothalamus. This is just one example of the homeostatic mechanisms that work outside of the individual's control to protect his or her health by regulating his or her internal environment to maintain a stable condition.

Even in situations in which the individual's weight might not be attributable to forces outside of her conscious control, weight is not usually the problem, nor is eating. Even if the person is overeating, why is she overeating? Why did she change her eating? Eating may be a symptom of a problem, and it may contribute to the individual being overweight. Dietary restriction, or dieting as it is typically called, is not an effective way to lose weight and maintain the loss because as we have discussed, weight involves several complex processes—not just eating. Even if the individual can diet and lose weight, that weight is apt to return because the problem has not been determined and resolved. Until the problem is resolved, it will continue to affect eating and eventually weight.

When a sportsman or woman has been identified as being medically overweight, and possible medical conditions that could account for the weight or weight gain have been excluded, the individual should be asked if he or she wants to try to "improve his or her eating." Because of the sometimes sensitive and personal nature of weight and eating-related problems, it is important that this decision be made by the individual. It should be explained that the goal of improving eating is to improve health. Further, it should be explained that the goal is not to enhance athletic performance, and such performance may or may not change with a change in eating and health. If the individual does not want to pursue this course, the matter should be dropped. Managing eating-related issues is difficult enough when the individual wants to participate. If the individual agrees to participate, then further identification is warranted.

Ideally, a dietary/nutritional assessment should be conducted by a dietitian with expertise in working with eating disorders and experience working with sport participants. Such an assessment can provide information regarding a weight history in addition to possible eating and nutrition-related problems. This will help determine whether there are adjustments (other than dietary restriction) that can be made from a nutritional point of view. An additional assessment should be conducted by an eating disorder treatment specialist to determine whether the individual is engaging in frequent dysfunctional (nonhunger) or disordered eating (i.e., overeating, binge eating, etc.), as well as possible psychological and environment factors that may be affecting such eating. Following these assessments, if the individual is not judged to be eating in a manner that would indicate the need for change or adjustment through appropriate nutritional, psychological, or medical procedures, the individual's weight should be accepted as is. Obviously, if the assessments indicate the need for change or adjustment, appropriate treatment should be offered to the sport participant and arranged only with his or her consent.

A final comment involves the role of the coach in the identification of a sport participant as being overweight. It has been suggested that coaches are in an ideal position to identify disordered eating (Sherman, DeHass, Thompson, & Wilfert, 2005). At the same time, we strongly believe that coaches should not be involved in telling their sport participants that they need to lose weight. There are several reasons for this. First, because issues of weight are not usually part of a coach's formal training, there is no reason to expect coaches to know more about weight and weight loss than other members of the lay public. That is, they are just as apt to make some of the same mistakes that other people make regarding weight decisions. For example, their decisions about a sportswoman's weight tend to be subjective; that is, they make their weight determinations based more on appearance than on objective measures (Griffin & Harris, 1996). Second, our review of the literature in Chapter 3 suggested that many athletes diet and use unhealthy weight loss techniques because their coaches indicate that they need to lose weight. This provides evidence for our contention that coaches have considerable power and influence with their sport participants, and for that reason, being approached by the coach regarding this issue may be too difficult for an individual, who may fear displeasing the coach. As a result, we believe coaches should not be directly involved in this process. If a coach feels that one of his or her team is overweight and is concerned from a health or performance standpoint, it is recommended that the coach express that concern to a medical professional who works with the team, such as a team physician, sport psychologist, athletic trainer, or dietitian.

Body-Shaping Drugs in Young Female Sport Participants

The term *body-shaping drugs* includes substances that are used to suppress appetite, decrease weight, or promote leanness or muscularity. In addition to anabolic steroids, these are typically central nervous system stimulants such as amphetamines and amphetamine-like substances, including drugs prescribed for the treatment of attention-deficit/hyperactivity disorder (Adderall, Dexadrine, and Ritalin), nicotine, and ephedrine. Stimulant use by an eating disorder patient often begins in an effort to control appetite and weight (APA, 2000; Sansone & Sansone, 2007). Of course, an additional risk is that sport participants may also use these substances as ergogenic or performance-enhancing aids. Sport participants may view them as doubly helpful in that they may perform better due to increased energy or muscularity but also due to being thinner or leaner. Most of these drugs (nicotine being an exception) tend to be on banned drug lists by various sport governing bodies (e.g., National Collegiate Athletic Association).

An in-depth discussion of body-shaping drugs and their effects on health and performance is well beyond the scope of this book. Also, male and female sport participants who compete at higher levels of competition are apt to be drug tested. Thus, our focus will be on substance use that can play a role in the female athlete triad for younger female sport participants, and who, because of their age, gender, and competition level, may be less apt to be drug tested. Specifically, we will discuss caffeine ingested through diet drinks, and nicotine through smoking (Sherman & Thompson, 2004), as well as anabolic steroids.

Caffeinated Diet Drinks

Many eating disorder patients ingest numerous diet drinks daily for a variety of purposes. Often, these drinks are ingested for the caffeine. These individuals are apt to be low on energy because of caloric restriction. As a stimulant, caffeine is used for energy. Caffeine also suppresses appetite and is a diuretic that can make the individual feel thinner due to dehydration. Frequently, these drinks are used by the patient to fill the stomach and to feel full in order not to eat. Excessive ingestion of caffeinated drinks may be symptomatic, especially when the individual admits, "I don't drink my calories." This common refrain from eating disorder patients reflects the restrictive nature of their eating. That is, they may allow themselves a small number of calories daily, and they do not want to "waste" them on liquids when they could eat.

Striegel-Moore et al. (2006) found anorexic patients' relative caffeine intake from soda increased from 25% before onset of the disorder to 54% during the year of onset and 65% after onset. Excessive caffeine ingestion, especially in the absence of adequate ingestion of calcium, can contribute to bone loss because the phosphoric acid in diet sodas can inhibit calcium adsorption (Otis & Goldingay, 2000). Thus, an assessment of possible weight loss aids should include questions related to ingestion of caffeinated diet drinks.

Smoking

In their efforts to suppress appetite, many girls and young women are smoking (Crisp, Sedgwick, Halek, Joughin, & Humphrey, 1999; Welch & Fairburn, 1998; Wiseman, Turco, Sunday, & Halmi, 1998). The highest rates of smoking among women with eating disorders have been found in patients engaging in bulimic behaviors (Anzengruber et al., 2006).

Believing that smoking can suppress appetite, girls aged 12 to 15 who valued thinness more strongly were more apt to become smokers than those who valued thinness less (Honjo & Siegel, 2003), and eating pathology and body dissatisfaction were predictive of smoking (Stice & Shaw, 2003). Related to our previous discussion on ingestion of caffeine, cigarette smoking in eating disorder inpatients was also associated with caffeine abuse (Haug, Heinberg, & Guarda, 2001). But do sport participants smoke knowing the potential health effects, as well as the potential effect on sport performance? In a recent NCAA survey, smoking prevalence varied by sport: 22.6, 17.0, 16.8, 10.9, and 6.2 of collegiate athletes in softball, tennis, swimming, basketball, and track/field, respectively, with more than 20% of the smokers reporting smoking at least one pack of cigarettes per day, and the majority reporting that they began smoking before college (NCAA, 2005). Thus, assessments of weight loss aids should include questions related to smoking, especially regarding the individual's motivation for smoking. Regarding the triad, smoking can suppress appetite and contribute to bone loss. With respect to other symptoms, smokers with bulimia nervosa reported more symptoms of depression and alcohol abuse (Sandager et al., 2008).

Anabolic Steroids

Our discussion here will focus on girls and young sportswomen who may be using anabolic steroids to perform better in addition to attempting to be leaner. Yesalis, Barsukiewicz, Kopstein, and Bahrke (1997) found adolescent girls using steroids in order to be thinner or leaner in addition to enhancing sport performance. Steroid use by girls in this age group is illustrated in a more recent study (Elliot, Cheong, Moe, & Goldberg, 2007) that looked at the general population of high school girls rather than sport participants per se. In this study, prior or current anabolic steroid use was reported by 5.3% of U.S. high school females, more than two-thirds of whom used steroids in an effort to change their weight. Related to disordered eating and smoking, these girls were also more likely to use vomiting, laxatives, and diet pills, powders, or liquids to lose weight, and were more apt to smoke cigarettes.

Given the use of anabolic steroids in girls who may also be engaging in other risky behaviors related to weight loss (i.e., use of other body-shaping drugs, smoking, disordered eating, etc.), girls believed to be at risk for the female athlete triad should be assessed for steroid use. Amenorrhea can result from the use of anabolic steroids (Yates, 1999). Theoretically, for the triad, amenorrhea is diagnosed as "functional hypothalamic amenorrhea" when all possible medical conditions (i.e., pregnancy, polycystic ovary syndrome, pituitary tumors, etc.) that could explain the problem have been excluded (ACSM, 2007). Even if the sportswoman's menstrual dysfunction is determined to be a result of one of these medical conditions, it would still be prudent for her to be evaluated regarding the triad components related to eating and bone health.

Final Thoughts

The use of body-shaping drugs, especially caffeine and nicotine, may be more prevalent in female participants under the age of 18 because of their gender, but also because they are at an age in which body concerns are most critical and the risk of the development of eating disorders is highest (Sherman & Thompson, 2009). As we have said previously, any complications regarding identification put an individual at additional risk. Athletes in youth sports may be doubly at risk due to having fewer and less sophisticated coaches and other sport personnel caring for them with the knowledge and expertise available to identify triad components.

In reviewing the literature regarding the lifetime prevalence of a substance abuse disorder in eating disorder patients, Pearlstein (2002) found prevalence rates ranging from a low of 12% in anorexia nervosa to a high of 70% in bulimia nervosa. Thus, when evaluating sport participants who abuse body-shaping drugs, the individual who is abusing such drugs in an attempt to lose weight or perform better should be assessed for a substance abuse disorder in addition to an eating disorder. If the individual has both disorders, these assessments can be helpful in determining whether the disorders are best treated concurrently, or the order of treatment if treated consecutively. We will discuss such issues in more depth in Chapter 7.

Vegetarianism Versus Pseudovegetarianism

In terms of the health advantages, as well as its ethical concerns related to the humane treatment of animals, vegetarianism is certainly a reasonable lifestyle choice for many individuals. Part of its attractiveness is the avoidance of dietary fat that comes with eating meat and other animal products. Much, if not most, of the dietary fat contained in the diet of non-vegetarians comes from meat and animal products.

The motivation for choosing vegetarianism is not always related to improving health or based on the ethical treatment of animals. A vegetarian diet is also attractive for an individual who wants to eliminate fat from his or her diet in order to lose weight, such as a person with an eating disorder. Avoidance of eating meat and animal products can look like an acceptable or even admirable choice based on health or ethics rather than on a fear of "getting fat" from eating dietary fat. Research with vegetarians indicates that they not only score higher than nonvegetarians on measures of eating disorder attitudes and behaviors (Bas, Karabudak, & Kiziltan, 2005; Klopp, Heiss, & Smith, 2003), but at least one study (Neumark-Sztainer, Story, Resnick, & Blum, 1997) found that adolescent vegetarians compared to nonvegetarians were twice as likely to report frequent dieting, four times as likely to report induced vomiting, and eight times as likely to report laxative use. With respect to eating disorders, vegetarianism appears to be overrepresented in eating disorders, with one study reporting a prevalence of 45% (Kadambari, Gowers, & Crisp, 1986).

Gilbody, Kirk, and Hill (1999) suggested that vegetarianism is probably best seen as a complication to normalization of eating rather than a risk factor for an eating disorder. We would agree but add that pseudovegetarianism may be a sophisticated way for a person with an eating disorder to avoid identification. If the individual engages in possible eating disorder symptoms or is significantly underweight and claims to avoid the ingestion of meat and animal products because he or she is vegetarian, have the individual see a dietitian who is experienced in working with eating disorder patients. Have the dietitian assess the individual's nutritional needs for his or her health and sport, and then provide him or her with a vegetarian meal plan designed to meet dietary/nutritional requirements. If the individual cannot or will not follow it, the individual is likely a pseudovegetarian who is using a vegetarian diet to practice disordered eating or an eating disorder. Additionally, for those who claim to be vegetarian based on the ethical treatment of animals, one simple assessment is to check to see if they are wearing leather shoes, belts, or jackets.

FORMAL ASSESSMENT MEASURES AND SYMPTOM CHECKLISTS

Assessment measures used with eating disorder patients typically include measures regarding attitudes and behaviors characteristic of such disorders and more general measures of psychopathology (Garner, 2002). We will address only the former. Assessment measures regarding eating disorder attitudes and behaviors typically include self-report inventories or questionnaires and (semi)structured interviews. Such measures alone should not be the basis on which the diagnosis of an eating disorder is made. When used, they should be used as part of a full assessment that would include an in-depth clinical interview by a mental health professional experienced in working with eating disorder patients, a dietary/nutritional assessment by a dietitian/nutritionist experienced with eating disorders, and a physical examination. Although most of the instruments discussed have demonstrated reasonable validity and reliability in the general population, such characteristics have not been adequately examined regarding their use with sport participants.

Self-Report Questionnaires/Inventories

The primary advantages of self-report instruments are that they tend to be relatively inexpensive, reasonably quick and easy to administer, objectively scored, and free of interview bias (Garner, 2002). Their biggest drawback is that they are self-report; that is, they rely on the accuracy and honesty of the individual's report. A discussion of all of the self-report inventories is beyond the scope of this book, but for such a discussion the reader is directed to Olmsted, McFarlane, Carter, and Trottier (2007). We will confine our discussion to the ones most frequently used clinically and in research.

Eating Attitudes Test

The Eating Attitudes Test (EAT; Garner & Garfinkel, 1979; Garner, Olmsted, Bohr, & Garfinkel, 1982) in its original form was a 40-item screening instrument for anorexia nervosa. It has been shortened to 26 items and has been translated into many languages with norms for different cultures. In general, it has reasonable validity and reliability. Despite the fact that the EAT has not been evaluated as appropriate for use with sport participants, it has been used extensively in research with such individuals. An advantage of the EAT-26 is that it is in the public domain, which means it is easily accessible to almost anyone and free of charge to use.

Eating Disorder Inventory

The Eating Disorder Inventory (EDI; Garner & Olmsted, 1984) in its original form was a 64-item screening instrument for attitudes and behaviors characteristic of anorexia nervosa and bulimia nervosa. It had eight subscales, three of which related specifically to eating and weight (Drive for Thinness, Bulimia, and Body Dissatisfaction), and five scales relating more to general psychopathology (Ineffectiveness, Perfectionism, Interoceptive Awareness, Interpersonal Distrust, and Maturity Fears). The EDI-2 (Garner, 1991) resulted from expanding the EDI to 91 items with an additional three subscales (Asceticism, Impulse Regulation, and Social Insecurity). The EDI-3 (Garner, 2004) now has 12 primary scales and 6 composite scales. Again, these instruments have good validity and reliability with clinical and nonclinical populations, and they have been used extensively in research with sport participants despite not being examined as to their appropriateness for such individuals.

Structured Interview

The measure in this category that is most frequently used clinically and in research is the Eating Disorder Examination (EDE; Fairburn & Cooper, 1993). The EDE is administered by a clinician and is designed to assess specific psychopathology characteristic of eating disorders. The EDE has good validity and reliability. The advantage of this and other interview measures is that it permits the clinician to explain and elaborate the questions to the patient, allowing for the attainment of more specific information, thus decreasing the likelihood of false positive diagnoses (Peterson & Miller, 2005). Additionally, Torstveit, Rosenvinge, and Sundgot-Borgen (2008) suggested that a clinical interview is especially important when assessing lean sport participants for eating disorders because of the likelihood of false-negatives that may result from the underreporting of disordered eating behaviors. Torstveit et al. used the EDE as an interview guide to determine the presence of DSM-IV eating disorder criteria in elite sportswomen.

Before moving on to formal assessments specific to sport, we want to reiterate the importance of early assessment and identification. For more on the assessment of eating disorders, refer to Mitchell and Peterson (2005).

Formal Assessments for the Sport Environment

As we mentioned earlier, most eating disorder assessment tools have not been standardized for use with sport participants. However, this is not to imply that their use with such individuals is inappropriate. Instruments have been developed specifically for use with sport participants, such as the Athletic Milieu Direct Questionnaire (Nagel, Black, Leverenz, & Coster, 2000) and Female Athlete Screening Tool (McNulty, Adams, Anderson, & Affenito, 2001). A more in-depth discussion of such instruments is beyond our purposes here, but for more information on these and other such instruments, refer to Bonci et al. (2008). One approach to screening sport participants for eating disorders and disordered eating, however, is novel in its conception and warrants at least a brief description. Black, Larken, Coster, Leverenz, and Abood's (2003) 18-item Physiologic Screening Test (PST) has the advantage of including physiological signs and symptoms, in addition to interviewer questions and self-report items.

Symptom Checklists

Perhaps the easiest way to begin the identification process of sport participants is with a simple checklist of signs and symptoms of eating disorders and disordered eating. A checklist is a screening measure. It is an appropriate first step because it can be used by virtually all sport personnel, and it is not apt to be intrusive to the person in question. Its primary drawback is that the signs and symptoms are open to the interpretation of the observer. As with most symptom checklists, one symptom does not indicate the presence of a disorder. However, the presumed risk to the individual in question increases as the number of observed signs and symptoms increases. Several of these checklists for sport participants have appeared in the literature (Bonci et al., 2008; NCAA, 2005; Rosen, McKeag, Hough, & Curley, 1986). We prefer to divide characteristics both by disorder—anorexia nervosa and bulimia nervosa—and by type of sign or symptom, physical/medical and psychological/behavioral (Thompson & Sherman, 1993a). Those lists can be found in Tables 5.3 to 5.6.

Table 5.3   Physical/Medical Symptoms of Athletes With Anorexia Nervosa

- Amenorrhea
- Dehydration, especially in the absence of training or competition
- Fatigue beyond that normally expected in training or competition
- Gastrointestinal problems (i.e., constipation, diarrhea, bloating, postprandial distress)
- Hyperactivity
- Hypothermia (cold intolerance)
- Lanugo (fine hair on face and arms)
- Muscle weakness
- Overuse injuries
- Significant weight loss beyond that necessary for adequate sport performance
- Stress fractures
- Weight significantly lower than necessary for adequate sport performance

Table 5.4 Physical/Medical Symptoms of Athletes With Bulimia Nervosa

- Callus on back of hand from inducing vomiting
- Dehydration, especially in the absence of training or competition
- Dental and gum problems
- Edema, complaints of bloating, or both
- Electrolyte abnormalities
- Frequent or extreme weight fluctuations, especially with resultant mood fluctuations (i.e., mood worsens as weight goes up)
- Gastrointestinal problems
- Low weight despite eating large volumes
- Menstrual irregularity
- Muscle cramps, weakness, or both
- Swollen parotid glands

Table 5.5 Psychological/Behavioral Characteristics of Athletes With Anorexia Nervosa

- Anxiety, both related and unrelated to sport performance
- Avoidance of eating and eating situation
- Claims of feeling fat despite being thin
- Compulsiveness and rigidity, especially regarding eating and exercise
- Depression
- Excessive or obligatory exercise beyond that required for a particular sport or coach
- Exercising while injured despite prohibitions by medical and training staffs
- Insomnia
- Obsessiveness and preoccupation with weight and eating while being at a low weight and engaging in minimal eating
- Resistance to weight gain or maintenance recommended by sport support staff
- Restlessness—relaxing is difficult or impossible
- Restrictive dieting, especially when self-imposed and unnecessary for, or detrimental to, sport performance
- Social withdrawal from teammates and sport support staff, as well as from people outside sports
- Unusual weighing behavior (i.e., excessive weighing, refusal to weigh, negative reaction to being weighed)

Table 5.6 Psychological/Behavioral Characteristics of Athletes With Bulimia Nervosa

- Binge eating
- Agitation when bingeing is interrupted
- Depression
- Dieting that is unnecessary for health or sport performance
- Evidence of vomiting unrelated to illness
- Excessive exercise beyond that required for the athlete's sport
- Excessive use of the restroom
- Going to the restroom or "disappearing" after eating
- History of sexual abuse
- Self-critical, especially concerning body, weight, and sport performance
- Secretive eating
- Stealing, especially when items taken are related to bulimia (i.e., food, laxatives, etc.)
- Substance abuse—whether legal, illegal, prescribed, or over-the-counter drugs, medications, or other substances
- Use of laxatives, diuretics, or both that is unsanctioned by medical or training staffs

FINAL THOUGHTS ON IDENTIFICATION

We began this chapter with a discussion related to the importance of identification. To reiterate, identification is perhaps the most important part of the process that leads to recovery, in large part because it is the first step in the process. We consider anything that interferes with, or complicates, identification as an additional risk factor. A delay in identification increases the risk of additional medical and psychological risks to the eating disordered individual. Once the symptomatic or at-risk individual has been identified, we can move to the next step—management.

6

Management of Eating Problems in the Sport Environment

Once the symptomatic or at-risk sport participant has been identified, several management decisions must be made regarding how best to communicate with the individual, as well as how to arrange for the necessary evaluation and possible treatment. However, before going further, we should describe what we mean by management, and explain why sport personnel should be involved. We make a distinction between management and treatment. Management is broader than treatment and refers to a process that begins with identification of an at-risk individual and continues through the individual's treatment and aftercare (Thompson & Sherman, 1993a).

Although sport personnel play a less significant role or no role at all in treatment, they may play a critical role in managing the sport participant within the sport environment. Healthcare professionals often question why sport personnel should be involved in any capacity. Some even suggest that coaches and sport participation are part of the problem. On the contrary, we usually view their involvement as potentially positive. In many cases, there is little or no need to involve sport personnel. However, some cases may present more complex or complicated management issues, such as patient resistance, severe or dangerous symptoms, or the need for intensive treatment. In such cases, a "sport management team" consisting in large part of sport personnel can work directly or indirectly with the treatment team to facilitate patient management. The primary rationale for having them involved is that they are in an ideal position to identify, monitor, and support symptomatic sport participants because they spend so much time with them at practice, competitions, and traveling.

The role of the sport management team will be our primary focus in this chapter. We will first discuss the possible makeup of a sport management team. We will then discuss the roles of sport personnel on the management team in approaching the individual, making referrals to appropriate healthcare professionals, monitoring of symptoms, monitoring of specific therapeutic strategies, communications with teammates and the media, and even participating when necessary and appropriate in treatment as the sport participant's "sport family." Finally, we will examine the role of healthcare professionals on the management team and provide recommendations as to how they interface with sport personnel.

THE SPORT MANAGEMENT TEAM

Much has changed in the past 20-plus years regarding eating disorders in sport since we first recommended a sport management team approach to dealing with sport participants with such problems (Thompson, 1987). One thing that has not changed, however, is the critical role such a team can play in facilitating the identification, management, and treatment of symptomatic or at-risk sport participants. The size of the management team, as well as how active and involved it is, will vary given the complexity of issues. It could include almost any sport personnel in an authority or decision-making position who has contact with the individual in question. Typically, this would be coaches and athletic trainers. It could also include team physicians and sport psychologists for teams and sports that have them, but it might also include others, such as sport administrators (Bonci et al., 2008).

In assembling a sport management team, there are several considerations. First, the management team should be coordinated by a healthcare professional who is involved in the individual's treatment; second, involvement of each member must be therapeutic as defined by the coordinating health professional; and third, management team members' participation must occur within acceptable ethical guidelines (Sherman & Thompson, 2001).

Coaches

Unfortunately, coaches have often been associated with precipitating or perpetuating eating disorders, in both the popular press (e.g., Ryan, 2000) and the professional literature (e.g., Thompson, 1998). It has been suggested that pressure (at higher competition levels) regarding winning in order to maintain employment can create moral and ethical dilemmas for coaches with respect to the health of their charges (Flint, 1999). Our experience suggests that this represents a minority of coaches, and that most coaches understand and accept the seriousness of disordered eating symptoms regarding consequences to their sport participants' health and performance (Sherman, DeHass, Thompson, & Wilfert, 2005).

There are several reasons why coaches should be involved in the management of eating disordered sport participants. Coaches can be a good management team choice because they spend so much time with their team at practices, meetings, competitions, and traveling, thus giving them numerous opportunities to observe, monitor, or support a sport participant. Most important, coaches have significant power and influence with their charges. Their power and influence are such that any program or protocol related to the identification, management, treatment, and prevention of eating disorders most likely will not succeed without their support. Coaches' power and influence will be felt by the sport participant whether or not the coach is formally involved. By having coaches be a part of the team, the coordinating healthcare professional can be more aware of, and to some degree have more control over, their influence, which can provide greater assurance that it has a positive effect. Because of their power, the roles of coaches in management have to be selected and executed carefully. For example, a coach may or may not be the best person to approach a sport participant regarding identification and referral.

In the succeeding chapter regarding treatment, we will discuss the skepticism that some coaches feel regarding having their sport participants in treatment. Having coaches formally involved in the process affords them the opportunity to see how the management and treatment processes work. Hopefully, this can alleviate some of their skepticism, and increase the likelihood of a greater understanding of the complexity and seriousness of eating disorders and their relationship to sport, as well as increase the likelihood of their positive participation regarding future at-risk or symptomatic sport participants.

Athletic Trainers

Athletic trainers are essential in terms of managing eating disordered sport participants. It has been suggested that they are in the best position in the sport environment to first approach and manage these individuals (Petrie & Sherman, 1999), and are often the sport personnel who have the responsibility for managing them (Sherman et al., 2005). Additionally, athletic trainers are liaisons between the individual and the coaching staff. The relationship they have with sportsmen and women is facilitated by the fact that athletic trainers are healthcare professionals but also sport personnel. Although they have the advantages of being a part of the sport environment and understanding the demands of the individual's sport, they are more focused on, and concerned with, the sport participant's health than sport performance. Thus, when necessary, the athletic trainer can serve as an intermediary between the sport participant and the coach, especially regarding health issues. Because of the power of the coach, it may be too difficult for the individual in question to go to the coach with her problem. It might be easier for her to talk with the athletic trainer, who in turn could talk with the coach.

Because they are healthcare professionals, athletic trainers are also ideal liaisons between the sport personnel and the healthcare professionals who will be treating the sport participant. They can initiate and facilitate referrals in this regard. They are in an ideal position to monitor symptomatic behaviors and assess progress regarding treatment goals (i.e., weight, physical activity, etc.), as well as to talk with sport participants about the effects of their disordered eating symptoms on health (i.e., menstrual dysfunction) and sport performance. They can also be invaluable consultants to the treatment staff when decisions need to be made regarding training and exercise for the symptomatic sport participant. For example, they can make recommendations regarding the appropriate levels of exercise frequency, duration, and intensity for a particular individual who may not be ready for full training and competition.

Again, the importance of the management role of the athletic trainer cannot be overstated. For an excellent in-depth discussion of the athletic trainer's role in the management of the eating disordered sport participant, the reader is directed to a recent position statement on eating disorders in sport by the National Athletic Trainers' Association (Bonci et al., 2008).

A final note on athletic trainers involves the term *athletic trainer*. When we use the term *athletic trainer*, we are not referring to a personal trainer.

Rather, we are referring to a certified athletic trainer, who has met the educational, training, and experience requirements necessary for certification as defined by their parent professional organization (i.e., National Athletic Trainers' Association).

Team Physician

For those sport participants who are fortunate to have a team physician, the team physician can be one of the most important individuals in the sport environment to the individual with an eating disorder, and having a team physician provides several advantages. One advantage is that the team physician will probably know the sport participant because of yearly preparticipation physicals or treatment for previous injuries. Thus, she will not have to see a "stranger." Another advantage is that the team physician is viewed by the sport participant as being informed as to the special needs of sportsmen and women. That is, he or she does not have to be concerned that the team physician will not understand or appreciate the importance of sport in his or her life, as well as the special demands of a particular sport. Having the team physician involved also provides the advantage of communicating the medical nature of eating disorders, which can serve to emphasize the seriousness of their medical and psychological consequences. Finally, the team physician can function as a liaison between sport personnel and the eating disorder treatment team.

A final note on team physicians involves the importance of having a treatment team that can consult with the physician. There is no reason to expect that a team physician will have expertise or even much experience treating disordered eating in sport participants. This is one area in which the management team concept is beneficial in that the physician has the opportunity to consult with other team members (athletic trainer, psychologist, or dietitian) who may have the needed expertise or experience.

Sport Psychologist

If a particular team or department has the luxury of having a sport psychologist, he or she is an ideal member of the sport management team to respond to the sport participant in question. The psychologist may already know the individual, and should be comfortable in approaching her, as well as being able to manage possible resistance, answer the individual's questions, and provide referral information. Additionally, as both a healthcare professional and member of the sport world, the sport psychologist can also be an invaluable liaison between the treatment team and sport personnel.

(Sport) Dietitian

Regarding the inclusion of a dietitian as part of the management team, especially one with expertise or experience working with eating problems and sport participants, we believe that the services of a dietitian should be employed in virtually all cases that involve eating, weight, or nutrition. The dietitian is the expert in these areas. Although having a dietitian may seem like a luxury, we believe that it is a necessary luxury. For more information on how a sport dietitian can be helpful in managing and preventing eating problems in the sport environment, see Girard Eberle (2005).

Final Thoughts on the Management of Youth Sport Participants

The aforementioned sport management team is apt to function best with sport participants who compete at the secondary school and college levels, in addition to those who compete at elite levels for their national teams or compete professionally. Such a management team may not be available or even appropriate for participants at the youth sport (age 12 and under) level. Certainly, for children in this age group the parents need to be involved. In fact, the younger the sport participant, the more parents need to be involved, as they will be the primary decision makers, typically with less involvement by sport personnel. For such young sport participants, the primary role of sport personnel in management would be identification of at-risk or symptomatic youth and notification of parents. At the same time, our recommendations regarding the involvement of parents should not be misconstrued to imply that parents would not be involved at higher competition levels or with older sport participants.

ROLES OF SPORT PERSONNEL IN MANAGEMENT

Approaching the At-Risk/Symptomatic Sport Participant

Who should talk with the sport participant? The person designated to talk with the sport participant should have some authority in the sport environment. More important, however, is that this person should either have a good relationship with the sport participant, or at least be comfortable discussing sensitive and important issues (NCAA, 2007). This could be a coach, athletic trainer, team physician, or other sport personnel involved in the sport participant's life. As mentioned previously, an athletic trainer is in many ways an ideal person to approach an at-risk or symptomatic sportsman or woman. Depending on the sport or the level of competition, however, athletic trainers may or may not be available. The power of coaches may or may not make them good choices. It really depends on the relationship between the coach and sport participant, and the coach's comfort in discussing such issues. The team physician is often a good choice because the message is being communicated by a medical professional, suggesting the medical nature of the problem.

Actually, who approaches the individual is less important than *how* he or she is approached. Often, the biggest concern of the person approaching the symptomatic individual is saying the wrong thing and worsening the situation. Perhaps the biggest mistake that can be made in this circumstance is to respond to the individual in an insensitive or judgmental manner or imply that the difficulty is trivial or a sign of weakness.

The timing of the approach can be almost as important as what is to be communicated. In order to make the situation as easy on the sport participant as possible, the approach should occur privately. This will minimize the likelihood of embarrassment and discomfort. It also decreases the possibility of distraction. The designated person should tell the sport participant that individuals associated with her sport are concerned about her and her health. As a consequence, an evaluation with a medical specialist (i.e., team physician) will be arranged for her. If the individual questions the concern, she can be told that the concern involves her eating or her nutritional status. However, we have found that being too specific regarding her symptoms (i.e., self-induced vomiting) may be too threatening for her. Also, specific symptoms can too easily be fended off or denied. Less direct inquiries regarding whether her sport performance has decreased, or if she is having difficulty complying with the physical demands of her sport, can sometimes be helpful. If reassurance seems necessary, try to reassure her that you are only concerned for her welfare and want to make sure that she is healthy. We also recommend that the sport participant be involved in the referral process. That is, have her participate in making the necessary appointment for the evaluation.

Obviously, there are several scenarios that occur once the sport partic-ipant has been approached. Ideally, she will respond positively and accept the evaluation referral. In the event that the sport participant should express reluctance or refuse the evaluation, she should be told that until she is properly evaluated she will be considered to be "injured," and that injured sport participants must be cleared for training and competition by appropriate healthcare professionals. If she continues to refuse the evalu-ation, she should be told that she will be withheld from training and com-petition until she has the evaluation and is cleared to train and compete. Additionally, she should be told that, although the temporary suspension from training and competition may seem harsh, it is not a punishment. Rather, it is a statement regarding the importance of her health over her sport performance. This is a communication that will be expressed sev-eral times in this book. Health is never to be subordinated to sport per-formance. This is an important message to an individual with an eating disorder, who often believes, and has often been treated as if, her impor-tance to others is related to pleasing them by what she does rather than for who she is. If she is reluctant to accept the evaluation or, worse yet, refuses it, her reluctance or resistance may be related to a fear of displeasing sig-nificant others (i.e., coaches, teammates, family, friends, fans, etc.).

If the sport participant continues to refuse, she should be held out of training and competition until she agrees to the evaluation. However, she should be suspended only from training and competition. She should remain a part of the team and attend all practices and team meetings, as well as any other team functions. Maintaining an attachment to the team is important for many reasons that we will discuss in a later chapter regarding treatment.

The following vignette is offered as an illustration of such a situation with recommended responses.

Jennifer is a 20-year-old collegiate field hockey player. On road trips, she frequently makes excuses for not eating with the team. When she does eat, she often goes to the restroom immediately after eating. Her roommate on the last road trip expressed her concern to an assistant coach that Jennifer was vomiting after eating and complaining that she is too fat. The coach approached Jennifer privately, and the following conversation ensued:

Coach: Jennifer, some of your teammates, other coaches, and I are con-
    cerned about you and are wondering if you feel okay.
Jennifer: Concerned about what? I feel fine.

Coach: We're concerned about your health.

Jennifer: My health? There's nothing wrong with my health.

Coach: We're concerned about a possible eating problem and just want to make sure that you are okay. The only way we can do that is to have you see a healthcare professional for an evaluation.

Jennifer: I'm fine. I don't need an evaluation.

Coach: We hope that you are fine. Again, the only way to know for sure is to have you evaluated. We want to arrange your evaluation at soon as possible. When would you be available for an appointment?

Jennifer: I'm too busy to do it now. I've got exams coming up, not to mention practice every day. Maybe I could do it later.

Coach: Jennifer, until you are evaluated and cleared for training and competition, we will consider you to be injured. And, remember, we don't practice if we're injured.

Jennifer: I can't practice? That's not fair. You're forcing me to do something I don't want to do.

Coach: We can't force you to have the evaluation, but we can't allow you to train and compete until we know you are okay. Let's arrange the evaluation. We will hope, as you say, that you are fine. If you are, we will all breathe a sigh of relief and you can return to full training and competition. If you aren't okay, we will do whatever is necessary to get you well and back with us on the field as quickly as possible.

Jennifer: Okay, let's schedule it. Can I come to practice today?

Coach: Jennifer, you are still a part of the team. Yes, you are to come to practice, team meetings, and anything else associated with the team. The only exception to this is that you cannot miss any medical appointments to attend practice or meetings. Your health comes first.

The aforementioned responses by the coach are reasonably sensitive and direct. They are not necessarily ideal or ones that a professional counselor or psychotherapist would make, and that is the point. The goal is not to r ke counselors or therapists out of sport personnel. The goal is to appr i the individual in question and assist her or him in getting the assistance she or he needs with a minimum of discomfort or embarrassment. There are many ways to get the job done. However, sometimes the individual will refuse the evaluation no matter how sensitively or

117

appropriately the request is communicated. This situation obviously requires a different approach.

We will use the previous vignette as an illustration. We are returning to the segment in which the coach tells Jennifer that she is considered to be injured and cannot train or compete without an evaluation attesting to her health. She complains that not allowing her to practice is unfair and that she is being forced to do something she does not want to do. The coach reiterates that she cannot train or compete until medically cleared via the evaluation.

Jennifer: You can't make me do this. I won't do it. I don't need an evaluation!

Coach: As I said, I can't make you go to the evaluation. I want you to go, but it is your choice. If you choose not to have the evaluation, you leave us with no choice. You will not be allowed to train or compete. We won't risk your health.

Jennifer: It's not fair! You're punishing me because I won't do what you want.

Coach: It is not a question of fairness. It is a question of health, and we are not willing to risk your health, even if you are. If you still refuse, you will not train or compete until you are cleared to do so. Even though this may feel like a punishment, it is not intended to be a punishment. Rather, it is intended to get you the assistance you may need. If you don't need it, the evaluation is still not a waste. It will simply reassure all of us that you are healthy enough to train and compete. Now, are you ready to agree to the evaluation?

Jennifer: No!

Coach: Let me know when you are. Until then, you are still a part of this team even though you will not practice or compete, and you will be expected to be at practice and team meetings.

In this exchange, the coach maintains firmness, while explaining expectations and requirements without being critical or heavy handed. The coach continues to stress the importance of her health over her sport. It is a good exchange even though Jennifer still refused. It should be noted that a refusal for an evaluation or treatment by some eating disorder patients is not unusual. In fact, many such referrals by professionals are often rejected.

A final note here involves the information obtained even when the individual refuses. Resistance is a communication. Often, resistance increases with the seriousness of the problem and the fear associated with its detection. A person without a problem has little need or reason to defend, resist, or refuse. In *Hamlet*, Shakespeare could have been describing Jennifer when he wrote, "The lady protests too much, methinks."

The individual should be withheld from training and competition until she agrees to the evaluation. She will, in all likelihood, eventually agree to the evaluation, if she really wants to participate in her sport. Motivating the eating disorder patient in treatment is almost always a difficult prospect. Withholding sport participation can motivate the sport participant, providing she wants to continue playing. There is the possibility that she does not want to return to her sport, and her "resistance" may allow her to avoid returning. It may be a way out for her that is more acceptable to her than quitting. We will discuss this issue in greater detail in Chapter 7.

Getting the sport participant to the medical evaluation is the initial goal. Following the medical evaluation, however, further evaluation or treatment may be recommended, and the sport participant may again resist or refuse. The procedures for managing such a process as recommended by the IOCMC (2005) are presented in Figure 6.1. We will discuss these procedures in depth in Chapter 7, but suffice it to say that the resisting individual is considered to be injured and is withheld from training and competition until she is compliant with treatment recommendations.

Making the Referral

When the sport participant agrees to an evaluation, be prepared to make the referral. Referrals made to specific individuals are more apt to be accepted. This means knowing referral sources. It means doing your homework. Having an individual in need of treatment in your office is not the time to determine what treatment sources are available. For sport personnel who have the luxury or good fortune to have a team physician, the referral is made to him or her. For those who do not have a team physician, know your referral sources.

The importance of an immediate referral relates to the ambivalence many eating disorder patients experience. Their ambivalence may lead to obsessing about treatment, which in turn can lead to more resistance. Make the referral as soon as possible, and schedule an appointment as soon as possible. Call while the sport participant is in your office. Once making contact with the referral source, put the sport participant on the phone to make the appointment. Assist her in any way necessary. Offer

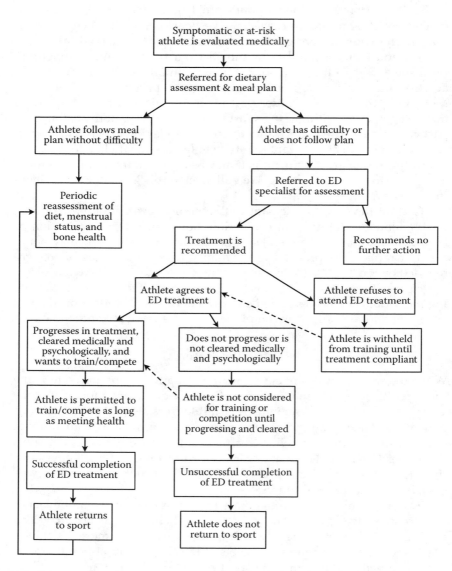

FIGURE 6.1   IOCMC decision tree for managing disordered eating.

to accompany her to the appointment, if necessary. This kind of commitment by sport personnel is a communication to the sport participant that her health is of paramount importance. Ask her how she feels about the appointment. She is apt to be anxious or afraid. Tell her what you know about the healthcare professional she will be seeing. Be positive and reassure her that you and others associated with her team are supporting her.

Monitoring of Symptoms and Treatment Strategies

Even though treatment providers cannot always share their information about the symptomatic individual with sport personnel because of confidentiality, it does not mean that they cannot listen to what sport personnel might want to report. Sport personnel are in an excellent position to notice and monitor symptoms. Treatment providers sometimes depend on the report of family members regarding a patient's symptoms. Sport personnel can sometimes function like the sport participant's sport family and provide helpful information regarding eating, exercise, and mood to those providing treatment. However, it is important to remember that this type of observation or monitoring must not be done with a vigilance that borders on being invasive or obtrusive. Monitoring does not mean spying, following her, or confronting her. For example, the patient should not be followed to the bathroom to try to catch her vomiting. Such behavior will only serve to embarrass her, and may evoke a need to hide and avoid those around her. The role of sport personnel here is not to intervene unless asked by the patient to intervene. The appropriate role is to monitor only, and to use discretion and sensitivity when monitoring. An illustrative example might be noting that the patient often went to the restroom immediately after eating while on a road trip, or usually avoided eating with others while on the trip.

Depending on treatment goals and the particular needs of the patient, sport personnel may play a similar role in monitoring and supporting therapeutic strategies. These might include assistance in following a meal plan, staying within recommended exercise guidelines, and not allowing sport participation to interfere with following treatment recommendations. Of course, it could also include being available and responsive when the patient is feeling at risk or symptomatic, or simply when she needs a good listener.

121

Sport Participant Unable to Train or Compete Remains on Team

Regardless of the reason for determining that the person should not train or compete (health or resistance), she should remain a part of the team and attend team functions, such as practice and team meetings (Sherman & Thompson, 2001). This allows her to maintain a sense of attachment, which can be very important to her because of issues related to her disorder. Remaining on the team also allows the sport participant to retain her identity as a sport participant, which may be the most important, if not the only, source of her self-esteem. Additionally, if she is removed from the team, she is essentially on her own. Having the patient remain on the team allows for better monitoring of symptoms by sport personnel.

Sport Personnel Attending Treatment Sessions

On rare occasions, sport personnel have participated in treatment sessions with the patient. On these occasions, it is usually a coach or athletic trainer participating. Sometimes we have arranged such meetings. Other times, the patient has asked the coach or trainer to attend with her. Obviously, confidentiality is a primary consideration in these cases, and such sessions cannot occur without the patient's consent, and should never occur without the patient fully understanding the possible consequences of having the other person(s) involved. Also, this consent should never be coerced. When we have arranged such meetings, the rationale is much the same as having family-of-origin members, spouses/partners, or friends involved. It may be arranged to resolve particular difficulties between the patient and the coach that appear to play a role in the eating disorder. We have sometimes recommended a session with the sport participant, a coach, athletic trainer, and medical staff early in treatment to ensure that all parties know their roles and responsibilities, as well as treatment goals and expectations.

Sport Personnel Communications With Teammates and the Media

If a sport participant has to miss a practice, or is withheld from training or competition, or worse yet, has to leave the sport environment to participate in more intensive (intensive outpatient, partial hospitalization, residential, or inpatient) treatment, her absence will be noticed by teammates.

Inevitable questions will be asked. This can be a delicate situation to manage. In many cases, teammates will know of their missing teammate's eating problems; in fact, they are often the first to know. Nonetheless, they are apt to ask coaches or athletic trainers about her status or health. Her privacy should be protected, and others should be told only what she wants them to know. If she requests that nothing is said regarding her absence, that request should be respected. In this event, teammates should be told that it is team policy not to comment on her absence. In the event that the person in question allows for a release of information to her teammates, they can be told specifically what information she wants to be released.

The media may also notice the absence of a particular sport participant. More care must be used with the media than with teammates. Even if the sport participant is willing to have information released, it is our recommendation that specific information not be released. In recent years, the release of information regarding a sport participant's injury status has become much more restricted, and the media seem to accept the innocuous statement that it is team policy not to release information in such instances. Another innocuous statement might be, "She is taking a much-deserved break from training and competition and will return when she is ready."

ROLES OF TREATMENT STAFF IN MANAGEMENT

In the next chapter, we will discuss the treatment team in more depth, but here we want to briefly suggest how certain treatment providers might interact with sport personnel to facilitate management of the patient. As mentioned previously, we recommend that a healthcare professional coordinate the management team. This might be a psychiatrist or nonpsychiatric physician because of potential issues related to physical health and the use of medication. This does not mean, however, that he or she would meet directly with sport personnel. For example, the psychotherapist who is working directly with the patient may consult with an athletic trainer to determine what might be an appropriate type, level of intensity, or duration of exercise for a sport participant who is allowed to train but not at a full level of participation. Or, the treating dietitian might consult with the athletic trainer regarding meal plan requirements for a patient who is allowed to compete on an upcoming road trip. The healthcare professional functioning as the coordinator would not need to meet directly with sport staff but would need to be apprised of, and agree with, such changes in the treatment plan regarding exercise and eating.

Treatment staff might also function in a less direct manner, that is, in ways that do not directly involve the patient. For example, eating disorders can create problems on a team and may even be "contagious" (as discussed in Chapter 4) and trigger concerns in teammates. One of these situations might involve the team's response to their teammate being in treatment or away from the team. In such an instance, team members may be upset, worried, curious about their teammate, or concerned about their own eating issues that arise in response to their teammate. In most of our cases, only one of us (RT or RS) meets directly with the patient. This arrangement leaves the other free to meet with the team (or sport personnel, including coaches) when necessary. With the consent of the treatment coordinator, and perhaps a consult with the coach, one of us would meet with the team. To protect confidentiality, the one of us (let's say RT in this case) who is not working directly with the patient would meet with the team. RT would meet with the team, not to discuss the patient, but to try to alleviate the concerns of her teammates. This is not only important for the team, but can be beneficial for the patient on her return to the team.

Final notes on the interaction of the treatment team with sport personnel involve the extent of interaction and, of course, confidentiality. From the aforementioned examples, it might appear that considerable interaction occurs in every case. In actuality, some cases require or need little interaction between treatment staff and sport personnel. Determining when to interact and the extent of interaction are primarily tasks of the coordinator. It goes without saying that confidentiality is always a relevant concern, and such interactions between treatment staff and sport personnel are not to occur without appropriate confidentiality safeguards. Confidentiality is a cornerstone of effective and appropriate treatment. It will be discussed in depth in the next chapter.

7

Treatment Issues

In this chapter, we will discuss the treatment process from the initial evaluation to termination of treatment. From the time we discussed treatment considerations for sport participants in *Helping Athletes With Eating Disorders* (Thompson & Sherman, 1993a) in 1993, eating disorder treatment options have increased. We will discuss those options as well as provide recommendations for increasing treatment efficacy. Specifically, we will cover special assessments for sport participants, various forms and modes of psychotherapy, dietary treatment considerations, and factors affecting treatment, such as comorbid conditions and treatment resistance, as well as necessary treatment conditions, such as confidentiality.

INITIAL EVALUATION

The initial evaluation should ideally be conducted by a physician having experience with eating disorder patients. He or she should obtain information of a general nature regarding medical history, perform a physical examination, order necessary laboratory tests and special procedures (e.g., electrocardiogram), and conduct an in-depth assessment of the "history of the present episode" (Yager, 2007a), focusing on specific eating and weight-related symptoms. Recommendations regarding the content of such history taking, examinations, tests, and procedures are presented in Chapter 8.

Perhaps the only difference in an initial evaluation with a sport participant would be to assess the role of sport participation in contributing to, or maintaining, the eating disorder. Related to this, we recommend that the healthcare professional conducting the evaluation also assess the potential positive role sport participation may play regarding the patient's identity (as a sport participant), self-esteem, and sense of attachment (to the team or teammates). Two additional goals of an initial evaluation are to determine what other special assessments are necessary and to determine the appropriate level or intensity of treatment and the appropriate treatment setting.

OTHER ASSESSMENTS

Regarding the female athlete triad (American College of Sports Medicine [ACSM], 2007), it has been recommended that the presence of one of the triad components indicates the need to assess for the others. Certainly, the presence of an eating disorder (or disordered eating) indicates a need to assess the patient's reproductive health. As we reviewed in Chapter 2, amenorrhea is a diagnostic criterion for anorexia nervosa, and menstrual irregularity is common in bulimia nervosa and eating disorder not otherwise specified (EDNOS). For this reason, a gynecological examination is warranted to assess the reproductive health of all patients without normal, regular menses. Questions to the patient regarding menstrual functioning must be specific. In our clinical practice, patients often report that they have no medical problems, despite experiencing menstrual irregularity if not amenorrhea, and as we discussed earlier, many sportswomen regard menstrual irregularity as "normal" or have a variety of reasons not to report it. Regarding the content of such an assessment and ordering the appropriate laboratory tests, we strongly recommend the evaluation procedure by Mountjoy that was discussed in Chapter 5.

Again, the presence of one triad component indicates the need to assess for the others. Menstrual dysfunction (and especially amenorrhea) indicates the need for assessment of the patient's bone health. As we discussed previously, inadequate estrogen levels can prevent bone accretion (growth) and accelerate bone resorption (turnover). Disordered eating (inadequate nutrition) resulting in the insufficient intake of calcium and vitamin D can exacerbate the process. Dual-energy x-ray absorptiometry (DEXA) is the recommended assessment for bone density. Early assessment is paramount given that many young anorexic patients experience osteopenia and even osteoporosis after having anorexia nervosa for only a short period (Mehler & MacKenzie, 2009).

Although our primary focus here is on sportswomen, it is important to remember that sportsmen, especially those in endurance sports, can experience low testosterone levels due to an eating disorder or excessive endurance training. Testosterone plays a role in bone health, and low testosterone levels can result in osteoporosis in males (Ongphiphadhanakul, Rajatanavin, Chanprasertyothin, Piaseu, & Chailurkit, 1998; Winters, 1999). Perhaps more important, at least two studies (Andersen, Watson, & Schlechte, 2000; Mehler, Sabel, Watson, & Andersen, 2008) found not only that male anorexic patients often suffer osteoporosis, but that it may be more severe than in their female counterparts. Thus, labs should include serum testosterone for male sportsmen, especially those with anorexia nervosa, as well as a DEXA to assess for abnormalities in bone density. For more information regarding the treatment of osteoporosis in anorexic patients, see Mehler and MacKenzie (2009).

PSYCHOTHERAPY

The topic of psychotherapy as it relates to the treatment of eating disorders is quite complex, and an exhaustive review is well beyond the scope of this book. The section that follows represents a very brief and broad overview. For more extensive reviews, the reader is directed to Brewerton (2004), Fairburn (2006), Fairburn and Brownell (2002), and Yager and Powers (2007).

Before discussing the specifics regarding the psychotherapeutic treatment of sport participants with eating disorders, we want to make some general comments and recommendations regarding the efficacy of that treatment. Treatment of sport participants is generally not significantly different than that of nonsport participants, although there are often special considerations for this group of patients (Powers & Thompson, 2007). In essence, the actual proceedings of a treatment session with a sport participant are not different from those of nonsport participants. We will begin the discussion by giving a brief overview of what we view as being an important part of the eating disorder treatment process for all patients, not just sport participants. That will be followed by recommendations designed to increase treatment efficacy with sport participants.

Why the Patient Might Not (Want to) Give Up the Disorder

For a variety of reasons, eating disorders are very difficult problems to overcome, even when the patient is motivated and wants to recover. Part of the difficulty involves the fact that eating disorders serve several functions or purposes for the patient. If they did not, the patient would not continue to practice his or her symptoms. Symptoms for a patient may seem more like "solutions." However, this should not be misinterpreted to mean that the patient likes the disorder. We simply mean that the disorder is "helpful" to the patient. By the term *helpful*, we do not mean ultimately helpful in terms of producing a healthy or happy state of affairs. Nonetheless, the disorder provides something for the patient, explains something for the patient, "protects" the patient, or is used by the patient. We are talking about what some might call secondary gain. A list of reasons not to give up an eating disorder is provided in Table 7.1. To illustrate how some of these reasons might be used by a patient, we will provide examples of some of the functions and purposes the disorder has served for many of our patients.

The use of the disorder for the purpose of controlling eating and weight is an obvious one and needs no explanation. The disorder can also

Table 7.1 Functions and Purposes of an Eating Disorder (or Reasons Not to Give up an Eating Disorder)

An eating disorder provides the patient with
- A means of distraction from difficult emotion
- A means to power and control
- A means to security/safety (through predictability)
- An excuse (for anything/everything)
- An explanation (for anything/everything)
- An identity
- A (safer) way to be angry
- A way to avoid (people, intimacy, difficult situations)
- A way to have others attend to him or her
- A way to be special
- A way to compete
- A way to deal with eating and weight
- A way to rebel
- A way to self-abuse/punish

---

provide the individual with an explanation or excuse for many things. For example, one of us (RT) had a sport participant who often felt stressed regarding practice. To help manage her stress, she used her bulimia nervosa by bingeing and purging before practice in order to be too sick to go to practice. Another sport participant would binge and purge after what she believed to be a poor sport performance in order to punish herself or deal with feelings of disappointment. A disorder can also serve the purpose of providing the patient with a sense of power and control. As one patient said, "I don't want to give up my disorder because it is the only thing that my mother can't control." An eating disorder can be a way to feel special and have significant others attend. As one young woman said, "My father has come to see me every day while I've been in the hospital. I'm afraid that he will go back to being the way he was if I get well."

Patients are sometimes aware of some of the reasons not to recover but not usually all of them. The number of these reasons used by a particular patient usually increases with the duration of the disorder. Such reasons are important in the treatment process. Patients usually know the reasons to recover from their disorder, and while these are important, reasons not to recover are usually more important. Reasons to recover do not usually interfere with or complicate the treatment process. The same cannot be said for reasons not to recover. Because the disorder serves functions and purposes for the patient, he or she is not apt to give up the disorder unless those same functions and purposes are managed in other ways that have nothing to do with eating disorder symptoms. Thus, one treatment goal is to teach the patient to deal with or manage whatever the disorder was providing in ways that have nothing to do with eating, food, weight, or exercise. Without such change, it is unrealistic to expect the patient to give up the disorder. When a patient is not progressing, it is a good strategy to assist him or her in determining the need for his or her symptom.

Recommendations for Increasing Treatment Efficacy With Sport Participants

Effective treatments with nonsport participants should also be effective with sport participants. It is the therapist rather than the therapy that needs to be different. Psychotherapy with sportsmen and women can be facilitated by a therapist who not only has expertise in treating eating disorders but also has experience with sport participants (Bonci et al., 2008; Petrie & Sherman, 1999; Sherman & Thompson, 2001). Equally important, however, are the therapist's beliefs regarding the importance of sport participation in the life of the individual. In our own clinical practice, we have had too many sportsmen and women tell us that they left a previous therapist because he or she did not value sport or understand its importance in their lives. In fact, these were usually sportsmen or women who had been told by their therapist that they had to leave their sport. Ideally, the therapist should have an understanding of, and appreciation for, the importance of sport participation in the patient's life. Finally, the "ideal" therapist would also have an understanding of the risk factors and pressures inherent in the sport environment that may have played a role in precipitating or maintaining the patient's disorder, or that may play a role during and following recovery from the disorder.

Types of Treatment

Typically, psychotherapy occurs in an individual, group, and family therapy format and may occur on an outpatient or inpatient basis.

Individual Therapy
In individual therapy, only the patient is participating with the therapist. The advantage of individual therapy is that the entire focus of treatment is centered on the individual patient. This allows for a focus on the unique and specific issues that predisposed, precipitated, and perpetuated the eating disorder in the individual. The disadvantages are that the patient does not have the opportunity to learn from others with similar concerns and issues, and has fewer direct opportunities to deal with relationships, both inside and outside of the family of origin.

Group Therapy
In group therapy, the patient is participating with other patients—in this case with other eating disorder patients. The advantages of group therapy are primarily cost effectiveness and the fact that group therapy also allows for opportunities to learn from other patients, as well as providing more opportunities than individual therapy regarding improving interpersonal communication and relationships. Our patients have acknowledged their initial fear of group therapy but admit that group support and understanding were beneficial to their recovery. They

have often remarked that in group therapy they did not have to explain anything because group members knew how they felt; they felt that they were immediately understood and accepted by group members.

Family Therapy
In family therapy, the patient is participating with one or more members of his or her family, and the focus is often on the family or family system as being the "patient," or that family members, especially parents with younger patients, become the agents of change as in newer family therapy approaches (Lock, le Grange, Agras, & Dare, 2001). The importance of family involvement is evidenced by the fact that recommended guidelines for treatment of eating disorders include the enlistment of family support and provision of family therapy, especially when the patient is a child or adolescent (American Psychiatric Association [APA], 2006; National Institute for Health and Clinical Excellence [NICE], 2004).

Effective treatment for a given patient might involve individual, group, or family therapy, in addition to pharmacotherapy (the use of medication as an adjunct to psychotherapy). Psychoeducational and self-help approaches may also be used.

Psychoeducation
Psychoeducational approaches involve the provision of information to patients with a psychological problem or disorder—in this case, eating disorders. Providing patients with information about their disorder can assist them in treatment and help prevent relapse. Psychoeducation can be provided to individuals, groups, and families on an outpatient or inpatient basis and may include information on any topic germane to the development, treatment, and prevention of eating disorders, such as risk factors, genetics, medical issues, exercise, and nutrition. Psychoeducational approaches have also been used with success in preventive efforts regarding eating disorders and characteristics (i.e., dieting, body dissatisfaction, etc.) associated with eating disorders (Yumamiya, Cash, Melnyk, Posavac, & Posavac, 2005).

Self-Help
The goals of self-help are to improve outcome by teaching patients skills necessary to overcome and manage their difficulties by following advice provided by self-help materials (Williams, 2003). Self-help treatments are used either independently of formal treatment or as an adjunct to

traditional treatment with a therapist. Self-help is referred to as guided when it is managed or provided by a therapist or other professional, and guided self-help is more helpful to bulimia nervosa patients than simply being on a waiting list (Perkins & Schmidt, 2005). The amount of guidance provided varies, as well as the type of guidance—face-to-face or media-based formats such as books or videos. For more information, refer to a recent review by Thiels and de Zwaan (2007).

Treatment Setting

The types of treatments that are needed and provided depend on several factors, including the treatment setting—outpatient, intensive outpatient, partial hospitalization, residential, or inpatient hospitalization.

Outpatient

Ideally, eating disorders should be treated on an outpatient basis (NICE, 2004). Outpatient treatment is advantageous in part because it allows the patient to maintain as normal a life as is possible while being in treatment, as it allows the patient to live at home and continue with school or work (APA, 2006). Eating disorder patients should be treated on an outpatient basis until medical and psychological risks increase to the point that inpatient treatment is warranted, as will be discussed in a later section.

Intensive Outpatient

In intensive outpatient treatment, the patient is typically in treatment for two to three hours daily, two to four days per week. Group therapy, psychoeducational groups, and dietary/nutritional guidance tend to be the treatments most often provided along with individual therapy. Pharmacotherapy may also be a useful adjunct for many patients. This level of treatment is appropriate for patients who need more than traditional once or twice weekly individual visits. It can also be a valuable "step-down" (lower level of care) for those patients who have been in partial hospitalization or 24-hour (residential or inpatient) programs.

Partial Hospitalization

Partial hospitalization or "day" treatment has become a popular treatment choice for eating disorder patients in recent years. It is designed for patients who do not need 24-hour care or supervision, but who are not yet ready for outpatient treatment. Partial hospitalization programs (PHPs) typically meet at least five days per week for six to eight hours daily. The day is typically structured with groups that are either therapy, psycho-educational, or nutritional/dietary in nature. Individual therapy will also occur on some days. Pharmacotherapy is also a part of the treatment protocol. Patients typically eat at least two meals daily in a partial program. Treatment in a PHP is cost effective when compared to 24-hour care, and it allows the patient to live outside a hospital setting. Dropout rates for PHP programs are lower than for inpatient hospitalization programs (Halmi, 2007). For more information regarding the structure, goals, and features of this type of treatment, the reader is directed to Olmsted (2002).

Outpatient Versus Inpatient Treatment
Ideally, eating disorder patients are treated on an outpatient basis, and in many cases they can be when the problem is identified early and appropriate treatment is provided in a timely manner. For many patients, unfortunately, identification occurs after the disorder is out of control or has become so severe as to result in dire medical or psychological consequences, requiring intensive and perhaps even inpatient treatment. Guidelines for when inpatient treatment is warranted have been recommended by several sources (Andersen, 1999a; APA, 2006; Birmingham & Beumont, 2004; Halmi, 2007; NICE, 2004; Yager, 2007a). Decisions regarding the need for hospitalization must be made on an individual, case-by-case, basis. However, recommendations for hospitalization typically involve significant weight issues (i.e., weight less than 85% of expected, significant rapid weight loss), cardiac symptoms (i.e., heart rate less than 40 beats/minute, blood pressure less than 80/50), potentially dangerous electrolyte abnormalities (i.e., hypokalemia, hypophosphatemia), or other significant medical symptomatology (unstable vital signs, severe malnutrition), suicidal risk, need for supervision regarding meals and bathroom use, and poor treatment compliance or lack of progress in outpatient treatment. Given the seriousness of the need for inpatient treatment, as well as the seriousness of the aforementioned criteria used to determine the need for such treatment, the need for experience and expertise by the treating healthcare professionals should be obvious. When a patient needs 24-hour supervision or monitoring due to the issues and problems just described, the best treatment options include residential treatment and inpatient hospitalization.

Residential

Residential treatment provides 24-hour supervision and monitoring but is not in a traditional hospital setting. Residential settings are typically more like a home or a dormitory. This type of treatment is recommended for those patients who may need 24-hour care but are not so medically compromised that a traditional hospital staff and procedures would be necessary. Individual, group, and family therapy are usually provided, as well as pharmacotherapy, with group therapy being the modality most often used. All meals and snacks are monitored, and nutritional guidance is provided on a regular basis. Patients who are successful at this level are often transitioned to lower levels of care such as day treatment, intensive outpatient, and transitional living programs (therapeutic living environment, usually with other patients who are moving to a less intense level of treatment).

Inpatient Hospitalization

Like residential treatment, inpatient hospitalization provides 24-hour supervision and monitoring but does so in a medical environment. Medical and psychiatric stabilization and nutritional rehabilitation are the primary goals of inpatient hospitalization. As with residential treatment, all meals and snacks are carefully monitored in addition to use of the bathroom to control purging. Physical activity is typically restricted to the point that complete bed rest (virtually no activity) may be used, especially early in treatment with severely malnourished patients. All forms of treatment described earlier are advisable in the inpatient environment (Halmi, 2007). As in residential treatment, patients who are successful in treatment at this level are transitioned to lower levels of care.

Treatment Goals

In general, treatment goals typically include the targeting of eating disorder symptoms for elimination, restoration of more normal eating and weight, elimination of factors that perpetuate or maintain the disorder, treating physical complications and comorbid conditions, family involvement, and relapse prevention. For more in-depth information related to these general goals, especially for inpatient treatment, the reader is directed to APA (2006) and NICE (2004). However, treatment goals can vary with the disorder, its severity, treatment availability, and the treatment setting. For the outpatient treatment of anorexia nervosa, see Kaplan and Noble (2007), and for outpatient treatment of bulimia nervosa, see Mitchell, Steffen, and Roerig (2007). The goals for binge eating disorder could be similar to those mentioned previously but might also be very different. For example, given that many patients with binge eating disorder tend to be overweight, they often want to focus on weight loss. Devlin, Allison, Goldfein, and Spanos (2007) suggest that weight stabilization and acceptance of a higher-than-average weight for height might be appropriate treatment goals for binge eating disorder. For more on the treatment of binge eating disorder, see Mitchell, Devlin, de Zwaan, Crow, and Peterson (2008).

The treatment goals for sport participants would not be different from those for nonsportsmen and women. However, regarding the elimination of factors that perpetuate or maintain the disorder, the special consideration for the sports participant would involve the factors in the sport environment that serve to maintain the disorder. These might be factors such as the emphasis on low weight in a sport like distance running, the pressures regarding cutting weight in a weight-class sport like wrestling, or a revealing uniform in an appearance sport like diving.

Treatment Outcome

Treatment outcome data for anorexia nervosa are not very encouraging. A recent review of the treatment literature related to anorexia nervosa (Bulik, Berkman, Brownley, Sedway, & Lohr, 2007) reported that studies employing randomized control trials (gold standard) were sparse and inconclusive, and male patients were underrepresented. Bulik et al. concluded that cognitive behavioral therapy (CBT) may reduce relapse risk for adults after weight is restored, but that less was known about its efficacy when the patient was in the underweight state. The reviewers reported that some forms of family therapy were effective for adolescents but not for adults. No pharmacological treatments were found to have a therapeutic effect on weight gain or psychological features of the disorder. Regarding outpatient treatment of anorexia nervosa, Pike, Attia, and Brown (2008) reported that 70% of patients either terminated treatment early or received little or no benefit from treatment.

Outcome data for bulimia nervosa are better than those for anorexia nervosa. In a recent review of randomized controlled trials regarding treatment of bulimia nervosa, Shapiro et al. (2007) reported that medication trials using fluoxetine (Prozac, 60 mg/day) decreased bingeing and purging and psychological features associated with bulimia nervosa in the short term, whereas CBT decreased these symptoms in the short and long term. Similarly, a review by Wilson and Bannon (2008) reported that manual-based CBT had the most empirical support for the treatment of bulimia nervosa. For more information on the treatment of bulimia nervosa, see Mitchell, Agras, and Wonderlich (2007).

Although most treatment research for bulimia nervosa has involved CBT, other treatments have been explored, such as interpersonal psychotherapy (IP), a form of psychotherapy developed originally for the treatment of depression (Klerman, Weissman, Rounsaville, & Chevron, 1984). The emphasis in treatment is on the patient's relationships rather than on specific eating symptoms. IP has been found to compare with CBT in terms of its effectiveness (Fairburn, Jones, Peveler, Hope, & O'Connor, 1993; Agras, Walsh, Fairburn, Wilson, & Kraemer, 2000). Dialectical behavior therapy, a form of psychotherapy developed initially for the treatment of borderline personality disorder (Linehan, 1993), has been adapted for the treatment of bulimia nervosa and binge eating disorder (Chen, Matthews, Allen, Kuo, & Linehan, 2008; Safer, Telch, & Agras, 2001; Safer, Telch, & Chen, 2009; Telch, Agras, & Linehan, 2001). Additionally, integrative cognitive affective therapy (ICAT; Wonderlich et al., 2008) is a new treatment for bulimia nervosa that utilizes interventions from CBT and emotion-focused therapies. In ICAT, the focus in treatment is on self-discrepancy, the disparity between how a patient views himself or herself and an ideal self. For a review of the literature related to outcomes of eating disorders, see Berkman, Lohr, and Bulik (2007).

Involvement of Coaches and Other Sport Personnel

In the previous chapter, we discussed the role of coaches and other sport personnel in the management of sport participants with eating disorders. We also briefly discussed having coaches and sport personnel on occasion participate in therapy sessions with their sport participant. Our recommendations in this regard are based on the belief that significant others can play a critical role in precipitating, perpetuating, or preventing eating disorders. In many cases, sport personnel, especially coaches, have a power and influence not unlike that of family members (Zimmerman, 1999). For this reason, we consider them to be the patient's "sport family." By having them involved, we increase the likelihood of their power and influence having a positive impact. Not only can they be involved in positively impacting a patient's treatment and recovery, but their inclusion provides them with an experience of what the treatment process is like. This experience can be helpful to them when subsequent sportsmen or women have similar difficulties. Additionally, the experience also helps them better understand the necessity and value of treatment, which could facilitate the referral of subsequent sports participants.

PHARMACOTHERAPY

Pharmacotherapy involves the use of medications and on rare occasions may be the primary form of treatment with eating disorders, but more often it is used as an adjunct to psychotherapy. Although several types of medication have been used with eating disorder patients, antidepressant medications have been used most with varying degrees of success. Although medications for the most part have not proven beneficial to anorexic patients during the acute (very low weight) stage of their disorder, fluoxetine (60 mg) has been of benefit to some patients in preventing relapse after weight restoration (Kaplan & Noble, 2007; Walsh, 2002). Preliminary work with atypical antipsychotic medications (i.e., olanzapine) may be helpful in promoting weight gain with less fear and resistance (Kaplan & Noble, 2007). For more information regarding pharmacotherapy with anorexic patients, see Crow, Mitchell, Roerig, and Steffen (2009), Pike et al. (2008), or Walsh (2002).

Although pharmacotherapy research with bulimia nervosa has included agents of several types with varying degrees of efficacy (i.e., anticonvulsants, 5-HT_3 antagonists, etc.), the majority of the work in this area has involved antidepressant medications. Such medications appear to be effective for many patients in that they contribute to reductions in binge eating and vomiting, as well as in related mood and anxiety symptoms associated with bulimia nervosa, but these drugs alone were never the most efficacious treatment (Mitchell et al., 2007). Despite the apparent efficacy of several antidepressant medications with bulimic patients, one such medication, bupropion (Wellbutrin), is contraindicated because of the possible side effect of seizures. An in-depth review of the pharmacotherapy research with bulimic patients is beyond the scope of this chapter. For such a review, however, the reader is directed to Mitchell et al. (2007) or Walsh (2002).

Pharmacologic treatments for binge eating disorder have been different from those for anorexia nervosa and bulimia nervosa in that they have included medications designed not only to decrease the frequency of binge eating but also to facilitate weight loss for overweight patients. Research in this area is somewhat limited, but preliminary studies suggest that medication in combination with appropriate psychosocial interventions adds little in terms of reducing binge eating, but may be helpful regarding weight loss or a reduction in depressive symptoms (Devlin et al., 2007).

Medication-Related Weight Changes

A final note on the use of medications with eating disorder patients involves their possible effects on the patient's weight, which will be briefly discussed in Chapter 8. As with many topics in this book, the issue of weight change—both up and down—is well beyond the purpose of this book. Suffice it to say that psychotropic medications are being used to help manage the many psychiatric comorbid conditions that are often found in eating disorder patients, and healthcare professionals using such medications must be aware that they can have significant effects on the development or course of an eating disorder (Powers & Cloak, 2007).

DIETARY/NUTRITIONAL COUNSELING AND NUTRITIONAL REHABILITATION

The importance of the dietary/nutritional component to the eating disorder patient's treatment cannot be overstated. It is also one of the more difficult aspects of treatment for many patients and for the dietitian who conducts it. It involves what the patient regards as the feared object—food. It may be the patient's most feared aspect of treatment, and the one that the patient most often resists or tries to avoid. Its importance lies not only in medical stabilization; depending on the condition of the patient, it may have to take place before psychotherapy can be meaningfully undertaken or even before the accurate identification of comorbid conditions can occur. In a semistarved state, starvation effects can affect virtually all aspects of normal functioning, including concentration, mood, personality, social behavior, and sexual interest/ drive, as well as hunger, eating, metabolism, and health. Interestingly, we have known this long before eating disorders became so prominent and prevalent.

Keys, Brozek, Henschel, Mickelsen, and Taylor (1950) were interested in how men in the U.S. military might respond to diminished food intake if taken captive by enemy forces. After establishing baselines for these men, the experimenters then restricted their eating to 50% of their baseline intake for six months while keeping them physically active. The changes that occurred in the test subjects were very similar to what is commonly seen in semistarved eating disorder patients. They became preoccupied with food, as well as depressed and anxious. They lost interest in sex and withdrew socially. Some engaged in binge eating. As they lost weight, their metabolism decreased significantly and they developed physical symptoms like hypothermia.

For reasons that should be obvious from Keys et al., eating disorder patients often must begin treatment by eating. By restoring more normal levels of nutrition, patients are often better able to concentrate. Sometimes depression and anxiety symptoms are decreased. Such changes not only increase the patient's ability to benefit from psychotherapy, but they also in part help the clinician decide what comorbid conditions exist and how best to treat or manage them. Nutritional rehabilitation and the dietitian who directs it are critical components in successful management and treatment of the eating disorder patient. When the patient is a sport participant, a dietitian with both expertise in treating eating disorders and experience in treating sportsmen and women is the ideal choice (Petrie & Sherman, 1999; Sherman & Thompson, 2001; Thompson & Sherman, 1993b).

Nutritional Rehabilitation/Management

Many, if not most, eating disorder patients have little sense of "normal" eating and seldom eat in response to hunger even if they have a recognizable hunger signal. Interestingly, many feel that they do not need eating or nutritional guidance and assistance from a dietitian, saying that they know what they need to eat. Typically, what they (think they) know are the calorie count and the number of fat grams in particular foods, and even these are often overestimates. Most have "fear" foods that they usually avoid. Given these issues, the goals for nutritional management should include the reeducation of the patient regarding nutrition and the restoration of normal eating behaviors (Beals, 2004). These can be accomplished through the replacement of countless myths and misinformation regarding eating, food, and weight with documented nutritional information and the gradual reintroduction of fear foods. Of equal importance to reestablishing normal eating is the reestablishment of normal thinking about eating because more normal eating behaviors cannot be maintained without *thinking* more normally. Although this aspect of nutritional management may sound like the province of the psychotherapist, it is also the province of many dietitians with experience working with eating disorder patients.

The need for a dietitian with experience with sport participants is evidenced by the myths regarding eating, food, and weight that are used by such individuals. Sportsmen and women with eating disorders are apt to use the same myths and misinformation as nonsport participants, but are also likely to use some that are specific to sport participation, such as whether to eat pre- or postcompetition meals, what to eat before a competition, or eating rituals or superstitious eating behaviors before a competition. The role of the sports dietitian will be discussed further in Chapter 9 regarding prevention of eating disorders in the sport environment.

WEIGHING THE SPORT PARTICIPANT/PATIENT

The weight of the sport participant/patient is obviously an important factor in treatment. It is so important that it must be obtained by appropriate healthcare professionals at appropriate intervals and in the appropriate manner. At the same time, it should not be the sole determinant of the appropriate level of treatment (APA, 2006; NICE, 2004). It must be remembered that weight is a very personal issue for many individuals, especially females. It is certainly a very personal issue for an eating disorder patient, and one that can generate considerable fear or anxiety for the patient. A patient may also be uncomfortable or even embarrassed for others to know her weight. It should be remembered that weighing has often become a compulsive and symptomatic behavior for many patients. For others, the scales may need to be avoided at all times. For these reasons, weighing (or scale avoidance) can become part of the patient's symptom complex. Thus, considerable care and sensitivity should be used when weighing such an individual.

The discussion that follows is clinical in nature and is intended primarily for the use of healthcare professionals involved in the treatment of the affected sport participant. At the same time, such a discussion could also be beneficial for those individuals not specifically involved in treatment, for whom an understanding of the complexity and importance of weighing could facilitate their role in management and support.

Symptomatic Versus Therapeutic Weighing

As we have indicated previously, the patient's weight should be obtained by a healthcare professional because we view it as a medical issue. Typically, this would be a physician, psychotherapist, or dietitian. It might also be an athletic trainer. As discussed previously, weighing has become symptomatic for most patients. Weighing by a medical professional facilitates weighing becoming therapeutic. That is, we want it to play a role in the patient's recovery, rather than as a symptom in her disorder. Thus, it must be used in treatment in such a way that it eventually plays a role in recovery.

Symptomatic Weighing
When used symptomatically, the patient is often using weighing to allay anxiety regarding her weight and may weigh when feeling anxious. If her weight is down, she may feel not only a sense of relief but also a feeling of accomplishment that serves to reinforce weighing. This often leads to more frequent weighing and a weighing goal of weight loss. Weighing can also be used by the patient to "motivate" (scare) herself to avoid eating (especially if her weight is up) because her weight is never low enough (to feel secure). The patient will reason that eating less has produced her weight loss (and is correct). Thus, she feels she must continue to eat less in order not to regain the weight.

Therapeutic Weighing
There are several ways to use weighing therapeutically. First, we ask the patient not to weigh herself and inform her that she is to be weighed only by healthcare professionals involved in her treatment. This is a communication to the patient that weighing is a medical issue. If the patient is in residential or inpatient treatment, compliance with the recommendation is not an issue, as it may be on an outpatient basis. If the patient can comply with the request not to weigh, the symptomatic behaviors and thoughts associated with weighing are not practiced and thus decrease in strength. If unable to comply, the patient may need a more controlled environment (i.e., residential, inpatient hospitalization).

When weighing the patient, it is important that the message about weighing be different from the ones the patient uses to maintain the disorder; that is, although weight is important, its importance needs to be communicated in a way that is different from the obsessive and symptomatic messages used by the patient. This issue speaks to the need for experience and expertise with eating disorders by those treating the patient. Critical mistakes by well-meaning but inexperienced healthcare professionals in the treatment of eating disorder patients often involve unknowingly reinforcing the patient's obsessions about weight and weighing (Thompson & Sherman, 1989). An example of such a mistake involves a nurse who in an attempt to help an anorexic patient not worry about being weighed, said to the patient, "A person as thin as you doesn't have to worry about her weight." Although this communication was intended to reassure the patient, it may have inadvertently confirmed her belief that she does not have to worry about her weight if it is low enough. Or, conversely, that she would have to worry if it was not low enough.

Even if the practitioner avoids making such a mistake as the nurse in our example, balance is still needed in the focus on weight. Thus, we want to focus on weight but not overfocus on it. Overfocusing on weight can confirm that her weight is as important as she has feared. (This is also one of many reasons to deemphasize weight in the sport environment.) We want to communicate that weight is important, but as one indicator of her health. As health is emphasized, this is an excellent opportunity to communicate to the sport participant patient that good health is a major factor in good sport performance and that good nutrition is a major contributor to good health.

Once the decision has been made to weigh the patient, several strategies for weighing can be used therapeutically. Weighing at the beginning of a therapy session communicates its importance, but it also allows the therapist to know how much time and emphasis need to be given to weighing during a particular session. If weight goals are being met, then less time and emphasis devoted to weight will be needed. A question about weighing the patient involves whether the patient should know her weight. The answer must be determined by the therapist or treatment team. In some cases, it may be better that the patient not know her weight, but it is probably naïve to think that she will not weigh herself if she is in outpatient treatment. If the treating professional or treatment team determines that the patient is not to know her weight, simply have her face away from the scale when being weighed. In such a case, try to be quick about determining the weight. Some patients have informed us that hearing the weighing professional move the sliding weights back and forth (on a manual or doctor's scale) makes them anxious. Taking such time also can confirm the patient's obsessive-compulsive beliefs about weighing that it must be exact and done with extreme care and precision.

We typically tell the patient why she needs to be weighed for health or medical reasons. Sometimes our decision about how often to weigh the patient has to do with how often the patient has been weighing herself. We tend to go in the opposite direction of her symptomatic weighing. If she has been weighing frequently, we tend to weigh her less often. If she is afraid to weigh and never weighs herself, we tend to weigh her more. The rationale for this strategy involves not having (allowing) the patient to practice her symptomatic and compulsive use of weighing. If the patient is weighing too frequently, we limit weighing to prevent her from practicing the behavior but also to have her begin to deal with her anxiety without resorting to her symptom (weighing). If she is afraid to weigh, we weigh her more to assist her in overcoming her fears related to weighing or weight. In essence, we are attempting to change her symptomatic weighing (or avoidance of weighing) to therapeutic weighing.

Another strategy for making weighing therapeutic is to ask the patient before and after weighing how she feels. This can not only give the treating professional information about the emotions driving her need to weigh, but also provides an opportunity to begin to desensitize the patient to weight and weighing. Additionally, the patient can be asked what she wants to see when weighed, that is, an increase in weight, a decrease, or no change. Again, this not only provides the treating professional with information about her thinking, goals, and feared outcome regarding weight, but also provides an opportunity to begin restructuring her irrational thoughts in this regard. Also, related to the patient's thinking, we often ask the patient before being weighed to estimate her weight. Often, the patient assumes (obsesses) that she weighs too much or has gained too much weight. Thinking in this regard usually leads to symptomatic behavior. Asking what she thinks she weighs provides information to the treating professional but also to the patient regarding the irrational and inaccurate nature of her (symptomatic) estimates. Over time we want the patient to become more accurate at estimating her weight without having to weigh. Obviously, when able to do this, the patient is less apt to practice the irrational thinking that often leads to compulsive and symptomatic weighing.

143

COMORBIDITY

Comorbidity refers to the psychiatric and medical conditions that co-occur with eating disorders. Many, if not most, eating disorder patients have one or more comorbid conditions (Braun, Sunday, & Halmi, 1994; Milos, Spindler, & Schnyder, 2004). The most common conditions co-occurring with an eating disorder are mood disorders (major depressive, dysthymic, and bipolar disorders), anxiety disorders (generalized anxiety, panic, obsessive-compulsive, and posttraumatic stress disorders), substance use disorders, and personality disorders (Yager, 2007a). These comorbid conditions can either be risk factors for the development of an eating disorder or can exacerbate an existing disorder. Additionally, they can greatly affect the course of treatment for an eating disorder patient. Some comorbid conditions can be (semi)starvation effects, and some may remit with successful treatment. Depending on their severity and relation to the eating disorder, some comorbid conditions can be treated concomitantly with the eating disorder, whereas others may need to be treated prior to or following eating disorder treatment. For more information on such conditions and recommended treatment modifications, see Sansone and Sansone (2007). For how these comorbid conditions might specifically affect sport participants, the reader is directed to the National Collegiate Athletic Association (NCAA; 2007).

CONFIDENTIALITY

Confidentiality involves maintaining the patient's privacy; that is, information obtained during treatment is to be protected and provided only to those individuals with a legitimate need to know. Confidential information can be given to others only with the patient's permission. To do otherwise is not only unethical but illegal, except in a few clearly defined instances (i.e., potential danger to self or others). Its importance to the process of psychotherapy involves creating a therapeutic environment in which the patient can feel safe and secure in discussing very sensitive and personal information—information that is so sensitive that it may not be known to anyone other than the patient. Although confidentiality is the "cornerstone" of psychological treatment, many coaches experience it as a "stumbling block." That is, a well-meaning coach, who is genuinely concerned about one of his sport participants, may become frustrated when unable to receive information about the player's condition and treatment. As one coach said, "When you send your players to the counseling center, it's like they disappear into a black hole."

There appear to be several reasons for frustrations related to confidentiality, but these do not have to occur if handled properly from the beginning of the treatment process. One reason involves the fact that those in the sport world are not aware of the ethical and legal nature of confidentiality. Healthcare professionals are not simply choosing to be withholding and difficult. Information cannot be released without the patient's consent. It is true that they can use their discretion about what or how much information to release once given permission to release information, and this may be part of the difficulty. Unfortunately, many healthcare professionals believe that sport participation or even a coach play a critical role in the precipitation or maintenance of the eating disorder. In such a situation, they are apt to be less likely to release information, believing that individuals in the sport environment cannot be trusted to use the information appropriately.

Coaches often report that confidentiality is a problem for them, not because they do not understand it, but because of the aforementioned issue of trust. Many assume that they are not being given health information because they cannot be trusted to use it in the patient's best interest. To use an analogous situation, many assume that our recommendation that they not weigh their sport participants is based on this same assumption—that they cannot be trusted to use the information therapeutically. However, many of these same coaches again assume that we are ascribing ulterior motives to them when they weigh their teams; that is, that we think they are "bad guys," as one coach described it. It is true that we fear that they will use the information in ways that are not therapeutic, but only because they do not usually know how to use it therapeutically. And without training, there is no way they could be expected to know how to use it therapeutically. The other reason is that coaches have so much power with their sport participants that some participants would worry about what the coach thought about their weight and what was to be done with their weight. Those who are predisposed to an eating disorder might try to decrease their weight in unhealthy ways in order not to "displease" the coach.

It appears that part of the difficulty related to confidentiality for coaches involves assumptions and biases on both sides of the issue. Part of the bias against coaches by healthcare professionals has been fueled by reports in the popular press (e.g., Ryan, 2000) as well as the professional literature (e.g., Thompson, 1998) in which coaches have been implicated in playing significant roles in sport participants' use of potentially dangerous pathogenic weight loss methods. The question is whether these incidents are a thing of the past or are still occurring too often. It is probably naïve to believe that they do not occur, and any occurrences are too many. However, with the information now available to coaches in this area (e.g., Eating Disorders Foundation of Victoria, 2005; International Olympic Committee Medical Commission [IOCMC], 2005; NCAA, 2005), coaches are more aware of the seriousness of eating disorders and disordered eating with regard to the health of their sport participants, and they report that they do not want their charges undereating (e.g., Sherman, DeHass, Thompson, & Wilfert, 2005). Thus, we believe that although abuses are occurring and will likely continue to occur, they are occurring less often. We anticipate that this positive trend will continue as educational and preventive efforts are increasing, efforts that will be discussed in Chapter 9.

Confidentiality does not have to be a problem if handled properly from the beginning. In the first stage of treatment, we ask our patients if they want anyone from the sport family to be informed as to their progress, stressing that it is their decision. Such a decision should never be coerced. In fact, there should not even be an implication or suggestion that they acquiesce to such a request or question. Most of our sport participant patients indicate a desire to have them be informed. Information in this regard could be simple to complex, depending on what the patient wants to be communicated. It might be as simple as informing the athletic training staff or coaches that the sport participant is or is not allowed to train and compete until further notice. It might simply be that the sportsman or woman is attending treatment and progressing. Sometimes the sport participant wants them to be not only informed but involved as well.

The patients are told that any information to be released to others will be thoroughly discussed with them prior to the release, including the exact content and to whom it is to be released. Also, they are told that only minimal information will be released (unless directed otherwise by them) and only information for which the intended recipient has a reasonable need to know. The patients are informed that the recipient will be told of the personal and sensitive nature of the information and will be told that they are to keep the information private. Patients are told that, even though the recipient has been given these instructions, he or she may choose to ignore them. They are also told that they can at any time revoke the permission to release information.

To provide the patient with additional options regarding the release of information, they can choose to have sport personnel come to a session in which the information is released in person. If they prefer that the information be released on the telephone, they can choose to be with the therapist when it is released. If it is their preference that it be released in written form, the patient reads it prior to release. If they choose this option, we recommend a letter rather than electronic sources such as a facsimile or an email.

Final Thoughts

We feel that it is time for healthcare professionals to consider decreasing their biases against coaches and other sport personnel and begin facilitating a better relationship with concerned individuals in the sport world to facilitate the treatment and health of sportsmen and women with eating disorders and other related health problems. Further, we feel the onus of such a process change falls primarily on mental health practitioners, in that improving communication and enhancing the quality of interpersonal relationships are generally a part of their training and hopefully a part of their expertise.

SPECIAL TREATMENT ISSUES AND PROBLEMS

Jamie is a 21-year-old rower who has struggled with bulimia nervosa for 4 years. Even though her weight is in a normal range for her height, she believes that she needs to lose weight. Her only medical problem involves menstrual irregularity. Because of her eating disorder, she is required to be seen in individual outpatient psychotherapy twice weekly. She is allowed to train and compete as long as she complies with all treatment recommendations, makes progress in treatment, and does not develop any medical or psychological problems that would increase her risk. Jamie does not like having the required therapy and readily admits that she would not be in treatment if she were not required to do so in order to continue in her sport.

Decisions Regarding Training and Competition

One of the more difficult and sometimes controversial decisions to be made in treatment involves whether the symptomatic sport participant will be allowed to train and compete. Those who oppose allowing the individual to train and compete while symptomatic argue that not only is it a health risk, but that treatment is being made subordinate to sport. In essence, the individual's sport performance is viewed as being more important than his or her health. We and others have suggested that there are advantages to allowing the sport participant to train and compete while in treatment as long as several important controls are in place (Powers & Thompson, 2007, 2008; Sherman & Thompson, 2001). We will discuss these advantages, but first we want to explain the conditions necessary to ensure the safety of the patient.

Conditions Necessary for Training and Competition
The first step in this process involves diagnosis. If the patient meets diagnostic criteria for anorexia nervosa, he or she does not train or compete. The medical risk is too great, and this is a communication to the patient that he or she is too ill to train or compete. For those who do not meet criteria for anorexia nervosa, it must be determined by the treatment team that training or competition will not increase the medical or psychological risk to the patient. This has sometimes been referred to as clearing the patient to play or return to play for those who may have been withheld from training or competition. Specifics should be provided regarding clearance for which activities and how much activity is acceptable. These specifics will also be discussed in the next chapter. Additionally, the patient must be in treatment and progressing. The patient should also want to train and compete, rather than participating in sport in order to please (or not displease) others. Before consideration for possible sport participation, the patient must be at a body mass index (BMI) of at least 18.5 and preferably 19, or be at 90% of expected body weight based on height for general population cohorts (not sport group cohorts). The patient must remain in full compliance with all treatment goals and recommendations. In addition to these aforementioned general requirements, each patient should also be required to meet maintenance criteria that are specific to his or her particular case. Finally, a decision to allow the patient to train and compete should be considered a tentative one that can be revoked at any time based on a lack of compliance with treatment goals and recommendations, a lack of progress in treatment, a negative change in the patient's medical or psychological condition, or simply at the discretion of the treatment team. The patient should be fully apprised of the criteria

necessary for sport participation, as well as the conditions under which sport participation is to be withdrawn.

Advantages of Training/Competing While Symptomatic

Allowing some sport participants with eating disorders to train and compete may seem incongruent with our requirement that health is not to be subordinate to sport. However, our recommendation to allow training and competition for some individuals is not related to sport performance. Rather, it is related to the individual's health. We think that when properly managed, sport participation can facilitate treatment. It allows patients to maintain their identity as a sportsman or woman. It allows them to maintain an important source (sometimes the only source) of self-esteem. That is, it allows them to do the thing they may do best. Not being able to participate may increase depression. Sport participation allows them to maintain a sense of attachment by being part of a team. Allowing them to train and compete may make it easier for them to make the necessary changes in eating and weight. The concern about having sport participants train and compete often focuses on the physical activity or exercise related to their sport. By having them continue with sport, they may be less at risk because, as part of the team, their condition and symptoms can be more easily monitored, and controlled by sport personnel if necessary. If not participating, they are apt to be less "visible" and may go against medical advice and lose more weight, engage in dangerous symptoms, or exercise without supervision. To reiterate, allowing them to train and compete is not about sport but rather about what is in the best interest of the individual.

A final note on allowing sport participants to train and compete relates to the potential positive effect of exercise. The concern about allowing symptomatic sport participants to train and compete often centers on the physical activity or exercise related to their sport. However, although higher levels of exercise are associated with greater eating pathology, sport participation may mediate this relationship; that is, the relationship may not apply to sport participants as it does to nonsport participants (Madison & Ruma, 2003). Also, at least one study with nonsport participant bulimic patients (Sundgot-Borgen, Rosenvinge, Bahr, & Schneider, 2002) found that exercise produced treatment effects that were greater than for a treatment group receiving cognitive behavioral therapy— effects that were maintained at 18-month follow-up. At follow-up, 8 of 15 (62%) patients in the exercise group had recovered from bulimia nervosa compared to 5 of 16 (36%) patients in the CBT group. An additional finding that might be of importance regarding the treatment of sport participants was the fact that the exercise group showed an increase in peak oxygen consumption and a healthy decrease in body fat.

Motivating the Resistant Sport Participant-Patient

Anyone who treats eating disorder patients is aware that such patients can be very challenging because of the resistance that is characteristic of many such patients, especially anorexic patients. Overcoming that resistance often occupies considerable time in treatment. Such resistance is not infrequently found in sport participants but may be dealt with more easily in some cases than in nonsport participants. As has been suggested earlier, the sport participant may resist an initial evaluation or resist participating in treatment following the evaluation, as well as resist change during treatment. Overcoming resistance often involves attempting to motivate the patient. Sport participation is one form of motivation that is not available to healthcare professionals when treating eating disorder patients who do not participate in organized sports. When sport participation is withheld (or threatened to be withheld), because of either health issues or a lack of treatment progress, many sport participants will worker harder in treatment to regain or maintain their sport participation. This form of motivation was discussed in Chapter 6 and will not be recounted here.

Using sport in this way also provides information regarding another important issue. Some individuals in sport are not participating in sport because they want to participate. Some are playing or participating in order to please others. In a study of successful sport participants, Hemery (1986) found a need to please others. The need to please significant others is a characteristic often found in eating disorder patients and is probably related to their need for approval (Garfinkel & Garner, 1982) and to their tendency toward being compliant (Bruch, 1973; Strober, 1986). Some have such a need to please that they are willing to sacrifice their own needs for the needs of others (which in sport can make them look like the consummate team player). Quitting a sport is not often viewed by them as an acceptable way out of their dilemma. Some of the sport participants with eating disorders who do not work to regain sport participation may do so as a more acceptable way to leave their sport. On occasion, we have told these patients that we will provide them with a way out by recommending that they no longer continue in their sport for health reasons (by taking responsibility for them not continuing), and on occasion we have had individuals accept such an offer.

Coaches' Concerns Regarding Treatment

On numerous occasions in this book, we have discussed the power and influence that coaches have with their sportsmen and women. How that power and influence is communicated by the coach can affect not only whether a sport participant seeks treatment but also the outcome of treatment. Thus, what coaches believe about treatment is of paramount importance. The following concerns of coaches have been made known to us primarily through our clinical, consulting, educational, and prevention work with coaches.

Confidentiality
We have already discussed the major concern of many coaches—not being given information regarding their sport participants' condition and treatment (confidentiality), and it will not be recounted here.

Valuing the Importance of Sport
Other concerns include the contention that the therapist will not value the importance of sport in the patient's life. This is not an irrational belief on the part of a coach. In our own clinical practice, we have worked with sport participants who have left other therapists because those therapists cavalierly recommended (sometimes insisted) that they leave their sport, as if sport participation were (should be) of little consequence. This concern by coaches relates to our earlier recommendation that healthcare professionals who work with sport participants would ideally have an understanding of and an appreciation for the importance of sport in the life of the sportsman or sportswoman.

Too Much Weight
Another concern of some coaches, especially those who coach sports that emphasize a thin body, size, or shape, or low weight, involves weight. The specific concern is that the patient will gain "too much weight." The question here is too much weight for what. We assume such coaches are suggesting that the individual might gain too much weight to perform well athletically. As discussed earlier in this chapter, one of the goals of treatment is the attainment and maintenance of a healthy weight. In essence,

151

this means a weight that allows the body to avoid the typical medical and psychological consequences of an eating disorder. The treatment team will likely have a target weight range that it is recommending in order to accomplish this goal. In actuality, it is most likely the patient's body that determines the appropriate weight. For example, the body generally determines when the right set of factors (i.e., general health, nutrition, appropriate training level, reduced stress, etc.) is in place to restore menstruation in an amenorrheic sportswoman. Restoration of menses, like the remission of other symptoms, is a message from the body that health conditions have improved.

A related issue regarding weight has to do with the risk of relapse. A "suboptimal" weight—a weight below that necessary for the body and mind to function healthfully—is an important factor determining whether the patient maintains her therapeutic gains, continues to struggle, or relapses. A risk factor for relapse is maintenance of a suboptimal weight (Strober, Freeman, & Morrell, 1997). Thus, a higher weight is not only healthier for the patient; it is also protective against relapse.

Treatment Decreases Competitiveness
Some coaches have been concerned about psychological treatment decreasing the sportsperson's competitiveness. This is perhaps related to a stigma related to treatment and the people who do therapy, as well as those who need therapy, that suggests such individuals are "soft" or lacking in "toughness." Certainly mental toughness and competitiveness are valued traits in the sport world.

Does treatment decrease competitiveness? We do not have an answer to this question, but it is hard to imagine successful treatment decreasing any positive behavioral or personality characteristic. Most likely, coaches are concerned about competitiveness because they feel that a decrease in competitiveness will likely result in a decrement in sport performance. Thus, the issue in which the coach is probably most interested is sport performance. From a physical/medical standpoint, many, if not most, individuals with an eating disorder are malnourished, dehydrated, fatigued, have difficulty sleeping, and are medically compromised. Psychologically, they tend to be depressed, distracted, obsessed, anxious, and have difficulty relaxing. As a consequence, concentration and motivation are apt to be decreased. With successful treatment, virtually all of these symptoms/complications are apt to be decreased if not eliminated. Given that, wouldn't the sport participants who have completed successful treatment perform better than the eating disordered sport participants without treatment? Not only will they perform better; they will perform better *longer*.

Treatment Takes Time Away From Sport

There is no argument here. Successful treatment takes considerable time. However, improvements in most or all of the symptoms/complications listed in the previous paragraph will allow sportsmen and women to get more out of their physical and mental preparation and training. Just reasoning from a psychological point of view, they will be able to focus and concentrate better; that is, they will be able to think, make decisions, and react faster. Their improved emotional state will allow them to "play with emotion" rather than being distracted or constrained by it. Yes, treatment takes time, but it can eventually result in a more effective and productive use of time.

Final Note

One of the best uses of a coach's power and influence with his or her team is the support and encouragement of timely and appropriate treatment.

Treatment Versus Sport

We want to end this chapter with one of the most important recommendations that we will make in this book: Treatment can never be subordinate to sport. That is, the patient cannot be allowed to miss or put off treatment in order to train or compete. A patient cannot be rushed through treatment to return quickly to sport competition, nor can the patient be allowed to engage in any sport-related activity that runs counter to the treatment plan. If sport takes precedence over treatment, a message is being communicated to the sport participant. The message is that sport performance is more important than the health of the player. Unfortunately, this is a message that is consistent with the beliefs of many eating disordered individuals. Their self-esteem is often low, and many feel that they have little worth other than through pleasing others by what they do—in this case, play sports. By placing sport above or before treatment (and health), this belief about self is being confirmed. This runs counter to the treatment goal of building self-esteem and learning to value oneself for who the patient is rather than for what he or she does (or looks like or weighs).

A FINAL THOUGHT ON TREATMENT

In previous chapters we have discussed the risk factors that appear to place sport participants at increased risk for developing disordered eating if not an eating disorder. In this chapter, we have examined many nuances of eating disorders in such individuals that can serve to complicate treatment. Although the treatment of eating disorders can sometimes be a challenging, stressful, and even daunting task, there is a positive aspect to treating sport participants. We previously discussed what we have called "good athletes"—sport participants whom coaches want and value because of the psychological traits that play a role in their success in the sport arena. In discussing their good athlete traits, we suggested that these same traits may increase their risk of developing an eating disorder. Ironically, those same traits can assist them in treatment if used properly by the therapist. Their mental toughness and willingness to "play with pain" can help them deal more effectively with the aspects of treatment that are apt to increase their fear or anxiety, such as eating, gaining weight, or giving up their symptoms. Their "coachability" probably allows them more often to follow therapist instructions and recommendations, in that the therapist is in some ways like a coach. One of our patients even remarked, "You're like my *head* coach." Their perfectionism/pursuit of excellence will likely lead them to want to excel in treatment. What is required from a therapist in order to use these good athlete traits in therapy? It takes a therapist who has taken the time and made the effort to understand and appreciate not only sport, but also the personal traits and characteristics involved, and most importantly the individuals who possess them.

8

Medical Considerations

Pauline Powers, MD, FAED

INTRODUCTION

Eating disorders are common conditions that are increasing in prevalence worldwide (Hay, Mond, Buttner, & Darby, 2008) and are beginning to affect a range of people at various ages (Mangweth-Matzek et al., 2006). At the same time, participation in sports is becoming much more popular (Mond, Myers, Crosby, Hay, & Mitchell, 2008). These two sets of events commonly intersect, and many sports participants are affected by eating disorders. Although there is disagreement as to whether or not participation in sport itself increases the risk for an eating disorder or whether an individual with an eating disorder is more likely to participate in sport, co-occurrence is common.

Role of the Physician

Physicians are likely to be involved in many ways, beginning with the often-required preparticipation evaluation of children and adolescents. Among adults who decide to participate in sports, particularly older adults, the primary care physician is expected to advise patients how to participate safely (Swinburn, Walter, Arroll, Tilyard, & Russell, 1997). For individuals with certain limitations (for example, hypertension or asthma) or other disabilities, the physician is typically asked to assess the safety of the planned sport activity and make recommendations for accommodation. Teams associated with schools from primary grades through college often have a physician as part of the sport management team. Leagues involving children or adolescents usually have a physician as an advisor or as part of the team. Among sports involving elite athletes, physicians are an integral part of the endeavor. The International Olympics Committee Medical Commission (IOCMC) includes physicians from many specialties; recommendations from this commission are taken seriously and implemented for Olympic athletes.

Medical personnel are involved when participants of any age develop sport-related problems, including cardiac, respiratory, orthopedic, and psychiatric complications. Eating disorders are now recognized as common among athletes, and healthcare professionals from many specialties are likely to be involved in prevention, assessment, and treatment, including physicians (psychiatrists, pediatricians, family practice physicians, internists, and sports medicine specialists), psychologists, social workers, and nutritionists.

Two Teams: Health Management Team and Sport Management Team

As noted in Chapter 1, there are two teams involved in the assessment and management of eating disorders in sport: the health management team and the sports management team. These teams have different agendas, responsibilities, and conflicts. For example, healthcare teams typically describe eating disorders in psychiatric and medical terminology utilizing specific diagnostic criteria for anorexia nervosa and bulimia nervosa (in the United States as specified in the American Psychiatric Association *Diagnostic and Statistical Manual* [2000]), but key sport management guidelines typically refer to the female athlete triad (which is defined as disordered eating, amenorrhea, and osteoporosis). Both the IOCMC (2005) and the National Collegiate Athletic Association (2005) have guidelines for the assessment and management of the female athlete triad. Although there are advantages and disadvantages to both descriptive systems, these differences may be relatively easily resolved. However, the goals of the two teams can be widely divergent. For example, the primary goal of the health management team is optimal health of the athlete, and the primary goal of the sport management

156

team is likely to be success in sport. Recently the National Athletic Trainers' Association issued a position statement aimed at preventing, detecting, and managing disordered eating in athletes (Bonci et al., 2008) that was written from the perspective of the athletic trainer. The athletic trainer is often the member of the sport management team who facilitates communication with the physician on the health management team.

Medical practitioners may be on either team or both teams. There are complex issues related to legal responsibilities and liabilities (Pearsall, Kovaleski, & Madanagopal, 2005). For example, physicians may be held legally liable for not performing a standard preparticipation examination if a problem develops during a sport activity, or for violating an individual's civil rights if participation is not recommended. Or, the practitioner may be held liable for not administering appropriate care at the sport event or afterward. Although these legal complexities have not been widely discussed in terms of the contribution of sport activity to the development of eating disorders and the role of the physician in preventing or detecting eating disorders, this is likely to become an important topic as eating disorders and sport participation continue to increase.

Chapter Topics

Despite some of the difficulties noted above, there are many opportunities for physicians to contribute to the health of patients participating in sport who are afflicted with eating disorders. In this chapter, the preparticipation evaluation will be described and the most common medical complications will be reviewed. The role of medications in the management of eating disorders and the effect on sport performance will be discussed. The antidoping movement and its impact on prescription of medications will be discussed. Finally, the controversial topic of medical clearance and the connection to medical risk will be reviewed and specific recommendations will be made for modification of this concept.

PREPARTICIPATION EVALUATION: CHILDREN AND ADOLESCENTS

Recommendations for evaluation of health status prior to participation in sport have been discussed for decades, and in the last few years there have been efforts to standardize this evaluation. Most schools now require a preparticipation assessment, and it is estimated that during a typical year over 12 million students in the United States alone are evaluated. One focus has been on young competitive athletes in schools, and another focus has been on young elite athletes.

The Proposed Sport and the Child or Adolescent

Childhood and adolescence is a time of dramatic growth and development, and the changes that occur do so at different chronological ages for different children. Although typically considered to be in good health, the reality is that children and adolescents often have physical, mental, and behavioral disorders. The preparticipation evaluation offers the clinician an opportunity to identify these problems and participate in health maintenance in the context of facilitating sport participation. For example, among children and adolescents, musculoskeletal development varies dramatically even among children at the same age. Epiphyseal growth plate considerations can be important in considering whether or not the child or adolescent can safely participate in certain types and intensities of sport-related activity.

The nature of the proposed sport is important. The American Academy of Pediatrics (2001) has provided a useful categorization now often used to evaluate the risk of participation in terms of the physical contact that occurs during the activity. Sports are divided into three categories: contact or collision sports (e.g., ice hockey, American football, and rugby), limited/incidental contact sports (e.g., skating, baseball, or cycling [due to the risk of falling]), and noncontact sports (e.g., running, sailing, or archery). In addition, the level of physical intensity of the proposed sport is important. Intensity has several dimensions, including dynamic demands on the cardiovascular system, volume of work, and pressure placed on these systems. Table 8.1 is a list of sports classified by type of contact.

The stress of competition may also be very important depending on the circumstances and the personal characteristics of the child. Anxiety in its myriad forms is common during childhood and adolescence and is known to be a factor that can predispose to the development of eating disorders. Anxiety associated with the stress of competition (and fear of failing to meet the expectations of others, including parents, teammates, and coaches) may also contribute to the development of eating disorders among young athletes. However, some anxious youngsters have

Table 8.1 Classification of Sports by Contact

Contact or Collision	Limited Contact	Noncontact
Basketball	Baseball	Archery
Boxing[a]	Bicycling	Badminton
Diving	Cheerleading	Bodybuilding
Field hockey	Canoeing or kayaking	Bowling
Football	(white water)	Canoeing or kayaking
Tackle	Fencing	(flat water)
Ice hockey	Field events	Crew or rowing
Lacrosse	High jump	Curling
Martial arts	Pole vault	Dancing
Rodeo	Floor hockey	Ballet
Rugby	Football	Modern
Ski jumping	Flag	Jazz
Soccer	Gymnastics	Field events
Team handball	Handball	Discus
Water polo	Horseback riding	Javelin
Wrestling	Racquetball	Shot put
	Skating	Golf
	Ice	Orienteering[b]
	In-line	Power lifting
	Roller	Race walking
	Skiing	Riflery
	Cross-country	Rope jumping
	Downhill	Running
	Water	Sailing
	Skateboarding	Scuba diving
	Snowboarding	Swimming
	Softball	Table tennis
	Squash	Tennis
	Ultimate frisbee	Track
	Volleyball	Weight lifting
	Windsurfing or surfing	

Source: American Academy of Pediatrics Committee on Sports Medicine and Fitness, 2001. With permission.

[a] Participation not recommended by the American Academy of Pediatrics.

[b] A race (contest) in which competitors use a map and compass to find their way through unfamiliar territory.

159

improvement in their self-esteem and lessening of anxiety as they participate in sports. The health practitioner can assist the child and his or her parents in deciding if the planned sport activity is consistent with the child's stage of growth and development physically, socially, and mentally. The IOC has included this very important parameter of health in its consensus statement on training the elite child athlete (http://www.olympic. org/uk/utilities/reports), which concludes as follows: "The entire sports process for the elite child athlete should be pleasurable and fulfilling" (November 16, 2005).

Multiple preexisting medical conditions need to be considered in the preparticipation evaluation, including orthopedic, cardiac, neurological, and endocrinologic disorders as well as eating disorders. Orthopedic problems that are not apparent during regular daily activities can become problematic during sport. For example, congenital weakness of certain muscles, differences in leg length, or osteoporosis may result in complications when sport is undertaken. In addition, a large minority of adolescents develop chronic illnesses during adolescence. For example, up to 20% of boys and 13% of girls have prehypertension or hypertension (Falkner, Gidding, Portman, & Rosner, 2008), and the impact of the planned sport on blood pressure needs to be considered. Both types I and II diabetes mellitus are now also seen in a significant percentage of children and adolescents and special precautions are required.

Cardiovascular Conditions

Sudden cardiac death during sport participation, although uncommon, is particularly disturbing when it occurs in a child or adolescent with previously unsuspected heart disease. These cardiac events have led to specific recommendations for the preparticipation evaluation by several leading medical associations, including the American Heart Association (Maron, Douglas, Graham, Nishimura, & Thompson, 2005) and the European Society of Cardiology (Corrado et al., 2005). As a consequence of several shocking sudden cardiac deaths among elite athletes, the IOC convened a panel that published the Lausanne Recommendations (http://multimedia.olympic.org/pdf/en_report_886.pdf).

Overall, the guidelines all emphasize that the physician should obtain a careful personal and family history and perform a thorough physical examination targeting specific cardiac components. Although a 12-lead electrocardiogram is often recommended as part of the standard preparticipation evaluation (especially for elite athletes), it is generally considered less important than the history and physical examination. Some authors have called for more detailed evaluations (for example, echocardiograms), and some small studies have found that abnormalities that may be significant are often found (Weidenbener, Krauss, Waller, & Taliercio, 1995; Shry, Leding, Rubal, & Eisenhauer, 2002). Nonetheless, more detailed evaluations have not been recommended unless there are specific risk factors identified in the standard evaluation.

Finally, to quote a joint position statement from the American College of Sports Medicine and American Heart Association (2007), it is helpful to remember that "strategies, such as screening patients before participation in exercise, excluding high-risk patients from certain activities, promptly evaluating possible prodromal symptoms, training fitness personnel for emergencies, and encouraging patients to avoid high-risk activities, appear prudent but have not been systematically evaluated" (p. 886).

Preparticipation Evaluation for Cardiovascular Screening for Competitive Athletes

The American Heart Association has recommended 12 elements for the preparticipation cardiovascular screening for competitive athletes, including five elements from the individual's personal history (for example, a history of exertional chest pain or discomfort), three elements from the family history (for example, premature death before age 50 in a relative), and four elements from the physical examination (for example, heart murmur). All 12 elements are itemized in Table 8.2 (Glover, Glover, & Maron, 2007). The Lausanne Recommendations under the umbrella of the IOC Medical Commission are very similar but include a recommendation for a 12-lead resting electrocardiogram after the onset of puberty and recommend that the investigations be repeated at least every second year. In addition, the Lausanne Recommendations include a specific personal history questionnaire that can be completed by the sport participant (see Table 8.3).

Preparticipation Evaluation for Eating Disorders

The physician who performs the preparticipation evaluation may be able to detect or prevent the development of an eating disorder. Many

Table 8.2   The 12-Element American Heart Association Recommendations for Preparticipation Cardiovascular Screening of Competitive Athletes

Personal History[a]

1. Exertional chest pain/discomfort
2. Syncope/near syncope
3. Excessive exertional or otherwise unexplained dyspnea/fatigue associated with exercise
4. Previous recognition of a precordial murmur
5. Elevated systemic blood pressure

Family History

6. Premature death (sudden or otherwise) before age 50 related to heart disease in one or more relatives
7. Disability from heart disease in a close relative aged less than 50 years
8. Specific knowledge of certain cardiac conditions in family members: hypertrophic or dilated cardiomyopathy, long QT syndrome or other ion channelopathies, Marfan's syndrome, or clinically important arrhythmias

Physical Examination

9. Heart murmur[b]
10. Femoral pulses to exclude aortic coarctation
11. Physical stigmata of Marfan's syndrome
12. Brachial artery blood pressure (sitting position)[c]

Source: Glover, D. W., Glover, D. W., & Maron, B. J., *American Journal of Cardiology,* 100, 1709–1712, 2007.
[a] Parental verification recommended for high school and middle school athletes.
[b] Auscultation should be performed in the supine and standing positions, in particular to identify murmurs of dynamic left ventricular outflow tract obstruction.
[c] Preferably taken initially in both arms.

individuals who participate in sports begin to do so in childhood, adolescence, or young adulthood, and this is the time of highest risk for an eating disorder. Some people may undertake an exercise regimen or a sport as part of their eating disorder, and for some people, participation in sport may precipitate an eating disorder. The medical history may reveal the presence of an eating disorder. For example, the Florida High School Athletic Association Preparticipation Physical Evaluation (www.fhsaa. org/forms/pdf/EL02_physical.pdf) includes several items that might permit the physician to detect the presence of an eating disorder. The relevant

Table 8.3 Participation in Cardiovascular Screening

Personal History: Questionnaire by Examining Physician

- Have you ever fainted or passed out when exercising?
- Do you ever have chest tightness?
- Does running ever cause chest tightness?
- Have you ever had chest tightness, cough, or wheezing that have made it difficult for you to perform in sports?
- Have you ever been treated/hospitalized for asthma?
- Have you ever had a seizure?
- Have you ever been told that you have epilepsy?
- Have you ever been told to give up sports because of health problems?
- Have you ever been told you have high blood pressure?
- Have you ever been told you have high cholesterol?
- Do you have trouble breathing or do you cough during or after activity?
- Have you ever been dizzy during or after exercise?
- Have you ever had chest pain during or after exercise?
- Do you have or have you ever had racing of your heart or skipped heartbeats?
- Do you get tired more quickly than your friends do during exercise?
- Have you ever been told you have a heart murmur?
- Have you ever been told you have a heart arrhythmia?
- Do you have any other history of heart problems?
- Have you had a severe viral infection (for example, myocarditis or mononucleosis) within the last month?
- Have you ever been told you had rheumatic fever?
- Do you have any allergies?
- Are you taking any medications at the present time?
- Have you routinely taken any medication in the past two years?

Source: Lausanne Recommendations. *Sudden Cardiovascular Death in Sport*, Preparticipation cardiovascular screening. Lausanne, Switzerland: IOC Medical Commission, 2004. Used with permission from the IOC Medical Commission.

items include: "Have you ever taken any supplements or vitamins to help you gain or lose weight or improve your performance?" "Do you want to weigh less than you do now?" "Do you lose weight regularly to meet weight requirements for your sport?" Questions about menstrual function (which are optional in the Florida form) also would be helpful. Although people with an eating disorder may not acknowledge the symptoms during an interview, a surprising number will candidly answer questions on a form.

A more difficult issue for the primary care physician (PCP) is detecting the eating disorder if it begins after the approved sport activity is started. The patient may not see his or her PCP for a year or more after beginning sports, and during this time an eating disorder can become very serious. During this time, the athletic trainer on the sport management team who has frequent contact with the athlete may be more likely to detect the eating disorder. This is one important reason for the PCP to understand and maintain open communication with members of the sport management team.

POSSIBLE MEDICAL COMPLICATIONS

The concept of the female athlete triad (disordered eating, amenorrhea, and osteoporosis) has been very successful in promoting recognition of the impact of eating disorders among athletes. Guidelines for the prevention, detection, and management of the triad have been developed by influential sport organizations, including the IOC, the NCAA, the National Athletic Trainers' Association, and the American College of Sports Medicine (ACSM, 2007). Although there are significant problems related to the concept, particularly in the area of diagnosis, two important common physiological complications of eating disorders are included in the definition: the negative consequences of disordered eating on bone health and reproductive function. These will be discussed later in the chapter.

Cardiac complications are also common among athletes with eating disorders and can be lethal. Gastrointestinal complications occur in the majority of patients who meet formal criteria for either anorexia nervosa or bulimia nervosa, and these conditions tend to be chronic problems that cause pain and impair the ability of patients to consume adequate calories. Some gastrointestinal problems (such as pancreatitis) occur rarely but can be life threatening.

Misinterpretation of medical findings is common. For example, although it is true that sport participants tend to have lower heart rates than age-matched controls, bradycardia can also be a sign of malnutrition. Another example is that some athletes (and some coaches) may see amenorrhea as a sign that the athlete is successful in his or her training when, in fact, changes in menstrual function are a key component of the potentially dangerous female athlete triad. A third example relates to sport performance. If the athlete is losing weight inappropriately or purging, there may be a decrease in performance that is misinterpreted as inadequate time devoted to training. In all three of these examples, the unconscious use of the defense mechanisms of rationalization and intellectualization by the athlete can interfere with early intervention in the treatment of the eating disorder.

Cardiac Complications

Cardiac complications are common among patients with eating disorders, including sport participants with eating disorders. These complications include arrhythmias (both rate and rhythm abnormalities), orthostatic hypotension, decreased ejection fraction, decreased exercise tolerance, mitral valve prolapse, and pericardial effusion (Casiero & Frishman, 2006). Anorexia nervosa has one of the highest premature mortality rates of any psychiatric disorder (Steinhausen, 2002); cardiac complications are one of the three leading causes of death. Cardiac complications account for one-fourth of the premature deaths, renal complications for another one-fourth, and suicide for half of the premature deaths among anorexic patients (Herzog, Deter, Fiehn, & Petzold, 1997).

Although bulimia nervosa has been less well studied, it is known that some unexpected sudden deaths are secondary to electrolyte abnormalities that can result in lethal cardiac arrhythmias. Purging by vomiting, laxative, diuretic, or enema abuse all can lead to electrolyte abnormalities, particularly hypokalemia. Some patients use ipecac to facilitate vomiting; it is directly cardiotoxic and has been lethal in a number of cases (Silber, 2005). Thyroid medication has also been abused by eating disorder patients (Woodside, Walfish, Kaplan, & Kennedy, 1991) and can increase heart rate and, in vulnerable eating disorder patients, be dangerous.

In addition, cardiac problems can occur during treatment, especially among individuals who are outpatients and not carefully monitored. Participation in sport may intensify the chance of this occurrence and is one of the main reasons that various organizations have developed guidelines that limit sport participation in athletes with eating disorders until certain physiological parameters have significantly improved. Even under supervision, multiple problems have been reported during the weight restoration period in patients with anorexia nervosa, especially when treatment has been overly aggressive. One of the most dangerous is the refeeding syndrome, which includes hypophosphatemia, hypokalemia, hypomagnesemia, hyperglycemia, fluid and sodium retention, and neurological and hematologic complications (Miller, 2008).

Researchers in the eating disorder field have identified "excessive exercise" as an important characteristic of many people who develop eating disorders. For some, participation in sport can be a precursor to the eating disorder or may represent the first sign of the condition. For others who have already developed the eating disorder, exercise may be added to a list of actions used to promote weight loss or to counter the effects of eating. The term *excessive exercise* is particularly problematic in sport, especially among elite athletes, because optimal performance often requires more physical activity than necessary to promote health. It may be more useful to assess the level of activity in terms of its appropriateness given the circumstances and its effect on health.

The cardiac complications of eating disorders can be intensified or unmasked during sport participation. The additional burden of sudden increases in vigorous activity on heart function in patients with decreased cardiac function can be dangerous. Patients with anorexia nervosa may have a decreased ejection fraction and decreased exercise tolerance that is worsened with sport activity. Semistarvation and electrolyte abnormalities can result in bradycardia and orthostatic hypotension and lead to syncope and falls, especially during position changes in sport. Chest pain can occur with mitral valve prolapse and be worsened with vigorous activity.

Although uncommon, sudden cardiac death among athletes with eating disorders does occur. Although this may be due to a previously undetected congenital abnormality, an association between sudden death and corrected QT prolongation in eating disorder patients has also been suggested. A recent meta-analysis found that the QTc interval in anorexics was significantly longer than in controls, although still within the normal range (Takimoto, Yoshiuchi, & Akabayashi, 2008). Certain potentially lethal arrhythmias, including torsades de pointes, is more likely with prolongation of the QT interval, bradycardia, and hypokalemia, all of which may occur in vulnerable eating disorder patients. Figure 8.1 illustrates this arrhythmia.

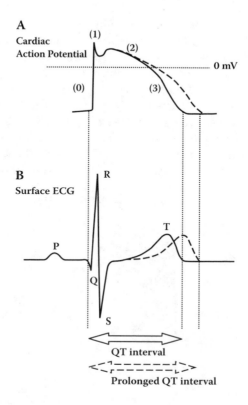

A
Cardiac
Action Potential
(0) (1) (2) (3)
0 mV

B
Surface ECG
P R Q S T
QT interval
Prolonged QT interval

Figure 8.1 Illustration of prolonged QT interval that can predispose to torsades de pointes arrhythmia. ECG = electrocardiogram. (Reprinted from Abriel, H., Schlapfer, J., Keller, D. I., Gavillet, B., Buclin, T., Biollaz, J., Stoller, R., Kappenberger, L., *Swiss Medical Weekly*, 27, 685–694, 2004. With permission.)

Menstrual and Reproductive Health

Menstrual irregularities, including delayed menarche, oligomenorrhea, and amenorrhea, are common among eating disorder patients and among sport participants. Although primary or secondary amenorrhea is currently a required criterion for females with anorexia nervosa in the current diagnostic scheme in the United States, most experts anticipate that this criterion will be changed in the next version of the *Diagnostic and*

Statistical Manual of Mental Disorders. This is because many people with the other typical signs and symptoms of anorexia nervosa still have menses (although not necessarily normal reproductive functioning). Loucks and her colleagues (Loucks, Stachenfeld, & DiPietro, 2006) working in the sport field have proposed the concept of "energy availability" to account for the finding that many significantly underweight female athletes continue to have menses. This group has proposed that when the energy consumed (calories) balances the energy expended (including obligatory energy expenditure, nonexercise adaptive thermogenesis, and physical activity; see Figure 8.2), menses are more likely to continue even at

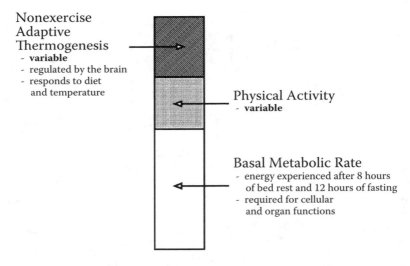

Total Energy Expenditure

Nonexercise
Adaptive
Thermogenesis
 - **variable**
 - regulated by the brain
 - responds to diet
   and temperature

Physical Activity
 - **variable**

Basal Metabolic Rate
 - energy experienced after 8 hours
   of bed rest and 12 hours of fasting
 - required for cellular
   and organ functions

Figure 8.2 Total energy expenditure includes basal metabolic rate, physical activity, and nonexercise adaptive thermogenesis. Basal metabolic rate (also called obligatory energy expenditure) accounts for the calories used to keep the body functioning at rest. Physical activities account for a minority of daily calories used and include the basic activities of daily life (e.g., walking or getting out of a chair) and planned exercise (e.g., running or lifting weights). Nonexercise adaptive thermogenesis refers to the calories used to maintain certain other fundamental activities (e.g., keeping the body warm or processing food). (From Yager, J. & Powers, P., Eds., *Clinical Manual of Eating Disorders,* American Psychiatric Publishing, 2007. With permission.)

significantly low (and potentially very dangerous) weights. Although this is an appealing idea, the evidence for it is not yet compelling and it probably only partly explains why some individuals retain menses even at very low weights. Paradoxically, the concept of the female athlete triad developed in response to the finding that many young female athletes had amenorrhea. Initially this was thought to be benign, but the association with osteoporosis and disordered eating was recognized as hazardous almost 20 years ago.

Late onset of menarche can be genetic or may be related to a variety of physical problems, but it can also be related to poor nutrition or to the stress of unhealthy and excessive exercise. Menses are notoriously susceptible to emotional stress, which can occur in many circumstances, including competitive sports as well as among individuals particularly prone to anxiety disorders. A combination of these factors is likely in the athlete with an eating disorder who may have a preexisting anxiety disorder, the stress of competition, and malnutrition.

Menstrual and Reproductive Health: Fertility

Fertility is sensitive to the availability of oxidizable metabolic fuels. When food intake is severely limited or available energy stores are expended in exercise, fertility is decreased or suspended in favor of the metabolic processes needed for survival. This has been observed in famines and in many patients with anorexia nervosa. However, there have been some dramatic reports of very underweight anorexic patients unexpectedly able to conceive.

Normal menstrual function and normal fertility do not always accompany weight restoration in anorexia nervosa patients. Several decades ago, Frisch and McArthur (1974) provided evidence for the theory that a certain minimum fat content was required for menarche (17% of body weight) and a higher percentage for normal fertility (22%). Although Loucks's energy availability theory conflicts with this idea, it is probable that normal fertility requires both a certain minimum level of fat content and a balance between energy consumed and energy expended. Although significant weight changes can occur over the course of days to weeks, usually changes in weight take longer, yet there is evidence that fertility can change quickly in response to nutritional or activity changes that are related to various hormonal changes, particularly gonadotropin releasing factor. These and multiple other factors may explain why some patients do not resume menses when at a seemingly normal weight and why some patients maintain menses at a very low weight.

Bulimia nervosa patients often have menstrual irregularities and changes in various hormones known to influence menses and thus fertility. In addition, many patients with bulimia nervosa have a past history of anorexia nervosa, which may have a lasting influence on fertility. However, most patients with bulimia nervosa are able to conceive. This may relate to the fact that most are not significantly underweight and, by definition, there are periods of overconsumption of calories that may provide the substrate for normal hormonal function and therefore normal fertility.

Menstrual and Reproductive Health: Pregnancy

In addition to difficulties with fertility, pregnancy can be problematic for patients with eating disorders, particularly if they are very invested in sport. For normal weight women, expected weight gain is about 25 lb (11.4 kg), and this can be frightening to a woman with a body image disturbance. When underweight, greater weight gain may be needed for a successful pregnancy. Although many women with bulimia nervosa are able to cease binge eating and purging when pregnant, a sizable minority cannot, and this can be risky to the fetus. Physical activity can be safe through much of pregnancy, and there is evidence that moderate physical activity improves a woman's sense of well-being and helps maintain fitness at a time when it typically declines. However, participation in some high-level sports may not be safe, and this limitation to a woman with an eating disorder may increase anxiety and worsen a preexisting body image disturbance. Certain sport activities that pose a risk of falling (cycling, for example) or those that might result in abdominal trauma should be curtailed, particularly after the first trimester. Scuba diving should be avoided because it puts the fetus at risk of developing decompression sickness ("the bends").

Pregnancy in individuals actively ill with their eating disorder has been associated with many complications in both the mother and baby. The problems with the baby include preterm delivery, low birth weight, intrauterine growth restriction, Cesarean birth, and low Apgar scores (James, 2001). Women with eating disorders are more likely to require Cesarean section and to develop postpartum depression (Franko et al., 2001). Full psychological recovery also seems to affect fertility. In one study (Brinch, Isager, & Tolstrup, 1988) of 151 patients with a former diagnosis of anorexia nervosa, none of the 11 males had children and 50 of the 141 women had given birth to 86 children. In addition, the prematurity rate was twice the expected rate and perinatal lethality six times the expected rate. The fertility rate was approximately one-third the expected fertility. More women in the group of mothers than in the group of nonmothers had better scores of general functioning at follow-up.

Ideally, the sportswoman with an eating disorder contemplating pregnancy should be in recovery from her eating disorder for at least one year. This would mean that she would be at her ideal body weight, have had no episodes of binge eating or purging, be able to moderate her sport activity consonant with good health, and have established a positive sense of identity free of troublesome obsessions about food, weight, and body size. Although each of these recommendations is difficult to quantify, ideal body weight may be the most controversial. Many sportswomen may be genetically likely to be slender and may have had later onset of menarche. Utilizing the individual's own growth chart and assessing her history of failed pregnancy attempts or miscarriages (including nutritional intake, weight, and exercise levels at those times) can help determine an ideal prepregnancy weight. However, weight is only one determinant of fertility. One group in London (Mason, Key, Allan, & Lask, 2007) has studied ideal weight in terms of ovarian structure, function, and size utilizing radiographic techniques and concluded that normal ovarian status may occur at lower weight than expected in some patients. Given the likely genetic disposition for some athletes to be slender, this may be particularly true for athletes in certain sports.

An important issue to discuss with the woman who plans to get pregnant is that fertility may be impaired even if she has recovered from her eating disorder. There may be as yet poorly understood long-term consequences of the eating disorder that impact fertility. The motivation for recovery may have been the wish to have children. Addressing the possibility that a successful pregnancy may not occur might assist in preventing relapse.

Osteoporosis and Bone Health

Closely related to reproductive health is osteoporosis and bone health. The concept of energy availability has contributed to our understanding of the relationship between these elements of the female athlete triad. Within this theoretical concept, the female athlete condition moves along each of the spectra of energy availability, menstrual function, and bone mineral density at different rates and in one direction or the other, depending on her diet and exercise habits. The goal is to have all female sport participants at optimal energy availability, optimal bone health, and eumenorrheic. This concept has the great advantage of integrating information from the well-established concept of energy homeostasis, which is widely accepted in several fields of medicine. However, there appear to be several problems with the theory: the research evidence for the theory is slim, weight is often not mentioned, and there appears to be an attempt to extricate the triad from the arena of mental health. Although it seems reasonable that some female athletes with the key element of the triad (decreased energy availability) might not have psychological or social problems, probably most affected individuals do.

Many athletes with eating disorders, especially those with anorexia nervosa, have decreased bone mass, and this is related to menstrual status. Multiple studies have shown that many patients with anorexia nervosa develop stress fractures and that the majority have decreased bone mass. A main problem has been trying to apply the well-known World Health Organization (WHO) criteria (1994) to athletes with eating disorders. There have long been standards for menopausal and postmenopausal women that utilize T scores (which compare the individual's scores to validated standards for young adults) from the dual-energy x-ray absorptiometry (DEXA). Recently, the International Society for Clinical Densitometry (ISCD) published an official position (Leslie et al., 2006) recommending that T scores not be used for premenopausal women or children and that instead bone mineral density (BMD) be expressed as Z scores (validated standards for age- and sex-matched controls). Since standards for children and adolescents are now available, this is feasible (Kalkwarf, et al., 2007). The ISCD also recommended that Z scores below –2.0 be termed "low bone density below the expected range for age" in premenopausal women and "low bone density for chronological age" in children. The ISCD also recommended that the term *osteopenia* not be used and that the term *osteoporosis* only be used if low BMD is present along with risk factors for short-term fractures (including chronic malnutrition, eating disorders, hypogonadism, gluocorticoid exposure, and previous fractures). These standards have been adopted by several organizations.

However, there is a problem in utilizing these standards for athletes with eating disorders. It is known that athletes in weight-bearing sports often have higher bone mineral density than nonathletes. Thus, waiting until there is a decrease in a Z score to –2.0 could be dangerous, particularly since elevated cortisol levels and chronic malnutrition are common findings in eating disorders. The American College of Sports Medicine (ACSM) position stand recommends that a BMD score less than –1.0 be investigated in sport participants.

Treatment of osteoporosis has several components. Nutritional intake should be adequate to support the level of energy expended in sport, weight should stabilize at an ideal weight for the individual, and purge behavior should cease. Generally, it is recommended that calcium intake be 1,500 mg per day, ideally in food (but supplemented if necessary), and that vitamin D intake be at least 400 to 600 IU per day. These levels may be a low estimate, as a recent study of female Navy recruits found that 2,000 mg per day of calcium and 800 IU per day of vitamin D compared to placebo reduced the frequency of stress fractures among 5,201 recruits (Lappe et al., 2008).

An important issue to consider in assessing sport participants is that males develop eating disorders and that elements of the triad also occur in males, including disordered eating and osteoporosis. Andersen, Watson, and Schlechte (2000) found that males with eating disorders were more likely to have low bone mineral density than females. Male athletes can develop low testosterone levels, often associated with weight loss or low energy availability. This may be associated with decreased libido, impaired fertility, or other reproductive health dysfunction. These problems can be even more serious among male athletes who may be even less willing to acknowledge eating problems since these problems are typically considered "female disorders." By the time males present for treatment they may have been ill longer. Unfortunately, there appears to be a trend with more boys and men affected by eating disorders, within both the sport world and the population in general.

Gastrointestinal Complications

Gastrointestinal symptoms are common in patients with eating disorders and also occur during aerobic exercise, particularly in runners. Eating disorder patients who are underweight or purge by vomiting frequently have abdominal discomfort, bloating, and early satiety associated with delayed gastric emptying (Benini et al., 2004). High-intensity running has also been associated with delayed gastric emptying of various sport drinks (Leiper, Nicholas, Ali, Williams, & Maughan, 2005). Therefore, it seems likely that sport participants (particularly runners) with eating disorders would be more likely to have dyspepsia associated with delayed gastric emptying.

Gastroesophageal reflux disorder (GERD) is common among patients who binge eat and purge, and aerobic exercise in healthy people can also induce esophageal acid reflux that increases with the intensity of exercise (Collings, Pierce Pratt, Rodriguez-Stanley, Bemben, & Miner, 2003). There is some evidence that chronic exposure to acid reflux can lead to cardiac arrhythmias, including atrial fibrillation (Gerson, Friday, & Triadafilopoulos, 2006). Chest discomfort or pain is the most common symptom of acid reflux and can also be a symptom of atrial fibrillation. There has been recent speculation that excessive exercise associated with acid reflux might facilitate the development of atrial fibrillation (Swanson, 2008).

Other Medical Concerns

Multiple other medical problems can occur in sportsmen and women with eating disorders, including a wide variety of problems associated with *muscle structure and function*. The semistarvation associated with anorexia nervosa has been shown to cause significant skeletal muscle changes associated with proximal muscle weakness, often reflected in difficulty standing from a sitting position (McLoughlin et al., 2000). Other muscles, particularly the thoracic diaphragm, can also be impaired and result in difficulty breathing. With weight loss, the heart, composed of specialized muscle cells (the cardiac myocytes), also may become smaller, resulting in what has been termed valvulventricular disproportion, increasing the risk for mitral or tricuspid valve prolapse. The decrease in cardiac size may also contribute to decreased exercise tolerance. These effects on the various muscle types of the body can be worsened by athletic activity in vulnerable individuals.

Orthopedic problems can affect athletes with eating disorders, but a detailed discussion is beyond the scope of this book. One issue, however, is the increased risk of female athletes to problems with the anterior cruciate ligament of the knee (Ireland, 2002). Women are particularly prone to injuries of this ligament, even without contact, and especially in the sports of basketball and soccer. It seems likely, although unproven, that the presence of eating disorder symptoms might increase the likelihood of such injuries.

MEDICATIONS

Introduction

Athletes with eating disorders are likely to require medications. The medications may be needed to treat the eating disorder, to treat associated comorbid psychiatric disorders, or to ameliorate physiological complications of the eating disorder. In the United States only one drug is approved by the Food and Drug Administration (FDA) for the treatment of any eating disorder: fluoxetine (trade name Prozac) in a dose of 60 mg for bulimia nervosa. However, many different drugs are used that have not been approved for that particular use by the FDA; this practice is called off-label use and is very common. For example, olanzapine (trade name Zyprexa) is frequently used for anorexia nervosa. A recent small double-blind placebo-controlled study of adult women with anorexia nervosa demonstrated that olanzapine was associated with a shorter time to achieve ideal body weight and a reduction in obsessive and compulsive symptoms (Bissada, Tasca, Barber, & Bradwejn, 2008).

Many medications may be needed to treat the common comorbid disorders that occur with eating disorders. The most common psychiatric conditions associated with anorexia nervosa are affective disorders (particularly depression) and anxiety disorders, including social phobia, obsessive-compulsive disorder, and generalized anxiety disorder. The most common comorbid disorders associated with bulimia nervosa are substance use disorders (particularly alcohol and cocaine use), affective disorders (depression and bipolar disorder), and anxiety disorders. The medications required for these conditions include various antidepressants, mood stabilizers, and antianxiety agents.

One problem in treating sport participants with eating disorders is that the disorder may be subsyndromal or atypical, thus complicating choice of possible medications. In addition, many affected individuals may be adolescents, and at present no medications are FDA approved for children or adolescents with eating disorders. Also, some symptoms of psychiatric disorders may be considered advantageous to sport participation and hence not be recognized. For example, amenorrhea may be inappropriately viewed as a sign of rigorous training and not recognized as a sign of a major mental illness.

A more subtle issue is related to energy level. It may be that some people who are particularly interested in sport have higher than usual energy levels. This may be adaptive and contribute to the enjoyment of sport or achievement of excellence as an elite athlete. But, sometimes increased energy levels can be a sign of the hypomanic or manic phase of bipolar disorder. Another issue is that increased activity level or participation in sport may be a means of coping with anxiety or depression. Often this is a helpful coping strategy, but when used excessively or in a way that endangers health, it can be problematic. For individuals with severe anxiety or depression, medications may be more appropriate than use of exercise to relieve symptoms.

Maintenance of physical health may also require medication in sport participants with eating disorders. For example, treatment of exercise-induced asthma (which is a common chronic condition) may require periodic use of inhalers such as short-acting beta-2-agonist bronchodilators, which can be associated with tachycardia and shakiness.

The physiological complications of eating disorders may also require the use of medications. For example, fractures associated with osteoporosis in a person with the female athlete triad may require use of medications such as alendronate, which can have gastrointestinal side effects.

Medication Effects on Weight

An important side effect of medications, particularly in people with eating disorders or among athletes, is weight change. Distorted cognitions about weight and sport performance can result in medication misuse or nonadherence. Multiple medications may be abused. These include thyroid medications, anorectic agents, orlistat, laxatives, diuretics, and Ipecac. Some athletes may be using various drugs purported to improve performance, including steroids, and these drugs can have serious deleterious systemic side effects.

Alternatively, medication-associated weight change can complicate management of the eating disorder. Since many sport participants with eating disorders require medication, it is helpful to be aware of the effect of any prescribed medication on weight. Table 8.4 illustrates the weight effects of some commonly used prescription medications. It is usually helpful to discuss possible effect on weight prior to prescription of any medication and to emphasize that an individual may respond differently than the statistically reported effect. For example, most studies have found that fluoxetine is weight neutral when mean weight change of all

Table 8.4 Weight Effects of Some Commonly Used Prescription Medications

	Weight Gain	Weight Loss	Weight Neutral
Antidepressants	Isocarboxazid	Bupropion	Desvenlafaxine
	Mirtazapine		Duloxetine
	Paroxetine		Lamotrigine
	Phenelzine		Most SSRIs
	Tricyclics		Nefazodone
			Tranylcypromine
			Venlafaxine
Mood stabilizers	Valproate		Lamotrigine
	Lithium		
	Carbamazepine		
Anticonvulsants	Carbamazepine	Felbamate	Lamotrigine
	Gabapentin	Topiramate	Tiagabine
	Pregabalin	Zonisamide	
	Valproate		
	Vigabatrin		
Antipsychotics	Clozapine	Molindone	Aripiprazole
	Most typical agents		Ziprasidone
	Olanzapine		
	Paliperidone		
	Quetiapine		
	Risperidone		
Other psychotropics	Cyproheptadine	Amphetamine	Buspirone
		Methylphenidate	Benzodiazepines
		Modafinil	
Antidiabetics	Insulin	Acarbose	Nateglinide
	Sulfonylureas	Exenatide	Repaglinide
	Thiazolidinediones	Metformin	
		Miglitol	
		Pramlintide	
Antihypertensives	Beta-blockers		All others
Gastrointestinal	Metoclopramide	H-2 blockers[a]	Anti-emetics
			Proton pump inhibitors
			Stool softeners

177

Table 8.4 Weight Effects of Some Commonly Used Prescription Medications (Continued)

	Weight Gain	**Weight Loss**	**Weight Neutral**
Hormonal	Corticosteroids		Contraceptives
			Tamoxifen

Source: Adapted from Powers, P. S., & Cloak, N. L., In Clinical Manual of Eating Disorders, American Psychiatric Publishing, Inc., Arlington, VA, 2007.
[a] Associated with weight loss in some but not all studies.

the study participants is considered. Nonetheless, some patients on fluoxetine lose weight and some gain weight.

Usually the major consideration is to avoid medications that cause weight gain, but drugs associated with weight loss can also be problematic. For example, in some vulnerable individuals, perhaps particularly very energetic athletes, weight loss secondary to a medication may precipitate an eating disorder. Weight loss with amphetamines and methylphenidate (commonly used in children or adolescents with attention-deficit/hyperactivity disorder) can also precipitate an eating disorder.

In general, however, weight gain rather than weight loss with various medications is more common. Medications utilized for psychiatric or neurologic conditions commonly cause weight gain. Among the commonly used antidepressants, mirtazapine (trade name Remeron) and paroxetine (trade name Paxil) both are associated with weight gain. Although bupropion (trade name Wellbutrin) is associated with weight loss, there is a relative contraindication to its use because it has been associated with an increased risk of seizures in patients with bulimia nervosa and it has a "black box" warning on the package insert for all patients with eating disorders. A black box warning means that the prescribing physician needs to be aware of the side effect and very carefully consider whether the possible benefit outweighs the significant risk listed in the black box. Most antipsychotics (except molindone [trade name Moban], ziprasidone [trade name Geodon], and aripiprazole [trade name Abilify]) are associated with weight gain. Except for lamotrigine (trade name Lamictal), the commonly used mood stabilizers are associated with weight gain. Of course, in underweight anorexia nervosa patients, weight gain may be desirable. However, because of the egosyntonic nature of weight loss in anorexia nervosa, perhaps particularly in sport participants, it is often difficult for patients to agree to take a medication for its side effect of weight gain. In addition, the atypical antipsychotics as a class may be associated with a variety of other side effects, such as elevation in lipids, that conceivably are dangerous aside from a possible beneficial effect of weight gain.

Since weight is such a focus among athletes, particularly elite athletes, it is recommended that the clinician prescribing medication take weight change into account during medication management. The potential for weight change should be discussed during the risk-benefit assessment prior to prescribing the medication and should be monitored during treatment. For patients taking antipsychotics, guidelines for metabolic monitoring (including blood glucose and lipid panel) should be done at least every four months. The potential for misuse of drugs that are associated with weight loss also needs to be carefully considered in athletes with eating disorders.

Medication Effects on Physical Activity

Although changes in physical activity level are not typically described as an adverse event during the evaluation process of drugs, certain side effects are probably related. Sedation and agitation, typically considered nervous system symptoms, are often associated with changes in physical activity that may be particularly problematic for sport participants. Some antidepressants cause sedation (e.g., mirtazapine), and some can cause agitation as part of the serotonergic syndrome (e.g., fluoxetine). Most of the atypical antipsychotics cause sedation.

Medication Effects on Sport Performance: Doping

Much attention has been paid to the effects of various illicit drugs and use of medications on sport performance. In the last decade a movement against doping in sport has crystallized in the World Anti-Doping Agency (Catlin, Fitch, & Ljungqvist, 2008). However, the practice of enhancing athletic performance by use of special diets and various potions has been around since the ancient Greek athletes (De Rose, 2008). The word *doping* is thought to be derived from the Dutch word *dop*, the name of an alcoholic beverage made of grape skins used by Zulu warriors to enhance their ability in battle. The term *doping* came into common use in the early 20th century to refer to the illegal drugging of racehorses. In 1904 Thomas Hicks ran to victory in the Olympic marathon with the help of raw egg, injections of strychnine, and doses of brandy administered to him during the race.

179

Several organizations attempted to ban the use of performance-enhancing substances, but few tests were available to document their use until the 1970s. Work was fragmented until the scandal of Ben Johnson, who won the 100 m competition at the Olympic Games in Seoul in 1988 and tested positive for stanozolol (an anabolic steroid). Following this event, testing became more common. In 1988 a police raid during the Tour de France found many prohibited medical substances, leading to another scandal that mobilized various groups to coordinate their efforts against doping in sports. The World Anti-Doping Agency (WADA), an independent international agency, was established and was fully operational by the 2000 Olympiad in Sydney.

WADA has established a list of prohibited substances and methods (including those termed blood doping) that are prohibited. Blood doping includes a variety of methods that increase the level of oxygen-containing hemoglobin. A comprehensive method has been developed to determine if any of these substances or methods is being utilized in national and international sports.

At the same time it was recognized that some medications are legitimately needed for various conditions, and a method was established to permit athletes to utilize approved medications (Hilderbrand, 2007). Permission must be obtained utilizing a system called therapeutic use exemption (TUE). The most common exemptions are those involving medications for asthma and its clinical variants and topical steroid medications. Exercise-induced asthma is common among sports participants (perhaps 10%), and use of inhaled short-acting beta-2-agonist bronchodilators is the most common treatment. These drugs are also stimulants, and some in the class (e.g., clenbuterol) may also enhance performance, particularly if used systemically. At present clenbuterol use is not permitted and only four beta-2 agonists are permitted, and these can only be used by inhalation. In addition, use requires approval via a detailed TUE application process. The exemption must be obtained prior to competition, and there are several detailed requirements for approval. For example, application for a TUE for a beta-2-agnonist bronchodilator requires a complete medical history, a report of spirometry with the measure of the forced expiratory volume in one second (FEV1). If airway obstruction is present, inhalation of a short-acting beta-2 agonist must demonstrate reversal of the bronchoconstriction (www.wada-ama.org/).

The global consensus that resulted in WADA is likely to result in fewer instances of misuse of performance-enhancing drugs, but as new opportunities to abuse potentially advantageous ways of enhancing performance become available, the guidelines will need to be changed. A process for achieving this is in place, and new guidelines are issued each year following careful consideration and agreement by multiple stakeholders. Not everyone agrees that the intense efforts made by WADA, which are often publicly funded, are beneficial to society as a whole (Smith & Stewart, 2008). Others have questioned the role of physicians in the antidoping efforts, arguing that these activities challenge principles of nonmalfeasance and privacy protection (Kayser, Mauron, & Miah, 2007). Physicians who provide care to sport participants will need to be aware of the changing requirements for use of medically required medications and consider some of the ethical questions involved.

ASSESSMENT OF MEDICAL RISK: MEDICAL CLEARANCE

The concept of medical clearance is important and can be misleading. To say only that someone has been "medically cleared" does not provide the information that is required. It is important to state what the person can and cannot do and what precautions are necessary. It is more helpful to discuss the risk-benefit ratio of certain activities. For example, if an athlete has developed anorexia nervosa and is in treatment and has started to gain weight and all of the physiological complications have improved, it may be appropriate to permit brief bouts of practice activity a few times a week. The specific recommendation might be as follows: "Nicole can participate in volleyball practice twice weekly for one half hour each time during the next two weeks. If her weight continues to improve, an increase in her activity will be considered. If she loses weight or weight gain does not continue, she will not continue to practice. If she becomes lightheaded or dizzy during practice, all practice should be discontinued until she is reevaluated by her physician. Her physician can be reached at the following phone number." The key elements are approved activity, including frequency and duration; precautions to be taken; and action to be taken if problems develop. To say that Nicole is medically cleared might mean to her (and her coach) that she can practice six days a week, participate in competition, and that there is no need to worry about possible complications.

181

FINAL THOUGHTS

A physician with experience assessing and treating sport participants with disordered eating is essential for an effective treatment team. As can be seen from this chapter, the medical considerations are complex, given the need to focus both on the physical demands of sport participation and on the possible seriousness of the medical complications of an eating disorder. Because individuals with eating disorders are not often forthcoming regarding their symptoms, the ideal physician would be one with both experience working with sport participants and expertise in working with eating problems. Unfortunately, there are not nearly enough physicians with such experience and expertise. Hopefully, there are physicians with expertise in either sports medicine or eating disorders who are willing to immerse themselves in the other world as well.

9

Prevention and Education

Although unique in many ways, eating disorders are like most disorders and problems in that they are more easily treated and the patient suffers less medically and psychologically if the problem is identified and treated early in the process. Preventive efforts aimed at early identification and treatment involve secondary prevention. Ideally, we would like to prevent eating disorders from occurring, or what has been called primary prevention. In primary or universal prevention, the goal is to decrease the incidence of eating disorders by decreasing exposure to risk factors and by increasing exposure to protective factors (Piran, 2002). This task is probably made more difficult, given the role of genetics in predisposing an individual to developing an eating disorder (Striegel-Moore & Bulik, 2007). We obviously cannot change one's genetics (at least not at the time of this writing); thus, we must work to reduce other risk factors, especially those that serve to precipitate or perpetuate eating disorders.

Another way to think about prevention programs involves how and to whom the program is presented. Levine and Smolak (2007) distinguish between universal-selective programs, which include very large groups such as high school-age females, and selective-targeted programs, in which the program participants involve a population that has been identified as being at high risk because of the presence of precursors to the development of eating disorders or mild symptoms.

Very little work has been done on the prevention of eating disorders in sport. One reason for this may be the rather exacting standards that are established for such work. Levine and Smolak indicate that the efficacy of preventative programs is demonstrated when the plan for implementation is followed, program participants show a lower incidence of eating disorders than the population incidence, the effect is probably due to the program based on comparison conditions, and the reduced incidence is mediated by a decrease in risk factors or an increase in protective factors. Those meeting these standards do not tend to use information alone but rather employ psychoeducation as part of a multidimensional, interactive/participatory approach that emphasizes consciousness raising and critical thinking about relevant cultural issues—what Levine and Smolak termed a "critical social perspective." Interestingly, they also suggest that prevention efforts need to be aimed at those individuals who are at moderate and low risk for developing eating disorders rather than simply at the high-risk group; more individuals from the medium- and low-risk groups will develop eating disorders because there are many more people in those groups than in the high-risk group.

This brief general introduction to prevention of eating disorders is not intended to be exhaustive but rather to provide background for a brief discussion of prevention efforts in sport. For more general information regarding prevention of eating disorders, the reader is referred to Levine and Smolak (2006, 2007).

Despite the fact that prevention of eating disorders (as well as disordered eating and the female athlete triad) among sport participants has been discussed and recommended frequently in the literature (e.g., Beals, 2004; Bonci et al., 2008; Otis & Goldingay, 2000; Powers & Johnson, 1996; Thompson & Sherman, 1993a, 1993b), there are very few prevention studies that involve this apparent high-risk group, and those that do involve only sportswomen. In this chapter, we will discuss innovative education and prevention programs with sport participants, the available research on the prevention of eating disorders in sport participants and in the sport environment, and what is needed to further prevention efforts.

PRIMARY PREVENTION

Ideally, we would prefer to discuss existing programs that have been formally evaluated. However, as we mentioned earlier, such programs with sport participants are limited in number. Therefore, we will begin our discussion with descriptions of two innovative programs that have been in existence for a reasonable period of time but have not been formally evaluated regarding their effectiveness—Athletes@Risk and the Female Athlete Triad Awareness and Prevention Program.

Athletes@Risk

Athletes@Risk is a prevention program based in Toronto designed to decrease the incidence and severity of the components of the female athlete triad. Specifically, Athletes@Risk aims to educate female sport participants as to the early establishment of good eating habits and training practices, in addition to developing positive self-esteem and a positive body image. The program consists of five workshop units that include informational content, interactive tools, and a teaching guide with a resource list, handouts, and workbook. Topics covered in the workshops include "Understanding the Health Consequences," "Food as Fuel," "My Body, My Sport," "Getting Strong, Getting Fit," and "Life Skills and Wellness." As mentioned previously, no data are available regarding the effectiveness of the Athletes@Risk program. For more information on this program, see www.womenscollegehospital.ca/programs/program105.html.

Female Athlete Triad Awareness and Prevention Program

In 1999, the New York State Public High School Athletic Association with the assistance of sport personnel, parents, athletes, and healthcare professionals developed the Female Athlete Triad Awareness and Prevention Program for girls in grades 6 to 12. Objectives of the program included increasing awareness of the triad, its risk factors, and triggers for disordered eating. A resource manual was developed that included guidelines and protocols for school personnel; information for educators, coaches, parents, and students; medical information for physicians; and classroom and team activities. Additionally, training sessions are available for schools in New York, and at the time of this writing 88% of the school districts have participated. For more information on this program, see www.nysphsaa.org/programs/triad.asp.

BodySense

BodySense is an educational initiative designed to promote positive body image in young female sport participants (Buchholz, Mack, McVey, Feder, & Barrowman, 2008) based in Ottawa, Ontario, Canada. Buchholz et al. evaluated the effectiveness of the program's attempt to reduce pressures regarding thinness, as well as promote positive body image and healthy eating behaviors in young female gymnasts aged 11 to 17. In this multi-dimensional, social ecological study, parents and coaches in addition to gymnasts were targeted. Participants were provided with information on eating attitudes/beliefs, accurate information about body health, unique body size/shape, resisting pressures to diet, physical activity for enjoyment, positive self-esteem, assertiveness, stress management, and balance between sport and life outside of sport. Participation resulted in the perception by the gymnasts of a reduction in pressure from their clubs regarding thinness, suggesting that the sport climate regarding thinness pressures could be altered.

ATHENA

Athletes Targeting Healthy Exercise and Nutrition Alternatives (ATHENA) is a universal-selective program that is scripted, coach facilitated, and peer led for female middle and high school sport participants (Elliot et al., 2006). The program was designed to decrease disordered eating risk factors and the use of body-shaping drugs. The curriculum focuses on factors that contribute to the risk of disordered eating and use of body-shaping drugs (mood/self-esteem, norms of behavior, health/normal body weight, media depictions of women, and societal pressures to be thin). The curriculum was designed to build skills for controlling mood, to counter media influences, and to provide information on sports nutrition and strength training. The curriculum was provided to sports teams in small groups led by an assigned peer leader during its season in eight 45-minute sessions. The ATHENA program significantly decreased the targeted risk factors, as well as reduced the ongoing and new use of body-shaping substances.

Health Education Approach

In an effort to decrease eating disorder risk factors in college sportswomen, Abood and Black (2000) devised a health education intervention designed to increase awareness and skills for developing positive health states and how such states can enhance sport performance. Seventy sportswomen from seven sports participated. Half from each sport were randomly assigned to either the intervention group or a control group. The 8-week intervention addressed self-esteem, performance pressure, nutrition knowledge and nutrition beliefs/myths related to sport performance, and stress management in 1-hour meetings. Two weeks were allotted for each topic. The control group attended academic study sessions at the times the intervention group met. Pre- and posttreatment measures included the Eating Disorder Inventory-2, the Rosenberg Self-Esteem Scale, the Sport Competition Anxiety Test, the Self-Rating Anxiety Scale, and a nutrition inventory. Findings indicated that intervention subjects scored lower than the control subjects on drive for thinness and body dissatisfaction, and the control group scored lower on self-esteem and nutrition knowledge.

Cognitive Dissonance Approaches With Sport Participants

Becker and colleagues (Becker, Smith, & Ciao, 2005, 2006) demonstrated an effective eating disorder prevention program for college sorority members that was adapted for female collegiate sport participants (Becker, Powell, & Bull, 2008). The Female Athlete Body Project is a multiyear program based on work by Stice, Trost, and Chase (2003) that employed a cognitive dissonance intervention with a healthy weight management program for eating disorder prevention. In a cognitive dissonance approach to eating disorder prevention, the individual engages in an experience that contradicts and challenges her beliefs about the thin ideal (Levine & Smolak, 2007). Sport participants in basketball, soccer, volleyball, cross country, tennis, golf, track, softball, and swimming/diving participated. The program was peer led and occurred in three sessions of 75 to 80 minutes. Topics covered included definitions of the sport-specific thin ideal and the athlete-specific healthy ideal, factors that enhance sport performance, and the female athlete triad. Comparisons of pre- and posttreatment measures indicated significant decreases in the thin ideal internalization, negative affect, eating pathology, and body dissatisfaction at posttreatment, and those changes were maintained at 6-week follow-ups for all measures except thin-ideal internalization. The Female Athlete Body Project is an ongoing prevention program that was continuing at the time of this writing.

Smith and Petrie (2008) also attempted to adapt a cognitive dissonance intervention to the prevention of eating disorder symptoms with collegiate female sport participants. The experimenters compared such an approach with a healthy weight program and a wait-list control group in terms of reducing the eating disorder risk factors of body dissatisfaction, negative affect, dietary restriction, and internalization of the thin ideal. The dissonance and healthy weight interventions were presented in three

1-hour meetings over 3 consecutive weeks. Each meeting involved an educational component, discussion, activity/practice, homework assignments, and review of homework. The dissonance intervention included writing about the costs associated with pursuing the thin ideal, participating in role-plays arguing against the thin ideal, and listing positive qualities about themselves while looking in a mirror. Inconsistent with research with nonsport participants, however, subjects receiving the dissonance intervention did not show significant reductions in the targeted risk factors compared to the other groups. The dissonance group did show a decrease in sadness/depression, a decrease in internalizing the importance of being physically fit, and an increase in body satisfaction. Also, it was the only group not to show more negative symptoms over the 3-week intervention period.

SECONDARY PREVENTION

In previous chapters, we have discussed the importance of coaches in the identification, management, and treatment of their sport participants with eating disorders. Similarly, their importance regarding prevention cannot be overstated. It is unlikely that any prevention program or initiative regarding sport participants can be successful without the support, endorsement, and participation of coaches. Perhaps for this reason, initial approaches in this area have focused on coaches.

National Collegiate Athletic Association

In a survey of collegiate coaches of women's sports (Sherman, DeHass, Thompson, & Wilfert, 2005) regarding the female athlete triad, respondents indicated that they needed training and information in order to better manage the triad. In response to that survey, the National Collegiate Athletic Association (NCAA, 2005) developed a manual to assist coaches with strategies to identify, manage, and prevent the triad. Regarding identification, information primarily focused on disordered eating and the aspects of the sport environment that complicate the identification process (i.e., sport body stereotypes, the purported relationship between leanness and performance, the similarity of "good athlete" traits and disordered eating symptoms, and the presumption of good health with good performance). With respect to managing the triad, information was provided on how to approach and talk with the affected sport participant, how to make a referral, how to make decisions regarding training and competition for a symptomatic sport participant, and how to manage the effect of a symptomatic team member on her teammates. Regarding prevention, coaches were informed as to the primary risks for disordered eating, but also were provided with strategies designed to decrease those risks, primarily through the de-emphasis on weight. As a follow-up to the coach's manual on managing disordered eating and the triad, the NCAA (2007) also developed a coach's manual designed to assist them in identifying and managing not only eating disorders, but also depression, anxiety, and substance use disorders in sport participants, conditions that often co-occur with eating disorders.

An Eating Disorders Resource for Coaches

This excellent resource was developed by the Eating Disorders Foundation of Victoria (Australia) and the Victorian Centre of Excellence in Eating Disorders (2005) to assist coaches and trainers in the prevention and early detection of eating disorders among sport participants, as well as the timely referral of such individuals for treatment with treatment specialists. Major content areas included identification (i.e., risk factors, warning signs, etc.), intervention (i.e., who should respond, how and when to respond, etc.), and support and prevention (i.e., reducing risk factors, promoting protective factors, etc.). This resource also provides several appendices that contain information on relevant topics such as excessive exercise, the female athlete triad, body mass index (BMI) and exercise guidelines, and referral information and resources.

Cheerleading Coaches

As reported in Chapter 3, cheerleaders are likely a high-risk group for the development of eating problems due to both appearance and performance pressures. Whisenhunt, Williamson, Drab-Hudson, and Walden (2008) targeted cheerleading coaches as change agents by training them to identify eating disorder symptoms and to reduce pressures to be thin. Specifically, coaches received training regarding negative coaching behaviors, eating disorder symptoms, and management techniques. They were then encouraged to participate in six intervention strategies: reading material, referral, video, parent and cheerleader handouts, and discussion format. At an 8-month follow-up, coaches were assessed regarding the effectiveness of the intervention. Although results indicated that the intervention had produced behavior change in the coaches, it was less successful in producing long-term change in knowledge about eating disorders.

FUTURE DIRECTIONS

The paucity of prevention and even educational programs designed to decrease the incidence and prevalence of eating disorders in sport is somewhat surprising and even alarming, given the fact that eating disorders appear to be more prevalent in the sport environment. Thus, our first recommendation should be obvious; we simply need more controlled prevention studies. Second, information alone is not likely to produce prevention of eating disorders. Nonetheless, education is still needed by sport participants, coaches, sport governing bodies, and parents.

Sport Participants

Before discussing the types of education that are needed by sport participants, we want to stress the need for preventive programming with all sport participants. Eating disorders are more prevalent in the high-risk sports for girls and women than in lower-risk (nonlean) female sports or sports for male participants. However, eating disorders are nondiscriminatory; they occur in all sports. Educational efforts with sport participants should include not only females in the high-risk sports (i.e., gymnastics, distance running, diving, figure skating, etc.) but also males and sportswomen in all sports. This recommendation is based on Levine and Smolak's suggestion that more individuals considered to be less at risk (sportsmen and women in nonlean sports in this case) will develop eating disorders than those from only the high-risk (women's) sports. There are more sport participants in men's sports and more in women's lower-risk (nonlean) sports than in the handful of high-risk women's sports. Even when the prevalence is higher among high-risk females, the actual numbers will be greater in the lower-risk sports based purely on the larger number of total participants.

Also, this recommendation to include all sportsmen and women, regardless of type of sport or gender, is based on our contention that most sportsmen and women with eating disorders would likely have had their disorders even without having participated in sport. That is, we do not view sport participation, even sport participation in lean sports, as the critical determinant for developing an eating disorder for most affected sport participants, but rather as another risk factor. Given this, what types of information should be provided to sport participants?

General Information

Some types of general information are appropriate for almost all sport participants, regardless of sport or gender. One of these involves nutrition and healthy eating.

Nutrition and Eating

This is actually an area in which individuals often claim (and perhaps actually believe) that they know how and what to eat. On examination, however, we find that sport participants (like most nonsport participants with eating disorders) make decisions about eating based on myths and misinformation. Additionally, sportsmen and women may also have unusual eating habits or engage in superstitious eating behaviors that may be idiosyncratic or related in some way to their particular sport. The idiosyncratic ones can be as individual as the number of participants. Some of the general ones include misinformation about carbohydrates, believing that they must cut or restrict carbohydrates, not realizing that carbohydrates, especially complex carbohydrates, provide the best energy source for most people, but certainly for sport participants. Regarding how nutrition affects sport performance, many sport participants seem not to understand that nutrition is important, while still others use nutritional information in ways that are unhelpful. As with the general population, many seem to lack balance. This lack of balance is not only in the choice of foods, but just as important, there often tends to be a lack of balance with respect to what is needed for general health and healthy sport performance.

In summary, eating and nutritional information should dispel common myths related to nutrition and sport and reflect not only a healthy balance of food choices, but also a healthy balance between eating and physical activity. On this last point, education should assist participants in understanding the proper relationship between eating and energy expenditure, that is, that energy expenditure requires a balanced energy intake, and that energy expenditure is not intended to legitimize eating (make it okay), nor should it be used to compensate for eating. Finally, sport participants with more knowledge of nutrition not only make better food choices, but also tend to have better physical and psychological health and perform better in sport (Quatromoni, 2008; Wiita & Strombaugh, 1996). Make reputable sources on nutrition readily available for sport participants and strongly encourage their use. There are several good sources in this regard, including Benardot (2006), Clark (2008), and Girard Eberle (2007).

Caution

Although many forms of general information are safe, there are some types for which caution should be used. Ironically, information designed to assist sportswomen and men in avoiding an eating disorder could be used by a sport participant to experiment with an eating disorder symptom (i.e., vomiting as a means to control weight). Because a priori it is difficult to know who might misuse information in such a manner, it is probably better to avoid specifically covering the symptomatic behaviors often found in eating disorder patients. Most notably, this would include the compensatory behaviors (purging techniques) frequently found in eating disorder patients (i.e., vomiting; abuse or use of laxatives, diuretics, diet pills, enemas, etc.).

Sport Performance

Nothing is more important than one's physical and psychological health. However, simply telling sport participants that they should eat well in order to be healthy is not apt to have great appeal. The best way to get the attention of sport participants is to talk performance. Thus, the information provided should indicate that poor or inadequate nutrition, including disordered eating, increases the likelihood of reduced sport performance (e.g., restrictive dieting leads to decreased running speed). Or, from a more positive perspective, the information provided should indicate that healthy eating can increase the likelihood of good sport performance. This can be accomplished in several ways.

One approach is to provide sportsmen and women with information related to the negative physical and psychological effects and consequences of disordered eating on sport performance, as shown in Table 9.1. Ideally, as Levine and Smolak suggested, we want to raise their consciousness and encourage critical thinking on relevant issues, which in this case would involve the relationship between nutrition and sport performance. In essence, we are challenging the myths and misinformation they may have regarding the effects of eating and weight on performance. Then ask them a series of questions (with obvious answers)

Table 9.1   Effects of an Eating Disorder on Sport Performance

- Many athletes can sometimes perform well despite having a serious eating disorder, but eventually the disorder begins to affect the athlete both physically and psychologically.
- Following a period of intense dieting, VO_2max and running speed usually decrease.*
- Inadequate carbohydrate intake results in early glycogen depletion and fatigue.*
- Inadequate carbohydrate intake results in increased use of protein as fuel.*
- Inadequate protein can lead to muscle weakness, wasting, and injury (increased risk of musculoskeletal injuries due to inability to build/repair muscle tissue damage).*
- Dehydration leads to fatigue, poorer performance, and earlier glycogen depletion.*
- Symptomatic athletes are apt to be malnourished, dehydrated, depressed, anxious, and obsessed (with eating, food, and weight), which serve to decrease concentration and the athlete's capacity to play with emotion, in addition to their negative effects on the athlete's physiology.

* Adapted from Beals, K. A., *Disordered Eating Among Athletes: A Comprehensive Guide for Health Professionals*, Human Kinetics, Champaign, IL, 2004.

regarding the sport performance of two sport participants—one who had engaged in disordered eating symptoms versus one who had been following a healthy, balanced eating regimen. Their answers serve two purposes. First, answers provide verification that participants learned (or did not learn) the information correctly. Second, they can serve to contradict previously held (mis)beliefs regarding the relationship between nutrition/disordered eating and performance, similar to the cognitive dissonance model that has been proven effective in eating disorder prevention. For example:

In the questions below, pick the sport participant who is apt to perform better.

1. One who has been undereating and is malnourished in an effort to lose weight or one who has been eating a healthy, balanced regimen?
2. One who is dehydrated or one who is adequately hydrated?
3. One who is distracted by thoughts of eating, food, and weight or one who is mentally focused?

For other activities that can be employed using the dissonance model with sport participants, see Becker et al. (2008) and Smith and Petrie (2008).

Information Specific to Gender/Sport

For sportswomen, information regarding menstrual functioning is of paramount importance. Despite efforts to educate sportswomen and sport personnel regarding the importance of menstrual functioning with respect to general, reproductive, and bone health (e.g., American College of Sports Medicine [ACSM], 2007; Medical Commission of the International Olympic Committee [IOCMC], 2005; NCAA, 2005), there is still the belief by many sportswomen that a menstrual cycle not only is unnecessary, but is viewed as undesirable by some because it interferes with training and performance. Still other sportswomen, as well as their coaches (Sherman et al., 2005), view amenorrhea (loss of menses) as normal. Worse yet, some view amenorrhea as indicative of an appropriate training level.

Information regarding menstrual functioning should first stress that a symptom is the body's way of communicating that something is wrong. Information should include all forms of menstrual dysfunction (i.e., amenorrhea, oligomenorrhea, luteal phase deficiency, etc.) as symptomatic and in need of medical intervention. As with other forms of information, in order to get the sportswoman's attention, talk performance, indicating that menstrual dysfunction can negatively affect performance both directly and indirectly. A negative performance effect could include the situation in which menstrual flow is heavy and the individual loses iron. In such a case, if the sportswoman does not get enough iron in her diet (i.e., such as might occur with disordered eating) to build red blood cells (which carry oxygen to exercising muscles), sport performance is apt to decrease (Otis & Goldingay, 2000). For sportswomen who have low estrogen due to menstrual dysfunction, such a condition serves to weaken bones and increase the likelihood of fractures, especially stress fractures. Emphasize that such fractures usually mean an interruption of training until healing occurs. Certainly, this information is important for sportswomen in all sports, and conventional wisdom would suggest that it is particularly important for sportswomen who participate in lean sports, especially the aesthetic sports. Also, because weight-bearing exercise is a requirement for building bone density (along with calcium, vitamin D, and estrogen), sportswomen in sports that are not weight bearing may be at increased risk. Studies investigating bone mineral density (BMD) of sportswomen found lower BMD in competitors in two non-weight-bearing sports: swimming (Duncan et al., 2002; Lee et al., 1995) and cycling (Duncan et al., 2002). With the likelihood of falls occurring in cycling, increased risk of fracture due to bone loss should get the attention of competitive cyclists.

While on the topic of bone health, it is important to mention that, although the relationships among and between sport training, testosterone levels, and bone health in males are not fully understood, sportsmen in endurance sports should be aware of the possibility of bone loss. Several studies have found decreased BMD in distance runners (Bennell et al., 1997; Bilanin, Blanchard, & Russek-Cohen, 1989; Hetland, Haarbo, & Christiansen, 1993) and again in the non-weight-bearing sport of cycling (Nichols, Palmer, & Levy, 2003; Smathers, Bemben, & Bemben, 2009; Stewart & Hannan, 2000). Low testosterone levels have sometimes been found in such sportsmen, which could result in bone loss and increased risk of fracture. Education in this regard is perhaps more important for these sport participants because a decrease in sex hormones is harder to detect in males. In females, we can rely on a change in menstrual functioning (i.e., amenorrhea) as a signal to the individual that her estrogen levels may be low, resulting in an increased risk of bone loss. Males do not have such a noticeable marker. The fact that osteoporosis is viewed by many as an "older woman's disease" is apt to increase the sportsman's risk because it may not be considered in males, simply because of their gender (and age). It may also not be a consideration if the sportsman is performing well because of the presumption of health that is often associated with good sport performance.

Coaches

Disordered Eating/Eating Disorders

There are several types of information coaches need in order to play a role in preventing eating disorders. First, they are in an excellent position to play a role in early identification. That is, they have numerous opportunities to observe their sport participants under a variety of circumstances (i.e., competition, practice, meetings, road trips, etc.). They must know which behaviors are possible symptoms, identify them as such, and then they must know how best to respond. At the same time, however, the goal in this regard is not to make coaches into psychologists; rather, the coach's role is *recognize* and *refer*. Additionally, coaches could benefit from more interactive approaches by responding to vignettes that involve identifying potential problems, and appropriately responding and referring. The following vignette is provided as an example:

Allison is 21 years old. She is quite coachable, trains very hard, and despite performing well, is never satisfied with her performance. Your assistant coach reported to you that Allison often tries to avoid eating with the team at team meals. A team member told you that Allison vomits if she thinks she has eaten too much. As a coach, I would ...

If coaches are going to be involved in decreasing the prevalence and incidence of eating disorders, they must not only be able to identify eating disorder symptoms, but also be aware of the risks for such disorders; they need to know those risk factors that are common to the sport environment in general, and those that are specific to their particular sport.

General Risk Factors

The most important risk factor (other than genetics) is pressure to lose weight or conform to a thinner ideal. The message for coaches in this regard is to recognize their power and influence with their sportsmen and women, and realize that they are so important that they can either promote or help prevent eating disorders. That influence and power must be used to deemphasize weight. As with sport participants, performance is the way to get the attention of coaches. Many believe that the thinner or leaner sport participant will perform better. From this, it may appear that weight is the issue. For most, however, the real issue is not weight but performance. They simply believe that losing weight or body fat is going to lead to enhanced performance. Thus, if we are going to ask coaches to deemphasize weight, we must give them reasonable alternatives to improve sport performance. That is, we have to provide them with ways to enhance sport performance without a weight focus. From an eating disorder prevention standpoint, we want to improve performance without the risks associated with an emphasis on weight.

In Table 9.2, we have listed factors that have been reported in the literature as related to sport performance, as well as the many factors that sport participants and coaches have suggested to us contribute to successful performance. Sport performance is like most human behaviors in that it has multiple determinants. Physical factors (i.e., speed, endurance, strength, etc.) establish a ceiling (top) as to the individual's physical potential, and a sport participant cannot exceed his or her potential. However, as one well-known coach suggested, "A guy with potential is a guy who hasn't done anything yet." Potential is nothing unless realized. The most important issue is how to get the sportsman or woman to realize that potential.

Table 9.2 Sport Performance Factors

- Like most human behaviors, athletic performance is determined by several factors.
- Performance is a product of genetics, training, practice, coaching, body composition, VO_2 max, physical health, mental health, nutrition, hydration, rest/sleep, mental toughness, balance, coordination, endurance, speed, quickness, strength, desire, determination, motivation, mental preparation, "heart," resilience, competitiveness, intelligence, concentration, confidence, commitment, composure, poise, pride, mood, relationship between sport participant and coach, relationship between/among teammates, teamwork, and hard work. Or as one coach said, "Everything is a performance issue."
- The important question is which of the aforementioned factors related to performance should be the focus for a particular sport participant.
- The factors that focus more on weight (loss) create a greater risk of triggering disordered eating.
- It probably makes more sense to focus on those factors that are more under the individual's control. One's genetic makeup, for example, is out of the sport participant's control.

Certainly, weight may be a factor in sport performance—even an important one. However, there are ways to work on these physical factors without focusing on weight. One way would be to focus on nutrition rather than weight. Even if weight is decreased, an increase in performance is less apt to occur or to be maintained with inadequate nutrition. Coaches could avoid this possibility by working with a dietitian when possible, especially a dietitian with experience and expertise not only with sport participants but also with eating problems.

Sport performance can also be enhanced by working with nonphysical factors. Coaches are forever telling their players to "concentrate," "focus," "play with emotion," and "give 110%." Coaches talk about a player needing to "step up." Sport participants have heard these exhortations many times, but how many sportsmen and women actually understand what they mean? More importantly, how many actually know what to do in order to comply with them? Whether they realize it or not, coaches are talking about psychological factors when referring to concentration, emotion, and effort. With proper instruction, training, and practice, sport participants can learn to use psychological factors (i.e., thoughts and emotions) in ways that improve their sport performance. They can learn such skills as the use of imagery, positive self-talk, mental preparation, and

197

relaxation training to eliminate negative psychological effects (i.e., choking, making mental mistakes, etc.), but on the positive side, these skills can increase motivation, concentration, and confidence. An exhaustive discussion of working with psychological factors to enhance sport performance is well beyond the scope of this book. Suffice it to say that physical factors determine a ceiling on performance, but it is often the psychological factors that determine how close to that ceiling the individual actually performs; that is, they determine the realization of potential. For more information in this area, refer to Burton and Raedeke (2008), Chamberlain (2003), and Orlick (2008).

Again, from a psychological point of view, improvement of the relationship between the coach and his or her sport participants is another area that could produce enhanced performance. This recommendation is based on information received from the female sport participants with whom we work clinically. We routinely ask about their relationship with their coach and if they believe that their performance could be enhanced by an improvement in their relationship with their coach. In virtually every case, the answer is yes. An additional advantage of an improved relationship might also include more openness and better communication about any problems, including those related to eating or weight. Improvement in this regard can also remedy some of the problems that coaches have regarding confidentiality when their sport participants are in treatment. That is, rather than relying on healthcare professionals for information (which may or may not be forthcoming), the coach might feel more comfortable asking the participant, who might in turn feel more comfortable talking with her coach about it.

Risk Factors for Particular Sports
Certain sports have the same general risk factors associated with them but also risk factors specific to a particular sport. For example, female athletes in aesthetic (appearance) sports are at risk for several reasons. One possible risk factor relates to revealing sport uniforms or costumes that seem to be a part of aesthetic sports, as well as other nonaesthetic sports that use revealing attire. Give consideration to body consciousness issues when uniforms are chosen for a particular sport. When possible, why not use the same uniform style for women as for men? For example, in track and field events, sportswomen are typically engaging in the same movements in a particular event as their male counterparts. There does not appear to be a good reason for them to wear more revealing

uniforms. The same could be said for other sports as well. If for some reason women cannot wear the same style or design as men in the same sport, provide them with more options within a particular sport, such as gym shorts or longer shorts in lieu of "bunhuggers" or bikini bottoms, or longer tops that reveal less midriff, or tops or bottoms that are less form fitting.

Risk of Binge Eating and Weight-Related Problems for Male Participants in Power Sports

For some sportsmen in power sports (American football, power lifters, throwers in field events, etc.), the goal is sometimes to increase size and weight in order to increase strength and power. At least one study found that sportsmen may be at risk for binge eating (Johnson, Powers, & Dick, 1999). It is important that these individuals have nutritional guidance rather than simply have them eating as much as possible. There are several reasons for such guidance. First, many of them will already be eating large quantities and may view binge eating as normal for sportsmen in their particular sports. Nutritional guidance would not only allow for the provision of necessary information regarding healthy weight gain practices, but also increase the likelihood of identification of binge eating. Second, some of the sportsmen who participated in sport at high weight levels (i.e., 300+ pounds) have been found to be at increased risk for metabolic syndrome (Miller et al., 2008) once their playing days are concluded. It is also imperative that these individuals learn how to moderate their intake to more normal levels once they have completed their competition in order to prevent weight-related health problems after leaving their active training schedules.

Menstrual Functioning

One area in which coaches need more information is in the area of menstrual functioning in terms of reproductive health, but also with its possible relationship with disordered eating. Many coaches still view amenorrhea as normal (Sherman et al., 2005). Because menstrual changes can be the first sign of disordered eating and the female athlete triad, it is important that coaches or at least their trainers know the menstrual status of their team members. Menstrual irregularity should be evaluated, but an assessment for disordered eating should also be conducted. Many coaches, especially male coaches, are not comfortable in discussing such issues with their sportswomen, feeling that such a discussion is too personal. For some young women, however, being told by a coach they need to lose weight is just as personal. Experiential training in talking with sportswomen about menstrual issues might be appropriate and helpful for some coaches. Also, as with disordered eating, coaches could benefit from interactive approaches that involve identifying problems related to menstrual functioning, and then responding and referring appropriately. The following vignette is provided as an example:

> Ann is 19 years old. She works harder than anyone else on the team and is willing to do whatever it takes to perform well. Your medical staff has notified you that Ann has been without a menstrual cycle for over a year, and suggested she decrease her training in an effort to restore her cycle. Ann has refused because she fears she will gain weight, resulting in poorer sport performance, which has been excellent to this point. As a coach I would ...

Other Information Needed by Coaches

We have mentioned many times the need for a deemphasis on weight and the personal nature of weight, especially for women. For this reason, we recommend that coaches not be involved in issues related to weight, and they should not be weighing their sport participants. As we have discussed previously, weight should be considered a medical or health issue and managed by medical professionals. It goes without saying that group weigh-ins should be avoided. Based on reports from patients, public weigh-ins are almost like public degradation for them. If an individual needs to be weighed for a legitimate medical reason, she should be weighed privately (and sensitively) by a healthcare professional, who explains the need for her being weighed and how the information is to be used.

Even though coaches should not be directly involved with a sport participant's weight, it does not mean that they cannot be of assistance to their sport participants regarding eating. Certainly, the sport dietitian is the expert in this area and his or her counsel should be the sport participant's first option regarding eating. Nonetheless, coaches are apt to be asked by their sportswomen or men for their advice or opinions regarding eating and nutrition, given their position of power and influence. For this reason, coaches need to be aware of the most recent, well-documented sources regarding nutrition and sport performance. One such source is Bonci (2009).

In a previous chapter, we discussed the issues related to competitive thinness and behavioral contagion among team members and how these issues can develop and reinforce norms regarding attitudes and behaviors that are associated with body dissatisfaction and disordered eating. Coaches can play a role in reducing the problems associated with behavioral contagion by discouraging "fat talk." Fat talk (Stice, Maxfield, & Wells, 2003) usually involves discussions or interactions between females in which they talk about their body dissatisfaction and need to lose weight. Fat talk can also involve talking about others' appearance and be related to eating pathology (Ousley, Cordero, & White, 2008). When hearing such talk, coaches need to discourage it by responding that such talk is negative, unhealthy, and has no place in sport. Coaches could also arrange for a healthcare professional to talk with the team about such issues.

Our final recommendation regarding coaches may run counter to what some coaches believe. It relates to recognizing the importance of individual differences. In sport, the emphasis has traditionally been on the team rather than the individual. We are not suggesting that team be deemphasized, but recognize that the team is made up of individuals. Regarding individual differences, there is no issue more important or more individual than that of weight. Each person has a unique set of genetic, familial, social, and psychological factors, as well as an eating and weight history that contribute to his or her weight. Some individuals will find being thin or lean to be relatively easy, whereas others will find it to be quite difficult if not impossible. For this reason, it makes little sense to believe that everyone should look the same. Nonetheless, there are beliefs about what a successful performer in a particular sport should weigh or measure with respect to body composition. For example, there are lists of body fat ranges that are associated with successful performance for participants in particular sports. As a result, some coaches believe that their sport participants must/should be in that range. This sounds reasonable, but is it as reasonable as it sounds?

There are several problems with this "reasoning." First, we do not know anything about the eating of the individuals whose body compositions were used to compute the body fat range for an elite sample of sportsmen or women in a particular sport. Were they healthy eaters? Did they engage in disordered eating or have eating disorders? Because we do not know anything about their eating, we cannot conclude much about the appropriateness of their body fat levels. Second, even if we did know about their eating, we still cannot conclude anything about how others will perform at that body fat level. Can we say, for example, that a sport participant with the same body fat level as participants who have been successful at the elite level of sport performance will perform at the same level? No, we cannot. These body composition levels may be descriptive of successful elite performers, but we cannot say with assurance that they are predictive. That would be like saying that a male swimmer with the same body composition as Michael Phelps (winner of eight gold medals in the 2008 Olympics) will swim like him, which of course is not reasonable. Additionally, Phelps was reportedly eating 8,000 to 10,000 calories daily during his heavy training days. Should all male swimmers eat at that level? And if they did, would they be Olympic champions? Not likely. Individual differences can be very important regarding sport performance. It would behoove a coach to consider them.

Sport Governing Bodies

Sport governing bodies are in a position to be impactful regarding prevention of eating disorders, but some (e.g., NCAA) have been more active than others. We cannot expect most coaches to take seriously the potential harm of eating disorders if their parent organizations do not take a proactive, strong stance in that regard. This type of commitment must not only be apparent in their official communications, but should also be reflected in the funding provided for such prevention efforts for sport participants and education and training for coaches.

A commitment from a governing body is a communication, but the message of the communication needs to be clear regarding the importance of the health of the sport participant. For example, certainly most have taken a strong stance against the use of steroids and other performance-enhancing drugs. Even though there has sometimes been disagreement on the seriousness of the health risks of such drugs, most organizations that govern sports would most likely agree that the use of such substances can have significant health consequences for some users, especially for women regarding reproductive and bone health. But is the purpose of that stance against steroids to protect the participant's health, or is it to protect the fairness of competition? That is, are sport governing bodies concerned about the health of the participant or about not giving one participant an unfair sport advantage over the other? These substances are not referred to as potentially health-compromising or dangerous drugs. Rather, they are referred to as performance enhancing. The name *performance enhancing* might entice a sportsman to try them. The participants who are "caught" using them are not usually provided with appropriate treatment but rather are sanctioned or banned from competition. What is the message?

As long as the communication is performance related rather than health related, the message can be interpreted to mean that sport performance is more important than the participant's health. This is not the message we want to give to individuals with eating disorders, who are not usually concerned with the health consequences of their disorder. Such a message may actually increase the likelihood of use by some sport participants, such as those who are willing to do whatever is necessary to perform well, including taking health risks. That message will not help prevent eating disorders, as some participants are willing to do anything to perform better, even engage in dangerous symptoms associated with eating disorders. An illustrative example involves the approach taken by the International Ski Federation to prevent male ski jumpers from losing too much weight. As you may recall from our discussion in Chapter 3, jumpers were aware that less weight allowed them to fly farther. The Ski Federation acted by establishing a minimal BMI for contestants. Skis were shortened for those under the BMI standard in order to nullify the sport performance advantage of low weight. This change was effective in the sense that it decreased the number of jumpers with low BMIs, but the message was related to sport performance. Why not disqualify those with low weights because they did not meet a healthy standard to be competing? By doing so, the message would be about health. What most likely will happen if the message is not changed to more of a health focus is that jumpers will still be attempting to lose weight and may use unhealthy weight-loss techniques in order to "make weight"; that is, they will try to be at the lowest weight possible without being penalized. We will see jumpers of the same height record the same weights—the exact BMI limit. The emphasis is still on weight as it relates to performance. The message must be clear. As we have discussed previously, one can get the attention of sport participants by talking performance. However, the message that is sent is not always the one that is received. Make sure the message about performance is not that the participant's performance is more important than his or her health, but rather that health is important in its own right, and that it is also the means to good, long-standing sport performance.

One specific recommendation we have for sport governing bodies is for the education of judges regarding the appearance standards that may be affecting their scoring. Coaches of aesthetic sports may feel that they must have their participants conform to weight, size, or shape standards of their sport that they feel are affecting judges' scoring. The responsibility here for governing bodies might be to educate not only their coaches with respect to their influence on sport participants' pressures to lose weight, but also their judges, whose scoring (judgments) of sport performances may not only determine the winners, but may also lead to unhealthy weight-loss attempts by the nonwinners. Sport governing bodies might also push for more objectivity in judges' scoring. This would be more helpful to judges and perhaps also safer for contestants. A related possible safeguard for participants in judged sports relates to uniform choices, as previously discussed in Chapter 4. Governing organizations could play a crucial role in recommending less revealing uniform options.

Parents

Parents are the most important people in the life of a child or adolescent. Thus, parents must have the necessary information to protect their children regarding the possible risk factors often associated with sport participation. First, it is important for parents to understand that it is not sport participation that is the risk. Rather, the risks reside in the unhealthy aspects of the sport environment that have been discussed throughout this book. Parents need to know how to identify these risks. Second, sport participation for children and adolescents may be riskier than for older participants at higher levels of participation (i.e., college, elite), because sports at lower levels tend not only to have less experienced and less informed coaches, but also to have less medical oversight. For that reason, the risk may be greater. This underscores the parents' need to be aware of risks and symptoms. Third, parents should get involved when concerned about their son or daughter. Parents generally know their children better than anyone. They should be assertive about their concerns with the sport personnel involved with their child.

FINAL THOUGHTS

It should be clear from previous chapters that the desire for weight loss/ thinness and its pursuit play a critical role in increasing the risk of an individual developing an eating disorder. In the nonsport environment, this desire and pursuit relate more to appearance. Also, as discussed previously, sport participants are at greater risk because they are exposed to the same risk factors as nonsportsmen, but also to those that are unique or specific to sport. In the sport environment, this desire and pursuit can relate to appearance for almost all sport participants, and especially those in the aesthetic sports. When the belief related to leanness and performance is added to the appearance-related one, the pressures, and thus the risks, can be significant.

One of the biggest impediments to the prevention of eating disorders among sport participants is the continued emphasis on the purported relationship between weight or leanness and sport performance; that is, the leaner competitor will perform better. It is true that some leaner individuals in some sports perform better some of the time. But, it is also true that many do not. If fact, some perform less well after losing weight or body fat. Additionally, there are many lean sportsmen or women who do not perform as well as they or their coaches believe they should, despite their leanness. This suggests that weight is not the critical factor, or at least there are other significant factors that contribute to successful sport performance. (For a list of factors believed to be related to sport performance, see Table 9.2.) Nonetheless, the "belief" that "thinner is the winner" in the sport environment is still held firmly by many sport participants and their coaches. For prevention efforts with sport participants to be successful, this "thinner/winner" mentality must be supplanted. Of necessity, the mentality that replaces it must include performance to get the attention of coaches and sport participants, but performance that is enhanced through health and nutrition.

Given the power and influence coaches have with their sportsmen and women, coaches are perhaps the only individuals who can assist preventive efforts in moving past the emphasis on weight and leanness. Their players will likely follow their lead if we can get coaches on board. We need coaches, through nondieting, non-weight-focused strategies, to make the link between good nutrition and health and good sport performance for their sport participants. By doing so, they reduce the risk to their sport participants.

EPILOGUE

We hope that the reader now has a better sense of the complexity of eating disturbances that much too often affect participants in the world of sport. Much of our discussion has been general in nature, pointing to factors and suggestions that are applicable in most cases. At the same time, we have also stressed individual differences. An affected sport participant who comes to the attention of sport personnel or a healthcare professional is not a person "in general," but rather a special individual who may or may not fit all of the characteristics or experience all of the symptoms described in this book. Sport participants with eating problems are special individuals who need specialized approaches to identification, management, and treatment.

Just as there is an emphasis on enhancing performance in sport, we need to enhance our performance in identifying, managing, and treating affected sportsmen and women by developing expertise through quality training, increased knowledge, and supervised experience. We have several recommendations regarding developing that expertise. Because the risks, causes, and consequences of eating problems are multidimensional, we need to think and work from a multidimensional perspective. In conceptualizing and responding to an eating disorder, sport personnel should not be so "ethnocentric" to assume that the only (or even the primary) contributing factor to the disorder involves a need to be lean solely for the purpose of performing better. Eating disorders serve multiple functions and purposes in the patient's life. In our clinical practice, sport participation plays little if any role in the disorders of many of our sport-participant patients. In essence, their eating disorders would have developed without participating in sport. In similar fashion, the healthcare professional should not be so biased as to assume that sport participation is the problem and thus should be eliminated. As we have emphasized throughout this book, it is not sport participation per se that is the problem, but rather the risks that are sometimes found in the sport environment. Medical professionals should not ignore psychological issues that can affect treatment response. Mental health professionals must be aware of the potential medical complications and how starvation can affect psychological functioning. Sport personnel, medical professionals, and mental health practitioners should not underestimate the need and importance of proper nutrition and nutritional guidance from a dietitian in the sport participant's recovery. The fact that each discipline brings its own set of experiences, expertise, and knowledge, not to mention its own set of biases and deficits, underscores the need for a comprehensive sport management team.

The management of a sport participant with an eating problem also needs to be met with unbiased acceptance and a positive but realistic outlook. It is not only unhelpful but inaccurate to view individuals with eating disorders as weak. Many of these individuals are some of the psychologically strongest people you will have the privilege to meet. The fact that they compete in the sport arena only adds to their strength. At the same time, some of the characteristics that help them perform well in the sport arena will increase their risk for developing or maintaining an eating disorder. However, as their eating becomes more disordered, they will have less and less control over their symptoms, and that strength that serves them so well in the other areas of life will need to be used in treatment. It is ironic that characteristics that facilitate sport performance can at the same time increase the risk of developing an eating disorder. But those same characteristics, if used properly by skilled and knowledgeable practitioners, can facilitate treatment. Even with the best treatment, sport participants' responses to treatment will again be individual. Although some will recover quickly, others may struggle for years, and still others may not survive their disorders. Just as people come in all shapes and sizes, so too do these problems and the complexity of their treatment. Usually, the duration and intensity required in treatment depends on the severity and chronicity of the problem. Given this, early identification and timely, effective treatment are paramount.

Finally, most of our insights provided in this book come as a result of our clinical experiences, and we thank our patients, who have taught us most of what we know. The rest of what we know we owe to research. Though we are not primarily researchers, we value the research contributions that thankfully have burgeoned in this area during the past 15 years. However, despite clinical advances and significant research productivity in this area, there are still too many sport participants being affected by eating and body image disturbances. In fact, the prevalence and incidence of such difficulties have increased in the past 15 years. Obviously, considerable research regarding eating disorders in sport is still needed. The most pressing needs include longitudinal studies investigating eating disorder risk factors for sport participants, studies related to eating disorder education and prevention, and research in the area of youth and adolescent sports, the time of life when the risk of eating disorders developing is greatest.

GLOSSARY

Aesthetic sports: Sports usually thought of as "appearance" sports in which the sport participant's appearance as well as her sport performance is being judged. Included in this group are diving, figure skating, gymnastics, and synchronized swimming.

Affective instability: Emotional lability; moods/emotions can change widely and quickly.

Amenorrhea: Absence or cessation of menstruation. Amenorrhea is either primary (menstruation has not occurred by age 16) or secondary (cessation of menstruation).

Anabolic: Of or related to the synthetic phase of metabolism.

Anabolic steroid: Hormone related to testosterone that increases protein synthesis in cells, resulting in increased cell tissue in the muscles.

Anorexia athletica: Disordered eating in female athletes involving fear of gaining weight/becoming fat when underweight and weight loss of at least 5% of body weight due to dietary restriction and excessive exercise; binge eating and the use of pathogenic weight control methods (i.e., self-induced vomiting or use of laxatives or diuretics) may be present.

Anorexia nervosa: Eating disorder in which the patient weighs less than 85% of expected weight, has an irrational fear of being fat, has body image disturbance, and is amenorrheic.

Anovulation: Menstruation without ovulation; a condition in which the ovary does not release a ripened egg each month as part of a woman's normal cycle in her reproductive years. Thus, anovulation is a prime factor in infertility.

Anterior cruciate ligament: One of four major ligaments that support the knee.

Antigravitation sports: Sports whose primary activity involves jumping (i.e., high jump, long jump, pole vault, etc.).

Anxiety disorders: The predominant symptom for this group of disorders is anxiety or fear (i.e., panic disorder, phobias, obsessive-compulsive disorder, posttraumatic stress disorder, etc.).

211

Apgar score: The Apgar score is a simple repeatable method to quickly assess the health of newborns immediately after childbirth. The score is determined by evaluating the newborn on five simple criteria on a scale from 0 to 2, then summing up the five values thus obtained. The resulting Apgar score ranges from 0 to 10. The five criteria (appearance, pulse, grimace, activity, respiration) are used as a mnemonic device.

Atrial fibrillation: The most common cardiac arrhythmia that involves the two upper chambers (the atria) of the heart. Its name comes from the fibrillating (i.e., quivering) of the heart muscles of the atria, instead of a coordinated contraction.

Binge eating disorder: A variant of EDNOS characterized by recurrent eating of large amounts of food associated with a perceived lack of control; binge eating is not usually followed by compensatory behaviors as in bulimia nervosa.

Body dissatisfaction: Most eating disorder patients experience body dissatisfaction, with either the entire body or certain body parts. Typically, the dissatisfaction relates to the belief that their body or body parts are to "too big" or are "fat." Body dissatisfaction usually plays a critical role in the development and maintenance of an eating disorder.

Body image disturbance: Most eating disorder patients experience body image disturbance in that they (mis)perceive their bodies or body parts as being larger than they actually are.

Body mass index (BMI): Body weight divided by the square of body height (kg/m^2); sometimes used as an estimate of body composition.

Bone accretion: The bone formation process of bone metabolism and remodeling of bone.

Bone mineral density: Refers to the strength of bone as represented by calcium content.

Bone resorption: The breaking-down process of bone metabolism and remodeling of bone.

Bradycardia: A slow heart rate.

Bulimia nervosa: Eating disorder characterized by episodes of binge eating followed by compensatory behaviors (i.e., vomiting, laxative abuse, etc.).

Cardiac arrhythmias: A term for abnormal electrical activity in the heart. There are two main types of arrhythmias: those of rate (for example, too rapid or too slow) and those of rhythm (any of many irregular patterns, including torsades de pointes).

Coachability: Sport participant's willingness to do what his or her coach wants.

Cognitive behavioral therapy: A form of psychotherapy that primarily involves restructuring irrational thoughts by the patient to assist in changing maladaptive behaviors; it is the most researched form of treatment for eating disorders, and thus is the one most often recommended and used.

Comorbidity: The co-occurrence of at least two medical or psychological disorders.

Compensatory behaviors/purging: Behaviors that are used by eating disorder patients to compensate (undo) the effects of eating to prevent weight gain (e.g., induced vomiting; use of laxatives, diuretics, enemas, or emetics; fasting; exercise, etc.).

Competitive thinness: A competition usually between or among females regarding who is thinner. The perception of a person being thinner can generate the perceiver to experience body dissatisfaction and "motivate" her to attempt to lose weight through a variety of weight-loss methods.

Confidentiality: The maintenance of a patient's privacy; patient records are released only with the patient's consent to individuals with a specific and legitimate need to know.

Contagion effect: Social pressure in a group (team) can lead group members to engage in behaviors that are consistent with the norms or expectations of the group (i.e., dieting among team members).

Cortisol: A hormone produced by the adrenal gland. It is involved in stress and is sometimes called a stress hormone. It can negatively affect blood pressure and immune function.

Decreased ejection fraction: A decrease in the normal amount of blood pumped out of a ventricle of the heart with each heartbeat.

DEXA: Dual-energy x-ray absorptiometry; a method for determining bone mineral content.

Dialectical behavior therapy: Form of psychotherapy that involves treatment strategies based on acceptance or validation. Patients are taught to use the coping strategies of mindfulness, emotion regulation, distress tolerance, and interpersonal effectiveness.

Disordered eating: A term probably first used regarding the female athlete triad; a spectrum of eating behaviors used to lose weight or

213

achieve a lean appearance, ranging in severity from restricting food intake to clinical eating disorders.

Dyspnea: Shortness of breath.

Eating disorder not otherwise specified (EDNOS): The residual eating disorder category for disorders that do not meet full criteria for the diagnosis of anorexia nervosa or bulimia nervosa; it is the most prevalent disorder, and it includes binge eating disorder.

Echocardiogram: A noninvasive ultrasound test that shows an image of the inside of the heart, which can be used to identify structural problems.

Egosyntonic: Behaviors, feelings, values, and thoughts that are acceptable to (liked by or in harmony with) the individual.

Electrolyte: Any substance containing free ions that behave as an electrically conductive medium. Potassium, phosphate, and magnesium are examples of electrolytes that may be out of balance in the body.

Energy availability: Dietary energy intake minus exercise energy expenditure, or the energy that is left (available) after the energy cost of exercise has been spent.

Energy balance: Energy (calories) ingested versus energy (calories) burned.

Epiphyseal growth plate: A hyaline cartilage plate near the end of a long bone. This plate is found in children and adolescents; in adults, who have stopped growing, the plate is replaced by an epiphyseal line.

Estrogen: Any of several steroid hormones produced chiefly by the ovaries and responsible for promoting estrus and the development and maintenance of female secondary sex characteristics.

Eumenorrhea: Normal, regular menstruation.

Excessive exercise: Term that is often used to describe unhealthy or unbalanced exercise. It can be used in a quantitative sense, referring to the frequency, intensity, or duration of exercise. It may also be used in a qualitative sense, such as a judgment of the appropriateness of exercise by a person under a specified set of circumstances (e.g., health status, age, energy balance, etc.).

Fear food: Food that is typically avoided by an eating disorder patient because of fear of weight gain.

Female athlete triad: Initially, the triad consisted of disordered eating, amenorrhea, and osteoporosis; in the 2007 revision, the triad was changed to spectrums of health regarding energy availability, menstrual function, and bone mineral density.

Fluoxetine (Prozac): The first antidepressant medication to be FDA approved for the treatment of bulimia nervosa.

Gastroesophageal reflux disorder (GERD): GERD occurs when the valve separating the esophagus and stomach does not close properly, allowing stomach contents (i.e., stomach acid) to move up into the esophagus.

Gonadotropin releasing hormone: A hormone made by the hypothalamus and secreted by the pituitary gland to make luteinizing hormone (LH) and follicle stimulating hormone (FSH), which are involved in reproduction.

Hypercholesterolemia: Elevated serum cholesterol.

Hyperglycemia: High blood sugar in which an excessive amount of glucose circulates in the blood.

Hypokalemia: Low serum potassium levels that can result in cardiac abnormalities and complications, including death.

Hypomagnesemia: A low magnesium level.

Hypophosphatemia: Low serum phosphate levels that can play a critical role in refeeding syndrome, which can result in death to the patient.

Hypothalamus: The area of the brain that controls body temperature, hunger, and thirst.

Hypothermia: Body temperature is below normal (35 to 37°C/95 to 98.6°F).

Integrative cognitive affective therapy: A form of psychotherapy being applied to the treatment of bulimia nervosa. The focus in treatment is on the discrepancy between the patient's actual self and ideal self, the emotions experienced as a result, and how these emotions are related to eating disorder symptoms.

Interpersonal psychotherapy: A form of psychotherapy for the treatment of bulimia nervosa that focuses on interpersonal problems (interpersonal deficits, interpersonal role disputes, role transitions, and grief) rather than on specific eating symptoms.

Lean sports: Sports for which there is a weight-class requirement or sports in which leanness is thought to confer a competitive advantage either from a biomechanical standpoint (i.e., moving the body through space) or from a judging standpoint based on appearance.

Low energy availability (LEA): Occurs when the physically active female ingests insufficient calories to fuel her physical activity and support normal bodily processes of growth and development.

Luteal deficiency: A deficiency in the progesterone-secreting mass of cells that forms from an ovarian follicle after the release of a mature egg.

Luteinizing hormone pulsatility: Pulsatility of this reproductive hormone is affected by energy availability; amenorrhea thus occurs when dietary intake is inadequate to fuel both the energy costs of exercise and body processes such as reproduction.

Luteinizing releasing hormone: A hormone that controls sex hormones in men and women.

Medical clearance: Such clearance indicates that appropriate healthcare professionals have determined that the individual/patient/sport participant's health risks will not increase as a result of participating in a particular activity (e.g., running). Medical clearance should be as specific as possible and reviewed periodically.

Menarche: First menstrual period.

Metabolic syndrome: A combination of medical problems (i.e., hypertension, insulin resistance, obesity, etc.) that can increase an individual's risk of developing diabetes or cardiovascular disease.

Mitral valve prolapse: Occurs when the valve between the left upper chamber of the heart (the left atrium) and the left lower chamber (the left ventricle) doesn't close properly and the valve's flaps bulge (or prolapse) back into the atrium.

Mood disorders: These disorders involve a disturbance in mood; this group of disorders includes all forms of depression (i.e., major depressive disorder, bipolar disorder, etc.).

Muscle dysmorphia: A preoccupation with not being muscular enough despite having very highly developed muscularity; found primarily in males.

Nonlean sports: Sports in this group usually do not emphasize the leanness or thinness of a sport participant regarding appearance or sport performance. Sports other than those regarded as aesthetic, endurance, and weight-class sports are usually included in this group.

Obesity: Medical disorder characterized by a BMI of at least 30.0.

Olanzapine (Zyprexa): Antipsychotic medication that has been used in trials with anorexic patients to increase eating and weight.

Oligomenorrhea: A reduction in number of menstrual periods or amount of menstrual flow.

Orthostatic hypotension: An abnormal decrease in blood pressure when a person stands up. This may lead to fainting.

Osteopenia: Bone density measured to be between 1.0 and 2.5 standard deviations below the mean of a healthy reference population.

Osteoporosis: The word *osteoporosis* means "porous bones" and is a result of excessive loss of protein and mineral content within the bones. Osteoporotic bones break easily. Bone density measured to be more than 2.5 standard deviations below the mean of a healthy reference population.

Overtraining syndrome: This syndrome is sometimes referred to as "staleness." Symptoms can include fatigue, amenorrhea, weight loss, sleep disturbance, depression, and a decrement in sport performance.

Overweight: BMI of 25.0 to 29.9.

Pathogenic weight control methods: Weight control methods viewed as being unhealthy. Included would be all compensatory methods used by eating disorder patients (i.e., vomiting; abuse of laxatives, diuretics, enemas, and emetics; fasting; unhealthy exercise; etc.).

Pericardial effusion: The accumulation of excess fluid around the heart.

Personality disorders: Group of disorders characterized primarily by patterns of behavior that are often maladaptive, self-defeating, and relatively resistant to change. Personality disorders commonly found in eating disorder patients include obsessive-compulsive, dependent, and borderline.

Pharmacotherapy: The use of medications as a primary or adjunctive treatment.

Pituitary: Often called the master gland because it produces hormones that control other glands and many body functions, including growth.

Polycystic ovary syndrome: Hormonal irregularity in women that is characterized by anovulation and hyperandrogenism.

Precordial: Portion of the body over the heart and lower chest.

Primary prevention: The goal of primary prevention is to decrease the incidence of a disease/disorder by decreasing exposure to risk factors and increasing exposure to protective factors.

Prodromal: Early symptoms that may mark the onset of a disease.

Pseudovegetarianism: Individuals whose decision to avoid eating animal products has more to do with their need to avoid dietary fat and calories than it does with ethics or animal rights.

QT interval: A measure of the time between the start of the Q wave and the end of the T wave in the heart's electrical cycle, as shown in the electrocardiogram.

QTc: The QT interval is dependent on the heart rate (the faster the heart rate, the shorter the QT interval), and QTc is calculated using a formula devised by physiologist Henry Cuthbert Bazett. Other factors may also influence the QT interval, but there is less agreement about these factors.

QT prolongation: When the QT interval is longer than established norms, it is called QT prolongation. This can occur from congenital or genetic conditions and is then called the long QT syndrome, but QT prolongation can occur with semistarvation, certain medications, or in a variety of other situations. When QT prolongation does occur, there is a risk for cardiac arrhythmias, which (rarely and often unpredictably) can be lethal.

Reverse anorexia: A condition in which individuals (mis)perceive their body as being much smaller than it actually is.

Secondary prevention: Secondary prevention goals are to identify and treat early in the disease process to minimize medical and psychological complications/consequences.

Sport family: The sport participant's "family" that includes coaches, other sport personnel, and teammates.

Sport management team: This team usually consists of both healthcare professionals and sport personnel. The team's goal is the appropriate and effective management of the sport participant with disordered eating, from identification through successful treatment.

Starvation effects: These effects are probably more accurately named semistarvation effects and are a result of inadequate caloric intake; they can involve virtually every system of the body; they usually remit with adequate nutrition.

Stress fracture: A fracture caused by a nontraumatic, cumulative overload on a bone.

Syncope: Fainting.

Tachycardia: A rapid heart rate.

Thermogenesis: A process that involves calories being used to maintain fundamental body activities, such as keeping the body warm and the processing of food.

Triiodothyronine (T_3): A thyroid hormone.

RESOURCES

The following resources are intended to provide further information and contacts. The Web sites are current at time of publication. However, many change over time, so please check for the most current site.

This list is not complete, as new sites are added yearly. In addition, inclusion of a Web site is for your convenience and does not constitute an endorsement.

EATING DISORDER INFORMATION

AED (Academy for Eating Disorders): www.aedweb.org
An international organization providing eating disorder information as well as a list of eating disorder treatment providers.

ANAD (National Association of Anorexia Nervosa and Associated Eating Disorders): www.anad.org
Provides eating disorders information and support groups, and is active in legislative advocacy within the United States.

ANZAED (Australia and New Zealand Academy for Eating Disorders): www.anzaed.org.au

NEDA (National Eating Disorders Association): www.nationaleatingdisorders.org
Provides eating disorders information and a referral line (800-931-2237). This website's primary focus is on prevention. In addition, it includes tips for coaches.

NAMED (National Association for Males with Eating Disorders): http://www.namedinc.org
NAMED is dedicated to offering support to and public awareness about males with eating disorders.

IAEDP (International Association of Eating Disorder Professionals): www.iaedp.com
Provides eating disorder information and referrals.

BANA (Bulimia Anorexia Nervosa Association): www.bana.ca
   Provides eating disorder assistance for Ontario, Canada.

NEDIC (National Eating Disorder Information Centre): www.nedic.ca
   A program of the University of Toronto, Canada Health Network, which provides information and resources about eating disorders, as well as a list of intervention resources throughout Canada.

ECED (European Council on Eating Disorders): www.eced.co.uk
   Offers a biannual meeting in Europe of eating disorder professionals.

BEAT (Beating Eating Disorders): www.b-eat.co.uk
   The Eating Disorder Association of the UK. In addition to extensive general information about eating disorders, there are information sheets in their publications section that focus on athletes and coaches.

EDANZ (Eating Disorders Association of NZ): www.ed.org.nz
   This site offers general information about eating disorders as well as a list of treatment facilities in New Zealand.

SPORT INFORMATION

Australian Institute of Sport: www.ais.org.au
ACSM (American College of Sports Medicine): www.acsm.org
CASM (Canadian Academy of Sport Medicine: www.casm-acms.org
IOCMC (International Olympic Committee Medical Commission): www.olympic.org/en/content/The-IOC/Commissions/Medical
NATA (National Athletic Trainers' Association: www.nata.org
NCAA (National Collegiate Athletic Association) www.ncaa.org/health-safety

SPORT NUTRITION INFORMATION

SCAN (Sports, Cardiovascular and Wellness Nutrition): www.scan-dpg.org
To locate a sports dietitian.

Australian Institute of Sport: www.ausport.gov.au/ais/nutrition
Gatorade Sports Science Institute (GSSI): www.gssiweb.com
Peak Performance: www.pponline.co.uk
Sports Dietitians Australia: www.sportsdietitians.com.au
USDA (United States Department of Agriculture) Nutrient Data Laboratory: www.ars.usda.gov/nutrientdata

FEMALE ATHLETE TRIAD

Female Athlete Triad Coalition: www.femaleathletetriad.org
International Olympic Committee Position Stand on the Female Athlete Triad: http://multimedia.olympic.org/pdf/en_report_917.pdf
NCAA coaches' handbook for managing the female athlete triad (follow link to female athlete triad prevention): http://www.ncaa.org/wps/ncaa?ContentID=1446

FILM

Beauty Mark: www.beautymarkmovie.com
A documentary about an elite triathlete's struggle with and recovery from an eating disorder.

BOOKS

Gürze Books: www.bulimia.com
Gürze Books publishes and distributes a wide variety of book titles dealing with eating and body image issues.

REFERENCES

Abood, D. A., & Black, D. R. (2000). Health education prevention for eating disorders among college female athletes. *American Journal of Health Behavior, 24,* 209–219.

Ackard, D. M., Brehm, B. J., & Steffen, J. J. (2002). Exercise and eating disorders in college-aged women: Profiling excessive exercisers. *Eating Disorders: The Journal of Treatment and Prevention, 10,* 31–47.

Adkins, E. C., & Keel, P. K. (2005). Does "excessive" or "compulsive" best describe exercise as a symptom of bulimia nervosa? *International Journal of Eating Disorders, 38,* 24–29.

Agras, W. S., Walsh, T., Fairburn, C. G., Wilson, G. T., & Kraemer, H. C. (2000). A multicenter comparison of cognitive-behavioral therapy and interpersonal psychotherapy for bulimia nervosa. *Archives of General Psychiatry, 57,* 459–466.

Allison, K. C., Grilo, C. M., Masheb, R. M., & Stunkard, A. J. (2005). Binge eating disorder and night eating syndrome: A comparative study of disordered eating. *Journal of Consulting and Clinical Psychology, 73,* 1107–1115.

Allison, K. C., Stunkard, A. J., & Thier, S. (2004). *Overcoming night eating syndrome: A step-by-step guide to breaking the cycle.* Oakland, CA: New Harbinger.

American Academy of Family Physicians, American Academy of Pediatrics, American Medical Society of Sports Medicine, American Orthopedic Society for Sports Medicine, American Osteopathic Academy of Sports Medicine. (2004). *Preparticipation physical evaluation* (3rd ed.). New York: McGraw-Hill.

American Academy of Pediatrics Committee on Sports Medicine and Fitness. (2001). Medical conditions affecting sports participation. *Pediatrics, 107,* 1205–1209.

American College of Sports Medicine (ACSM). (1997). Position stand: The female athlete triad. *Medicine & Science in Sports & Exercise, 29,* i–ix.

American College of Sports Medicine (ACSM). (2007). Position stand: The female athlete triad. *Medicine & Science in Sports & Exercise, 39,* 1867–1882.

American College of Sports Medicine and American Heart Association Joint Position Statement. (2007). Exercise and acute cardiovascular events: Placing the risks into perspective. *Medicine & Science in Sports & Exercise, 39,* 886–897.

American Psychiatric Association. (1994). *Diagnostic and statistical manual of mental disorders* (4th ed.). Washington, DC: Author.

American Psychiatric Association. (2000). *Diagnostic and statistical manual of mental disorders* (4th ed., text rev.). Washington, DC: Author.

American Psychiatric Association. (2006). Practice guidelines for the treatment of patients with eating disorders (3rd ed.). *American Journal of Psychiatry, 163,* 4–54.

Andersen, A. E. (1999a). The diagnosis and treatment of eating disorders in primary care medicine. In P. S. Mehler & A. E. Andersen (Eds.), *Eating disorders: A guide to medical care and complications* (pp. 1–26). Baltimore: Johns Hopkins University Press.

Andersen, A. E. (1999b). Males with eating disorders: Medical considerations. In P. S. Mehler & A. E. Andersen (Eds.), *Eating disorders: A guide to medical care and complications* (pp. 214–226). Baltimore: Johns Hopkins University Press.

Andersen, A. E., Watson, T., & Schlechte, J. (2000). Osteoporosis and osteopenia in men with eating disorders. *Lancet, 355,* 1967–1968.

Andersen, R. E., Brownell, K. D., Morgan, G. D., & Bartlett, S. J. (1998). Weight loss, psychological, and nutritional patterns in competitive female bodybuilders. *Eating Disorders: The Journal of Treatment and Prevention, 6,* 159–167.

Annus, A., & Smith, G. T. (2009). Learning experiences in dance class predict adult eating disturbance. *European Eating Disorders Review, 17,* 50–60.

Annus, A. M., Smith, G. T., Fischer, S., Hendricks, M., & Williams, S. F. (2007). Associations among family-of-origin food-related experiences, expectancies, and disordered eating. *International Journal of Eating Disorders, 40,* 179–186.

Anzengruber, D., Klump, K. L., Thornton, L., Brand, H., Crawford, S., Fichter, M. M., et al. (2006). Smoking in eating disorders. *Eating Behaviors, 7,* 291–299.

Arce, J. C., & De Souza, M. J. (1993). Exercise and male factor infertility. *Sports Medicine, 15,* 146–169.

Bachner-Melman, R., Zohar, A. H., Ebstein, R. P., Elizur, Y., & Constantini, N. (2006). How anorexic-like are the symptom and personality profiles of aesthetic athletes? *Medicine & Science in Sports & Exercise, 38,* 628–636.

Barkley, L. C. (2001). Prevalence of eating disorders among competitive ice skaters. *Medicine & Science in Sport & Exercise, 33,* S96.

Barrack, M. T., Rauh, M. J., Barkai, H. S., & Nichols, J. F. (2008). Dietary restraint and low bone mass in female adolescent endurance runners. *American Journal of Clinical Nutrition, 87,* 36–43.

Barrack, M. T., Rauh, M. J., & Nichols, J. F. (2008). Prevalence of and traits associated with low BMD among female adolescent runners. *Medicine & Science in Sports & Exercise, 40,* 2015–2021.

Bartok-Olson, C. J., & Keith, R. E. (1996). Prevalence of eating disorder symptoms in female collegiate cyclists. *Medicine & Science in Sports & Exercise, 28,* S105.

Bas, M., Karabudak, E., & Kiziltan, G. (2005). Vegetarianism and eating disorders: Association between eating attitudes and other psychological factors among Turkish adolescents. *Appetite, 44,* 309–315.

Beals, K. A. (2002). Body dissatisfaction and disordered eating among triathletes [Abstract]. *Proceedings of the Southwest American College of Sports Medicine.*

Beals, K. A. (2004). *Disordered eating among athletes: A comprehensive guide for health professionals.* Champaign, IL: Human Kinetics.

Becker, A. E., & Fay, K. (2006). Sociocultural issues and eating disorders. In S. Wonderlich, J. E. Mitchell, de Zwaan, M., & Steiger, H. (Eds.), *Annual review of eating disorders 2006* (pp. 35–63). Oxon, England: Radcliffe.

Becker, C. B., Powell, M., & Bull. S. (2008, May). *Evidence-based eating disorders prevention in athletes: The female athlete body project.* Workshop presented at the meeting of the International Conference on Eating Disorders, Seattle, WA.

Becker, C. B., Smith, L. M., & Ciao, A. C. (2005). Reducing eating disorder risk factors in sorority members: A randomized trial. *Behavior Therapy, 36,* 245–254.

Becker, C. B., Smith, L. M., & Ciao, A. C. (2006). Peer-facilitated eating disorders prevention: A randomized effectiveness trial of cognitive dissonance and media advocacy. *Journal of Counseling Psychology, 53,* 550–555.

Benardot, D. (2006). *Advanced sports nutrition.* Champaign, IL: Human Kinetics.

Benini, L., Todesco, T., Dalle Grave, R., Deiorio, F., Salandini, L., & Vantini, I. (2004). Gastric emptying in patients with restricting and binge/purging subtypes of anorexia nervosa. *American Journal of Gastroenterology, 99,* 1448–1454.

Bennell, K. L., Malcolm, S. A., Khan, K. M.,Thomas, S. A., Reid, S. J., Brukner, P. D., et al. (1997). Bone mass and bone turnover in power athletes, endurance athletes, and controls: A 12-month longitudinal study. *Bone, 20,* 477–484.

Benson, J. E., Geiger, C. J., Eiserman, P. A., & Wardlaw, G. M. (1989). Relationship between nutrient intake, body mass index, menstrual function, and ballet injury. *Journal of the American Dietetic Association, 89,* 58–63.

Berg, S. L., & Andersen, A. E. (2007). Eating disorders in special populations: Medical comorbidities and complicating or unusual conditions. In J. Yager & P. S. Powers (Eds.), *Clinical manual of eating disorders* (pp. 335–356). Arlington, VA: American Psychiatric Press.

Berkman, N. D., Lohr, K. N., & Bulik, C. M. (2007). Outcomes of eating disorders: A systematic review of the literature. *International Journal of Eating Disorders, 40,* 293–309.

Berry, T. R., & Howe, B. L. (2000). Risk factors for disordered eating in female university athletes. *Journal of Sport Behavior, 23,* 207–218.

Beumont, P., Arthur, B., Russell, J., & Touyz, S. (1994). Excessive physical activity in dieting disorder patients: Proposals for a supervised exercise program. *International Journal of Eating Disorders, 15,* 21–36.

Biddle, S. J. (1993). Children, exercise and mental health. *International Journal of Sport Psychology, 24,* 200–216.

Bilanin, J. E., Blanchard, M. S., & Russek-Cohen, E. (1989). Lower vertebral bone density in male long distance runners. *Medicine & Science in Sports & Exercise, 21,* 66–70.

Birmingham, C. L., & Beumont, P. J. V. (2004). *Medical management of eating disorders.* London: Cambridge University Press.

Birmingham, C. L., Su, J., Hlynsky, J. A., Goldner, E. M., & Gao, M. (2005). The mortality rate from anorexia nervosa. *International Journal of Eating Disorders, 38,* 143–146.

Bissada, H., Tasca, G. A., Barber, A. M., & Bradwejn, J. (2008). Olanzapine in the treatment of low body weight and obsessive thinking in women with anorexia nervosa: A randomized, double-blind, placebo-controlled trial. *American Journal of Psychiatry, 165,* 1281–1288.

Black, D. R., Larkin, L. J. S., Coster, D. C., Leverenz, L. J., & Abood, D. A. (2003). Physiologic screening test for eating disorders/disordered eating among female collegiate athletes. *Journal of Athletic Training, 38,* 286–297.

Blaydon, M. J., & Lindner, K. J. (2002). Eating disorders and exercise dependence in triathletes. *Eating Disorders: The Journal of Treatment and Prevention, 10,* 49–60.

Blouin, A. G., & Goldfield, G. S. (1995). Body image and steroid use in male body-builders. *International Journal of Eating Disorders, 18,* 159–165.

Boileau, R. A., & Lohman, T. G. (1977). The measurement of human physique and its effect on physical performance. *Orthopedic Clinics of North America, 8,* 563–581.

Bompa, T. (1983). *Theory and methodology of training: The key to athletic performance.* Toronto: Human Kinetics.

Bonci, C. M., Bonci, L. J., Granger, L. R., Johnson, C. L., Malina, R. M., Milne, L. W., et al. (2008). National Athletic Trainers' Association position statement: Preventing, detecting, and managing disordered eating in athletes. *Journal of Athletic Training, 43,* 80–108.

Bonci, L. J. (2009). *Sport nutrition for coaches.* Champaign, IL: Human Kinetics.

Bonogofski, S. L., Beerman, K. A., Massey, L. K., & Houghton, M. (1999). A comparison of athletic achievement and eating disorder behaviors among female cross country runners. *Medicine & Science in Sports & Exercise, 31,* S65.

Bouchard, C. (2002). Genetic influences on body weight. In C. G. Fairburn & K. D. Brownell (Eds.), *Eating disorders and obesity: A comprehensive handbook* (2nd ed., pp. 16–21). New York: Guilford.

Bratman, S., & Knight, D. (2000). *Health food junkies.* New York: Broadway Books.

Braun, D. L., Sunday, S. R., & Halmi, K. A. (1994). Psychiatric comorbidity in patients with eating disorders. *Psychological Medicine, 24,* 859–867.

Brewerton, T. D. (Ed.). (2004). *Clinical handbook of eating disorders: An integrated approach.* New York: Marcel Dekker.

Brewerton, T. D. (2005). Psychological trauma and eating disorders. In S. Wonderlich, J. Mitchell, M. de Zwaan, & H. Steiger (Eds.), *Eating disorders review* (Part 1, pp. 137–154). Oxon, England: Radcliffe.

Brinch, M., Isager, T., & Tolstrup, K. (1988). Anorexia nervosa and motherhood: Reproduction pattern and mothering behavior of 50 women. *Acta Psychiatrica Scandinavica, 77,* 611–617.

Brooks-Gunn, J., Warren, M. P., & Hamilton, L. H. (1987). The relation of eating problems and amenorrhea in ballet dancers. *Medicine & Science in Sports & Exercise, 19,* 41–44.

Brownell, K. D., Rodin, J., & Wilmore, J. H. (1988, August). Eat, drink, and be worried? *Runner's World,* 28–34.

Bruch, H. (1973). *Eating disorders: Obesity, anorexia nervosa, and the person within.* New York: Basic Books.

Buchholz, A., Mack, H., McVey, G., Feder, S., & Barrowman, N. (2008). BodySense: An evaluation of a positive body image intervention on sport climate for female athletes. *Eating Disorders: The Journal of Treatment and Prevention, 16,* 308–321.

Bulik, C. M., & Allison, D. B. (2002). Constitutional thinness and resistance to obesity. In C. G. Fairburn & K. D. Brownell (Eds.), *Eating disorders and obesity: A comprehensive handbook* (2nd ed., pp. 22–25). New York: Guilford.

Bulik, C. M., Berkman, N. D., Brownley, K. A., Sedway, J. A., & Lohr, K. N. (2007). Anorexia nervosa treatment: A systematic review of randomized controlled trials. *International Journal of Eating Disorders, 40,* 310–320.

Bulik, C. M., Sullivan, P. F., & Kendler, K. (1998). Heritability of binge-eating and broadly defined bulimia nervosa. *Biological Psychiatry, 44,* 1210–1218.

Burton, D., & Raedeke, T. D. (2008). *Sport psychology for coaches.* Champaign, IL: Human Kinetics.

Byrne, S., & McLean, N. (2001). Eating disorders in athletes: A review of the literature. *Journal of Science and Medicine in Sport, 4,* 145–159.

Byrne, S., & McLean, N. (2002). Elite athletes: Effects of the pressure to be thin. *Journal of Science and Medicine in Sport, 5,* 80–94.

Cash, T. F. (2002). The management of body image problems. In C. G. Fairburn & K. D. Brownell (Eds.), *Eating disorders and obesity: A comprehensive handbook* (2nd ed., pp. 599–603). New York: Guilford Press.

Cashdan, E. (1998). Are men more competitive than women? *British Journal of Social Psychology, 37,* 213–229.

Casiero, D., & Frishman, W. H. (2006). Cardiovascular complications of eating disorders. *Cardiology in Review, 14,* 227–231.

Catlin, D. H., Fitch, K. D., & Ljungqvist, A. (2008). Medicine and science in the fight against doping in sport. *Journal of Internal Medicine, 264,* 99–114.

Caulfield, M. J., & Karageorghis, C. I. (2008). Psychological effects of rapid weight loss and attitudes towards eating among professional jockeys. *Journal of Sports Sciences, 26,* 877–883.

Chamberlain, R. (2003). *Ready to play: Mental training for student-athletes.* Provo, UT: University Press, Brigham Young University.

Chen, E. Y., Matthews, L., Allen, C., Kuo, J. R., & Linehan, M. M. (2008). Dialectical behavior therapy for clients with binge-eating disorder or bulimia nervosa and borderline personality disorder. *International Journal of Eating Disorders, 41,* 505–512.

Clark, N. (2008). *Nancy Clark's sports nutrition guidebook* (4th ed.). Champaign, IL: Human Kinetics.

Clark, N., Nelson, M., & Evans, W. (1988). Nutrition education for elite female runners. *Physician and Sportsmedicine, 16,* 124–136.

Coleman, E. (1986). Good nutrition and female gymnasts. *Sports Medicine Digest, 8,* 6.

Collings, K. L., Pierce Pratt, F., Rodriguez-Stanley, S. Bemben, M., & Miner, P. B. (2003). Esophageal reflux in conditioned runners, cyclists, and weightlifters. *Medicine & Science in Sports & Exercise, 35*, 730–735.

Corrado, D., Pelliccia, A., Bjørnstad, H. H., Vanhees, L., Biffi, A., Borjesson, M., et al. (2005). Cardiovascular pre-participation screening of young competitive athletes for prevention of sudden death: Proposal for a common European protocol. Consensus statement of the Study Group of Sport Cardiology of the Working Group of Cardiac Rehabilitation and Exercise Physiology and the Working Group of Myocardial and Pericardial Disease of the European Society of Cardiology. *European Heart Journal, 26*, 516–524.

Costar, E. D. (1983, November). Gymnasts at risk. *International Gymnast*, 58–59.

Crandall, C. S. (1988). Social contagion of binge eating. *Journal of Personality and Social Psychology, 55*, 588–598.

Crisp, A., Sedgwick, P., Halek, C., Joughin, N., & Humphrey, H. (1999). Why may teenage girls persist in smoking? *Journal of Adolescence, 22*, 657–672.

Crow, S. J., Mitchell, J. E., Roerig, J. D., & Steffen, K. (2009). What potential role is there for medication treatment in anorexia nervosa? *International Journal of Eating Disorders, 42*, 1–8.

Crowther, J. H., Armey, M., Luce, K. H., Dalton, G. R., & Leahey, T. (2008). The point prevalence of bulimic disorders from 1990 to 2004. *International Journal of Eating Disorders, 41*, 491–497.

Cureton, K. J., & Sparling, P. B. (1980). Distance running performance and metabolic responses to running in men and women with excess weight experimentally equated. *Medicine & Science in Sports & Exercise, 12*, 288–294.

Currin, L., Schmidt, U., Treasure, J., & Jick, H. (2005). Time trends in eating disorder incidence. *British Journal of Psychiatry, 186*, 132–135.

Dale, K. S., & Landers, D. M. (1999). Weight control in wrestling: Eating disorders or disordered eating? *Medicine & Science in Sports & Exercise, 31*, 1382–1389.

Davis, C., & Cowles, M. (1989). A comparison of weight and diet concerns and personality factors among female athletes and non-athletes. *Journal of Psychosomatic Research, 33*, 527–536.

Davis, C., & Scott-Robertson, L. (2000). A psychological comparison of females with anorexia nervosa and competitive male bodybuilders: Body shape ideals in the extreme. *Eating Behaviors, 1*, 33–46.

DeBate, R. D., Wethington, H., & Sargent, R. (2002a). Sub-clinical eating disorder characteristics among male and female triathletes. *Eating and Weight Disorders, 7*, 210–220.

DeBate, R. D., Wethington, H., & Sargent, R. (2002b). Body size dissatisfaction among male and female triathletes. *Eating and Weight Disorders, 7*, 316–323.

De Bruin, A. P., Bakker, F. C., & Oudejans, R. R. D. (2009). Achievement goal theory and disordered eating: Relationships of disordered eating with goal orientations and motivational climate in female gymnasts and dancers. *Psychology of Sport and Exercise, 10*, 72–79.

230

De Bruin, A. P., Oudejans, R. R. D., & Bakker, F. C. (2007). Dieting and body image in aesthetic sports: A comparison of Dutch female gymnasts and non-aesthetic sport participants. *Psychology of Sport and Exercise, 8,* 507–520.

De Bruin, A. P., Oudejans, R. R. D., Bakker, F. C., & Woertman, L. (2009). *"Tell me about your eating history": Elite women athletes' narratives and the meaning of their eating disorder.* Manuscript submitted for publication.

DePalma, M. T., Koszewski, W. M., Case, J. G., Barile, R. J., DePalma, B. F., & Oliaro, S. M. (1993). Weight control practices of lightweight football players. *Medicine & Science in Sports & Exercise, 25,* 694–701.

De Rose, E. H. (2008). Doping in athletes—An update. *Clinics in Sports Medicine, 27,* 107–130.

De Souza, M. J., & Miller, B. E. (1997). The effect of endurance training on reproductive function in male runners: A "volume threshold" hypothesis. *Sports Medicine, 23,* 357–374.

Devlin, M. J., Allison, K. C., Goldfein, J. A., & Spanos, A. (2007). Management of eating disorders not otherwise specified. In J. Yager & P. S. Powers (Eds.), *Clinical manual of eating disorders* (pp. 195–224). Arlington, VA: American Psychiatric Press.

De Zwaan, M., & Mitchell, J. E. (1999). Medical evaluation of a patient with an eating disorder: An overview. In P. S. Mehler & A. E. Andersen (Eds.), *Eating disorders: A guide to medical care and complications* (pp. 44–62). Baltimore: Johns Hopkins University Press.

DiBartolo, P. M., & Shaffer, C. (2002). A comparison of female college athletes and nonathletes: Eating disorder symptomatology and psychological well-being. *Journal of Sport & Exercise Psychology, 24,* 33–41.

Dick, R. W. (1991). Eating disorders in NCAA athletic programs. *Athletic Training, 26,* 137–140.

Donini, L. M., Marsili, D., Gratziani, M. P., Imbriale, M., & Cannella, C. (2004). Orthorexia nervosa: A preliminary study with a proposal for diagnosis and an attempt to measure the dimension of the phenomenon. *Eating and Weight Disorders, 9,* 151–157.

Donini, L. M., Marsili, D., Gratziani, M. P., Imbriale, M., & Cannella, C. (2005). Orthorexia nervosa: Validation of a diagnosis questionnaire. *Eating and Weight Disorders, 10,* 28–32.

Dotti, A., Fioravanti, M., Balotta, M., Tozzi, F., Cannella, C., & Lazzari, R. (2002). Eating behavior of ballet dancers. *Eating and Weight Disorders, 7,* 60–67.

Drinkwater, B. L., Bruemner, B., & Chestnut III, C. H. (1990). Menstrual history as a determinant of current bone density in young athletes. *Journal of the American Medical Association, 263,* 545–548.

Drinkwater, B. L., Nilson, K., Chestnut III, C. H., Bremner, W. J., Shainholtz, S., & Southworth, M. B. (1984). Bone mineral content of amenorrheic and eumenorrheic athletes. *New England Journal of Medicine, 311,* 277–281.

231

Drinkwater, B. L., Nilson, K., Ott, S., & Chestnut III, C. H. (1986). Bone mineral density after resumption of menses in amenorrheic athletes. *Journal of the American Medical Association, 256*, 380–382.

Druss, R. G., & Silverman, J. A. (1979). Body image and perfectionism of ballerinas: Comparison and contrast with anorexia nervosa. *General Hospital Psychiatry, 2*, 115–121.

Duffy, A. (2008). *Perfectionism, perfectionistic self-presentation, body comparisons, and disordered eating in women's artistic gymnastics.* Unpublished master's thesis, Auburn University, Auburn, AL.

Dummer, G. M., Rosen, L. W., Heusner, W. W., Roberts, P. J., & Counsilman, J. E. (1987). Pathogenic weight-control behaviors of young competitive swimmers. *Physician and Sportsmedicine, 15*, 75–84.

Duncan, C. S., Blimkie, C. J., Cowell, C. T., Burke, S. T., Briody, J. N., & Howman-Giles, R. (2002). Bone mineral density in adolescent female athletes: Relationship to exercise type and muscle strength. *Medicine & Science in Sports & Exercise, 34*, 286–294.

Eating Disorders Foundation of Victoria. (2005). *An eating disorders resource for: Coaches.* Melbourne: Author.

Eddy, K. T., Crosby, R. D., Keel, P. K., Wonderlich, S. A., le Grange, D., Hill, L., et al. (2009). Empirical identification and validation of eating disorder phenotypes in a multisite clinical sample. *Journal of Nervous and Mental Diseases, 197*, 41–49.

Eddy, K. T., Dorer, D. J., Franko, D. L., Tahilani, K., Thompson-Brenner, H., & Herzog, D. B. (2008). Diagnostic crossover in anorexia nervosa and bulimia nervosa: Implications for DSM-V. *American Journal of Psychiatry, 165*, 245–250.

Elliot, D. L., Cheong, J., Moe, E. L., & Goldberg, L. (2007). Cross-sectional study of female students reporting anabolic steroid use. *Archives of Pediatrics & Adolescent Medicine, 161*, 572–577.

Elliot, D. L., Moe, E. L., Goldberg, L., DeFrancesco, C. A., Durham, M. B., & Hix-Small, H. (2006). Definition and outcome of a curriculum to prevent disordered eating and body-shaping drug use. *Journal of School Health, 76*, 67–73.

Engel, S. G., Johnson, C., Powers, P. S., Crosby, R. D., Wonderlich, S. A., Wittrock, D. A., et al. (2003). Predictors of disordered eating in a sample of elite Division I college athletes. *Eating Behaviors, 4*, 333–343.

Enns, M. P., Drewnowski, A., & Grinker, J. A. (1987). Body composition, body size estimation, and attitudes towards eating in male college athletes. *Psychosomatic Medicine, 49*, 56–64.

Fairburn, C. G. (2006). Treatment of bulimia nervosa. In S. Wonderlich, J. E. Mitchell, M. de Zwaan, & H. Steiger (Eds.), *Annual review of eating disorders 2006* (Part 2, pp. 144–156). Oxon, England: Radcliffe.

Fairburn, C. G., & Brownell, K. D. (Eds.). (2002). *Eating disorders and obesity: A comprehensive handbook* (2nd ed.). New York: Guilford Press.

232

Fairburn, C. G., & Cooper, Z. (1993). The Eating Disorder Examination (12th ed.). In C. G. Fairburn & G. T. Wilson (Eds.), *Binge eating: Nature, assessment, and treatment* (pp. 317–360). New York: Guilford Press.

Fairburn, C. G., Jones, R., Peveler, R. C., Hope, R. A., & O'Connor, M. (1993). Psychotherapy and bulimia nervosa. Longer-term effects of interpersonal psychotherapy, behavior therapy, and cognitive behavior therapy. *Archives of General Psychiatry, 50,* 419–428.

Falkner, B., Gidding, S. S., Portman, R., & Rosner, B. (2008). Blood pressure variability and classification of prehypertension and hypertension in adolescence. *Pediatrics, 122,* 238–242.

Falls, H. B., & Humphrey, L. D. (1978). Body type and composition differences between placers and nonplacers in an AIAW gymnastics meet. *Research Quarterly, 49,* 38–43.

Fasting, K., Brackenridge, C., & Sundgot-Borgen, J. (2003). Experiences of sexual harassment and abuse among Norwegian elite female athletes and nonathletes. *Research Quarterly for Exercise and Sport, 74,* 84–97.

Fasting, K., Brackenridge, C., & Sundgot-Borgen, J. (2004). Prevalence of sexual harassment among Norwegian female elite athletes in relation to sport type. *International Review for the Sociology of Sport, 39,* 373–386.

Federation Internationale de Ski. (2006). FIS news from Torino 2006. Retrieved October 2, 2006, from http://www.fis-ski.com/dat/document/whatisnew-comparedto2002.pdf

Ferrand, C., & Brunet, E. (2004). Perfectionism and risk for disordered eating among young French male cyclists of high performance. *Perceptual and Motor Skills, 99,* 959–967.

Ferrand, C., Magnan, C., & Philippe, R. A. (2005). Body-esteem, body mass index, and risk for disordered eating among adolescents in synchronized swimming. *Perceptual and Motor Skills, 101,* 877–884.

Fichter, M. M., Quadflieg, N., & Hedlund, S. (2006). Twelve-year course and outcome predictors of anorexia nervosa. *International Journal of Eating Disorders, 39,* 87–100.

Filaire, E., Rouveix, M., Pannafieux, C., & Ferrand, C. (2007). Eating attitudes, perfectionism and body-esteem of elite male judoists and cyclists. *Journal of Sports Sciences and Medicine, 6,* 50–57.

Fink, E. L., Smith, A. R., Gordon, K. H., Holm-Denoma, J. M., & Joiner, T. E. (2009). Psychological correlates of purging disorder as compared with other eating disorders: An exploratory investigation. *International Journal of Eating Disorders, 42,* 31–39.

Flint, F. (1999). Effective group health education counseling. In R. Ray & D. M. Wiese-Bjornstal (Eds.), *Counseling in sports medicine* (pp. 93–109). Champaign, IL: Human Kinetics.

Fogelholm, M., & Hiilloskorpi, H. (1999). Weight and diet concerns in Finnish female and male athletes. *Medicine & Science in Sports & Exercise, 31,* 229–235.

233

Forsberg, S., & Lock J. (2006). The relationship between perfectionism, eating disorders and athletes: A review. *Minerva Pediatrica, 58,* 525–536.

Franko, D. L., Blais, M. A., Becker, A. E., Delinsky, S. S., Greenwood, D. N., Flores, A. T., et al. (2001). Pregnancy complications and neonatal outcomes in women with eating disorders. *American Journal of Psychiatry, 158,* 1461–1466.

Fredrickson, B. L., & Roberts, T. (1997). Objectification theory: Toward understanding women's lived experiences and mental health risks. *Psychology of Women Quarterly, 21,* 173–206.

Fredrickson, B. L., Roberts, T., Noll, S. M., Quinn, D. M., & Twenge, J. M. (1998). That swimsuit becomes you: Sex differences in self-objectification, restrained eating, and math performance. *Journal of Personality and Social Psychology, 75,* 269–284.

Freischlag, J. (1989). More than a nice smile: A psycho-social analysis of high school cheerleaders. *Journal of Applied Research in Coaching and Athletics, 4,* 63–74.

Frisch, R. E., & McArthur, J. W. (1974). Menstrual cycles: Fatness as a determinant of minimum weight for height necessary for their maintenance or onset. *Science, 185,* 949–951.

Fulkerson, J. A., Keel, P. K., Leon, G. R., & Dorr, T. (1999). Eating-disordered behaviors and personality characteristics of high school athletes and nonathletes. *International Journal of Eating Disorders, 26,* 73–79.

Garfinkel, P. E., & Garner, D. M. (1982). *Anorexia nervosa: A multidimensional perspective.* New York: Brunner/Mazel.

Garner, D. M. (1991). *Eating Disorder Inventory-2 professional manual.* Odessa, FL: Psychological Assessment Resources.

Garner, D. M. (2002). Measurement of eating disorder psychopathology. In C. G. Fairburn & K. D. Brownell (Eds.), *Eating disorders and obesity: A comprehensive handbook* (2nd ed., pp. 141–146). New York: Guilford.

Garner, D. M. (2004). *Eating Disorder Inventory-3 professional manual.* Lutz, FL: Psychological Assessment Resources.

Garner, D. M., & Garfinkel, P. E. (1979). The Eating Attitudes Test: An index of the symptoms of anorexia nervosa. *Psychological Medicine, 9,* 273–279.

Garner, D. M., & Olmsted, M. P. (1984). *Eating Disorder Inventory manual.* Odessa, FL: Psychological Assessment Resources.

Garner, D. M., Olmsted, M. P., Bohr, Y., & Garfinkel, P. E. (1982). The Eating Attitudes Test: Psychological features and clinical correlates. *Psychological Medicine, 12,* 871–878.

Gerson, L. B., Friday, K., & Triadafilopoulos, G. (2006). Potential relationship between gastroesophageal reflux disease and atrial arrhythmias. *Journal of Clinical Gastroenterology, 40,* 828–832.

Gilbody, S. M., Kirk, S. F. L., & Hill, A. J. (1999). Vegetarianism in young women: Another means of weight control? *International Journal of Eating Disorders, 26,* 87–90.

Girard Eberle, S. (2005). Sports dietitians: Vital team players in any athletic setting. *Athletic Therapy Today, 10,* 58–60.

Girard Eberle, S. (2007). *Endurance sports nutrition* (2nd ed.). Champaign, IL: Human Kinetics.

Gleaves, D. H., Williamson, D. A., & Fuller, R. D (1992). Bulimia nervosa symptomatology and body image disturbance associated with distance running and weight loss. *British Journal of Sports Medicine, 26*, 157–160.

Glover, D. W., Glover, D. W., & Maron, B. J. (2007). Evolution in the process of screening United States high school student-athletes for cardiovascular disease. *American Journal of Cardiology, 100*, 1709–1712.

Goldfield, G. S. (2009). Body image, disordered eating and anabolic steroid use in female bodybuilders. *Eating Disorders: The Journal of Treatment and Prevention, 17*, 200–210.

Goldfield, G. S., Harper, D. W., & Blouin, A. G. (1998). Are bodybuilders at risk for an eating disorder? *Eating Disorders: The Journal of Treatment and Prevention, 6*, 133–157.

Gottlieb, A. A., Smith, P. D., Cleveland, E. E., Flick, E. L., & Capps, J. R. (1994). Eating disorders and alcohol use among adolescent female cheerleaders [Abstract]. *Journal of Adolescent Health, 15*, 80.

Greenleaf, C. (2002). Athletic body image: Exploratory interviews with former competitive female athletes. *Women in Sport and Physical Activity Journal, 11*, 63–88.

Griffin, J., & Harris, M. B. (1996). Coaches' attitude, knowledge, experiences, and recommendations regarding weight control. *Sport Psychologist, 10*, 180–194.

Haase, A. M., & Prapavessis, H. (2001). Social physique anxiety and eating attitudes in female athletic and non-athletic groups. *Journal of Science and Medicine in Sport, 4*, 396–405.

Hackney, A. C., Sinning, W. E., & Bruot, B. C. (1990). Hypothalamic-pituitary-testicular axis function in endurance-trained males. *International Journal of Sports Medicine, 11*, 298–303.

Hagmar, M., Berglund, B., Brismar, K., & Hirschberg, A. L. (2009). Hyperandrogenism may explain reproductive dysfunction in Olympic athletes. *Medicine & Science in Sports & Exercise, 41*, 1241–1248.

Hagmar, M., Hirschberg, A. L., Berglund, L., & Berglund, B. (2008). Special attention to the weight-control strategies employed by Olympic athletes striving for leanness is required. *Clinical Journal of Sports Medicine, 18*, 5–9.

Hallsworth, L., Wade, T., & Tiggemann, M. (2005). Individual differences in male body-image: An examination of self-objectification in recreational body builders. *British Journal of Health Psychology, 10*, 453–465.

Halmi, K. A. (2007). Management of anorexia nervosa in inpatient and partial hospitalization settings. In J. Yager & P. S. Powers (Eds.), *Clinical manual of eating disorders* (pp. 113–125). Arlington, VA: American Psychiatric Publishing.

Halmi, K. A., Tozzi, F., Thornton, L. M., Crow, S., Fichter, M. M., Kaplan, A. S., et al. (2005). The relation among perfectionism, obsessive-compulsive personality disorder and obsessive-compulsive disorder in individuals with eating disorders. *International Journal of Eating Disorders, 38*, 371–374.

235

Hamilton, L. H., Brooks-Gunn, J., Warren, M. P., & Hamilton, W. G. (1988). The role of selectivity in the pathogenesis of eating problems in ballet dancers. *Medicine & Science in Sports & Exercise, 20*, 560–565.

Harris, M. B., & Greco, D. (1990). Weight control and weight concern in competitive female gymnasts. *Journal of Sport & Exercise Psychology, 12*, 427–433.

Haug, N. A., Heinberg, L. J., & Guarda, A. S. (2001). Cigarette smoking and its relationship to other substance use among eating disordered inpatients. *Eating and Weight Disorders, 6*, 130–139.

Hausenblas, H. A., & Mack, D. E. (1999). Social physique anxiety and eating disorder correlates among female athletic and nonathletic populations. *Journal of Sport Behavior, 22*, 502–513.

Hausenblas, H. A., & McNally, K. D. (2004). Eating disorder prevalence and symptoms for track and field athletes and nonathletes. *Journal of Applied Sport Psychology, 16*, 274–286.

Hausenblas, H. A., & Symons Downs, D. (2002). How much is too much? The development and validation of the Exercise Dependence Scale. *Psychology & Health, 17*, 387–404.

Hay, P. J., Mond, J., Buttner, P., & Darby, A. (2008). Eating disorder behaviors are increasing: Findings from two sequential community surveys in South Australia. *PloS ONE, 3*:e1541. doi:10.1371 (journal.pone.0001541).

Hebebrand, J., Exner, C., Hebebrand, K., Holtkamp, C., Casper, R. C., Remschmidt, H., et al. (2003). Hyperactivity in patients with anorexia nervosa and in semi-starved rats: Evidence for a pivotal role of hypoleptinemia. *Physiology and Behavior, 79*, 25–37.

Hemery, D. (1986). *The pursuit of sporting excellence: A study of sport's highest achievers.* Champaign, IL: Human Kinetics.

Herzog, D. B., & Eddy, K. T. (2007). Diagnosis, epidemiology, and clinical course of eating disorders. In J. Yager & P. S. Powers (Eds.), *Clinical manual of eating disorders* (pp. 1–30). Arlington, VA: American Psychiatric Press.

Herzog, W., Deter, H. C., Fiehn, W., & Petzold, E. (1997). Medical findings and predictors of long-term physical outcome in anorexia nervosa: A prospective, 12-year follow-up study. *Psychological Medicine, 27*, 269–279.

Hetland, M. L., Haarbo, J., & Christiansen, C. (1993). Low bone mass and high bone turnover in male long distance runners. *Journal of Clinical Endocrinology and Metabolism, 77*, 770–775.

Hilderbrand, R. L. (2007). The world anti-doping program and the primary care physician. *Pediatric Clinics of North America, 54*, 701–711.

Hinton, P. S., Sanford, T. C., Davidson, M. M., Yakushko, O. F., & Beck, N. C. (2004). Nutrient intakes and dietary behaviors of male and female collegiate athletes. *International Journal of Sport Nutrition and Exercise Metabolism, 14*, 389–405.

Hoch, A. Z., Stavrakos, J. E., & Schimke, J. E. (2007). Prevalence of female athlete triad characteristics in a club triathlon team. *Archives of Physical Medicine and Rehabilitation, 88*, 681–682.

236

Hoek, H. W., & van Hoeken, D. (2003). Review of the prevalence and incidence of eating disorders. *International Journal of Eating Disorders, 34,* 383–396.

Holm-Denoma, J. M., Gordon, K. H., & Joiner, T. E. (2007). Classification of eating disorders. In S. Wonderlich, J. E. Mitchell, M. de Zwaan, H. Steiger (Eds.), *Annual review of eating disorders 2007* (pp. 125–136). Oxon, England: Radcliffe.

Holm-Denoma, J. M., Scaringi, V., Gordon, K. H., Van Orden, K. A., & Joiner, T. E. (2009). Eating disorder symptoms among undergraduate varsity athletes, club athletes, independent exercisers, and nonexercisers. *International Journal of Eating Disorders, 42,* 47–53.

Honjo, K., & Siegel, M. (2003). Perceived importance of being thin and smoking initiation among young girls. *Tobacco Control, 12,* 289–295.

Hopkinson, R. A., & Lock, J. (2004). Athletics, perfectionism, and disordered eating. *Eating and Weight Disorders, 9,* 99–106.

Howell, M. J., Schenck, C. H., & Crow, S. J. (2009). A review of nighttime eating disorders. *Sleep Medicine Reviews, 13,* 23–34.

Hudson, J. I., Hiripi, E., Pope, H. G., & Kessler, R. C. (2007). The prevalence and correlates of eating disorders in the National Comorbidity Survey Replication. *Biological Psychiatry, 61,* 348–358.

Hulley, A., Currie, A., Njenga, F., & Hill, A. (2007). Eating disorders in elite female distance runners: Effects of nationality and running environment. *Psychology of Sport and Exercise, 8,* 521–533.

Hulley, A. J., & Hill, A. J. (2001). Eating disorders and health in elite women distance runners. *International Journal of Eating Disorders, 30,* 312–317.

International Federation of Sport Climbing. (2009). Competition climbing history. Retrieved April 30, 2009, from http://www.ifsc-climbing.org

International Olympic Committee Medical Commission. (2005). Position Stand: The Female Athlete Triad. Retrieved September 12, 2009 from http://multimedia.olympic.org/pdf/en_report_917.pdf

Ireland, M. L. (2002) The female ACL: Why is it more prone to injury? *Orthopedic Clinics of North America, 33,* 637–651.

Isomaa, R., Isomaa, A. L., Marttunen, M., Kaltiala-Heino, R., & Bjorkqvist, K. (2009). The prevalence, incidence and development of eating disorders in Finnish adolescents—a two-step 3-year follow-up study. *European Eating Disorders Review, 17,* 199–207.

Jacobi, C. (2005). Psychosocial risk factors for eating disorders. In S. Wonderlich, J. E. Mitchell, M. de Zwaan, & H. Steiger (Eds.), *Annual review of eating disorders 2005* (pp. 59–85). Oxon, England: Radcliffe.

James, D. C. (2001). Eating disorders, fertility, and pregnancy: Relationships and complications. *Journal of Perinatal and Neonatal Nursing, 15,* 36–48.

Johnson, C., Powers, P. S., & Dick, R. W. (1999). Athletes and eating disorders: The National Collegiate Athletic Association study. *International Journal of Eating Disorders, 26,* 179–188.

Jones, R. L., Glintmeyer, N., & McKenzie, A. (2005). Slim bodies, eating disorders and the coach-athlete relationship. *International Review for the Sociology of Sport, 40*, 377–391.

Kadambari, R., Gowers, S., & Crisp, A. H. (1986). Some correlates of vegetarianism in anorexia nervosa. *International Journal of Eating Disorders, 5*, 539–544.

Kalkwarf, H. J., Zemel, B. S., Gilsanz, V., Lappe, J. M., Horlick, M., Oberfield, S., et al. (2007). The bone mineral density in childhood study: Bone mineral content and density according to age, sex, and race. *Journal of Clinical Endocrinology & Metabolism, 92*, 2087–2099.

Kaplan, A. S., & Noble, S. (2007). Management of anorexia nervosa in an ambulatory setting. In J. Yager & P. S. Powers (Eds.), *Clinical manual of eating disorders* (pp. 127–147). Arlington, VA: American Psychiatric Publishing.

Karlson, K. A., Becker, C. B., & Merkur, A. (2001). Prevalence of eating disordered behavior in collegiate lightweight women rowers and distance runners. *Clinical Journal of Sport Medicine, 11*, 32–37.

Katz, J. L. (1996). Clinical observations on the physical activity of anorexia nervosa. In W. F. Epling & W. D. Pierce (Eds.), *Activity anorexia: Theory, research, and treatment* (pp. 199–207). Mahwah, NJ: Lawrence Erlbaum Associates.

Kaye, W. H., Greeno, C. G., Moss, H., Fernstrom, J., Fernstrom, M., Lilenfeld, L. R., et al. (1998). Alterations in serotonin activity and psychiatric symptoms after recovery from bulimia nervosa. *Archives of General Psychiatry, 55*, 927–935.

Kayser, B., Mauron, A., & Miah, A. (2007). Current anti-doping policy: A critical appraisal. *BMC Medical Ethics, 29*, 2.

Kazdin, A. E., Kraemer, H. C., Kessler, R. C., Kupfer, D. J., & Offord, D. R. (1997). Contributions of risk-factor research to developmental psychopathology. *Clinical Psychology Review, 17*, 375–406.

Keel, P. K., Haedt, A., & Edler, C. (2005). Purging disorder: An ominous variant of bulimia nervosa? *International Journal of Eating Disorders, 38*, 191–199.

Keel, P. K., Heatherton, T. F., Dorer, D. J., Joiner, T. E., & Zalta, A. K. (2006). Point prevalence of bulimia nervosa in 1982, 1992, and 2002. *Psychological Medicine, 36*, 119–127.

Keel, P. K., & Klump, K. L. (2003). Are eating disorders culture-bound syndromes? Implications for conceptualizing their etiology. *Psychological Bulletin, 129*, 747–769.

Keel, P. K., Mayer, S. A., & Harnden-Fischer, J. H. (2001). Importance of size in defining binge eating episodes in bulimia nervosa. *International Journal of Eating Disorders, 29*, 294–301.

Kerr, G., Berman, E., & De Souza, M. J. (2006). Disordered eating in women's gymnastics: Perspectives of athletes, coaches, parents, and judges. *Journal of Applied Sport Psychology, 18*, 28–43.

Keys, A., Brozek, J., Henschel, A., Mickelsen, O., & Taylor, H. L. (1950). *The biology of human starvation* (Vol. 2). Minneapolis: University of Minnesota Press.

238

Kiernan, M., Rodin, J., Brownell, K. D., Wilmore, J. H., & Crandall, C. (1992). Relation of level of exercise, age, and weight-cycling history to weight and eating concerns in male and female runners. *Health Psychology, 11*, 418–421.

King, M. B., & Mezey, G. (1987). Eating behaviour of male race jockeys. *Psychological Medicine, 17*, 249–253.

Kirby, S., Greaves, L., & Hankivsky, O. (2000). *The dome of silence: Sexual harassment and abuse in sport.* London: Zed Books.

Kirk, G., Singh, K., & Getz, H. (2001). Risk of eating disorders among female college athletes and nonathletes. *Journal of College Counseling, 4*, 122–132.

Klerman, G. L., Weissman, M. M., Rounsaville, B. J., & Chevron, E. S. (1984). *Interpersonal psychotherapy of depression.* New York: Basic Books.

Klinkowski, N., Korte, A., Pfeiffer, E., Lehmkuhl, U., & Salbach-Andrae, H. (2008). Psychopathology in elite rhythmic gymnasts and anorexia nervosa patients. *European Child and Adolescent Psychiatry, 17*, 108–113.

Klopp, S. A., Heiss, C. J., & Smith, H. S. (2003). Self-reported vegetarianism may be a marker for college women at risk for disordered eating. *Journal of the American Dietetic Association, 103*, 745–747.

Klump, K. L., Miller, K. B., Keel, P. K., McGue, M., & Iacono, W. G. (2001). Genetic and environmental influences on anorexia nervosa syndromes in a population-based twin sample. *Psychological Medicine, 31*, 737–740.

Knechtle, B., & Schulze, I. (2008). Nutritional behaviours in ultra-endurance runners—Deutschlandlauf 2006. *Praxis, 5*, 243–251.

Krane, V., Stiles-Shipley, J. A., Waldron, J., & Michalenok, J. (2001). Relationships among body satisfaction, social physique anxiety, and eating behaviors in female athletes and exercisers. *Journal of Sport Behavior, 24*, 247–264.

Krones, P., Stice, E., Batres, C., & Orjada, K. (2005). In vivo social comparison to a thin-ideal peer promotes body dissatisfaction: A randomized experiment. *International Journal of Eating Disorders, 38*, 134–142.

Lamar-Hildebrand, N., Saldanha, L., & Endres, J. (1989). Dietary and exercise practices of college-aged female bodybuilders. *Journal of the American Dietetic Association, 89*, 1308–1309.

Lappe, J., Cullen, D., Haynatzki, G., Recker, R., Ahlf, R., & Thompson, K. (2008). Calcium and vitamin D supplementation decreases incidence of stress fractures in female navy recruits. *Journal of Bone and Mineral Research, 23*, 741–749.

Leahy, T. (2001). Feminist sport psychology practice. In A. Papaioannou, M. Goudas, & Y. Theodorakis (Eds.), *In the dawn of the new millennium. Programme and Proceedings of 10th World Congress of Sport Psychology, International Society of Sport Psychology* (pp. 234–242), Skiathos, Greece.

Leibel, R. L. (2002). The molecular genetics of body weight regulation. In C. G. Fairburn & K. D. Brownell (Eds.), *Eating disorders and obesity: A comprehensive handbook* (2nd ed., pp. 26–31). New York: Guilford.

Leiper, J. B., Nicholas, C. W., Ali, A., Williams, C., & Maughan, R. J. (2005). The effect of intermittent high-intensity running on gastric emptying of fluids in man. *Medicine & Science in Sports & Exercise, 37*, 240–247.

Lee, E. J., Long, K. A., Risser, W. L., Poindexter, H. B. W., Gibbons, W. E., & Goldzieher, J. (1995). Variations in bone status of contralateral and regional sites in young athletic women. *Medicine & Science in Sports & Exercise, 27*, 1354–1361.

Leslie, W. D., Adler, R. A., El-Hajj Fuleihan, F., Hodsman, A. B., Kendler, D. L., McClung, M., et al. (2006). Application of the 1994 WHO classification to populations other than postmenopausal Caucasian women: The 2005 ISCD official positions. *Journal of Clinical Densitometry, 9*, 22–30.

Levine, M. P., & Smolak, L. (2006). *The prevention of eating problems and eating disorders: Theory, research, and practice.* Mahwah, NJ: Lawrence Erlbaum Associates.

Levine, M. P., & Smolak, L. (2007). Prevention of negative body image, disordered eating, and eating disorders: An update. In S. Wonderlich, J. E. Mitchell, M. de Zwaan, & H. Steiger (Eds.), *Annual review of eating disorders 2007* (Part 1, pp. 1–13). Oxon, England: Radcliffe.

Levitt, D. H. (2008). Participation in athletic activities and eating disordered behavior. *Eating Disorders: The Journal of Treatment and Prevention, 16*, 393–404.

Levitt, J. L., & Sansone, R. A. (Eds.). (2007). Eating disorders in trauma. *Eating Disorders: The Journal of Treatment and Prevention, 15* (Special Issue).

Leydon, M. A., & Wall, C. (2002). New Zealand jockeys' dietary habits and their potential impact on health. *International Journal of Sport Nutrition and Exercise Metabolism, 12*, 220–237.

Lin, L. F., & Kulik, J. A. (2002). Social comparison and women's body satisfaction. *Basic Applied Social Psychology, 24*, 115–123.

Linehan, M. M. (1993). *Cognitive-behavioral treatment of borderline personality disorder.* New York: Guilford Press.

Lock, J., le Grange, D., Agras, W. S., & Dare, C. (2001). *Treatment manual for anorexia nervosa: A family-based approach.* New York: Guilford Press.

Loucks, A. B. (2003). Energy availability, not body fatness, regulates reproductive function in women. *Exercise and Sport Sciences Reviews, 31*, 144–148.

Loucks, A. B., Stachenfeld, N. S., & DiPietro, L. (2006). The female athlete triad: Do female athletes need to take special care to avoid low energy availability? *Medicine & Science in Sports & Exercise, 38*, 1694–1700.

Lundholm, J. K., & Littrell, J. M. (1986). Desire for thinness among high school cheerleaders: Relationship to disordered eating and weight control behaviors. *Adolescence, 21*, 573–579.

Lynch, S. M., & Zellner, D. A. (1999). Figure preferences in two generations of men: The use of figure drawings illustrating differences in muscle mass. *Sex Roles, 40*, 833–843.

Machado, P. P., Machado, B. C., Goncalves, S., & Hoek, H. W. (2007). The prevalence of eating disorders not otherwise specified. *International Journal of Eating Disorders, 40*, 212–217.

MacKelvie, K. J., Taunton, J. E., McKay, H. A., & Khan, K. M. (2000). Bone mineral density and serum testosterone in chronically trained, high mileage 40–55-year-old male runners. *British Journal of Sports Medicine, 34,* 273–278.

Madison, J. K., & Ruma, S. L. (2003). Exercise and athletic involvement as moderators of severity in adolescents with eating disorders. *Journal of Applied Sport Psychology, 15,* 213–222.

Maguire, J., & Mansfield, L. (1998). "No-body's perfect": Women, aerobics, and the body beautiful. *Sociology of Sport Journal, 15,* 109–137.

Maimoun, L., Lumbroso, S., Manetta, J., Paris, F., Leroux, J. L., & Sultan, C. (2003). Testosterone is significantly reduced in endurance athletes without impact on bone mineral density. *Hormone Research, 59,* 285–292.

Mangweth-Matzek, B., Rupp, C. I., Hausmann, A., Assmayr, K., Mariacher, E., Kemmler, G., et al. (2006). Never too old for eating disorders or body dissatisfaction: A community study of elderly women. *International Journal of Eating Disorders, 39,* 583–586.

Maron, B. J., Douglas, P. S., Graham, T. P., Nishimura, R. A., & Thompson, P. D. (2005). Task Force 1: Preparticipaton screening and diagnosis of cardiovascular disease in athletes. *Journal of American College of Cardiology, 45,* 1322–1326.

Marshall, J. D., & Harber, V. J. (1996). Body dissatisfaction and drive for thinness in high performance field hockey athletes. *International Journal of Sports Medicine, 17,* 541–544.

Mason, H. D., Key, A., Allan, R., & Lask, B. (2007). Pelvic ultrasonography in anorexia nervosa: What the clinician should ask the radiologist and how to use the information provided. *European Eating Disorders Review, 15,* 35–41.

Mazzeo, S. E., Slof-Op't Landt, M. C. T., van Furth, E. F., & Bulik, C. M. (2006). Genetics of eating disorders. In S. Wonderlich, J. E. Mitchell, M. de Zwaan, & H. Steiger (Eds.), *Annual review of eating disorders 2006* (pp. 17–33). Oxon, England: Radcliffe.

McGregor, M. (1998). Harassment and abuse in sport and recreation. *CAHPERD, 64,* 4–13.

McKnight Investigators. (2003). Risk factors for the onset of eating disorders in adolescent girls: Results of the McKnight longitudinal risk factor study. *American Journal of Psychiatry, 160,* 248–254.

McLoughlin, D. M., Wassif, W. S., Morton, J., Spargo, E., Peters, T. J., & Russell, G. F. (2000). Metabolic abnormalities associated with skeletal myopathy in severe anorexia nervosa. *Nutrition, 16,* 192–196.

McNulty, K. Y., Adams, C. H., Anderson, J. M., & Affenito, S. G. (2001). Development and validation of a screening tool to identify eating disorders in female athletes. *Journal of the American Dietetic Association, 101,* 886–892.

Mehler, P. S., & Andersen, A. E. (Eds.). (1999). *Eating disorders: A guide to medical care and complications.* Baltimore: Johns Hopkins University Press.

241

Mehler, P. S., & MacKenzie, T. D. (2009). Treatment of osteopenia and osteoporosis in anorexia nervosa: A systematic review of the literature. *International Journal of Eating Disorders, 42*, 195–201.

Mehler, P. S., Sabel, A. L., Watson, T., & Andersen, A. E. (2008). High risk of osteoporosis in male patients with eating disorders. *International Journal of Eating Disorders, 41*, 666–672.

Miller, M. A., Croft, L. B., Belanger, A. R., Romero-Corral, A., Somers, V. K., Roberts, A. J., et al. (2008). Prevalence of metabolic syndrome in retired national football league players. *American Journal of Cardiology, 101*, 1281–1284.

Miller, S. J. (2008). Death resulting from overzealous total parenteral nutrition: The refeeding syndrome revisited. *Nutrition in Clinical Practice, 23*, 166–171.

Milos, G., Spindler, A., & Schnyder, U. (2004). Psychiatric comorbidity and Eating Disorder Inventory (EDI) profiles in eating disorder patients. *Canadian Journal of Psychiatry, 49*, 179–184.

Milos, G., Spindler, A., Schnyder, U., Martz, J., Hoek, H. W., & Willi, J. (2004). Incidence of severe anorexia nervosa in Switzerland: 40 years of development. *International Journal of Eating Disorders, 35*, 250–258.

Mitchell, J. E., Agras, S., & Wonderlich, S. (2007). Treatment of bulimia nervosa: Where are we and where are we going? *International Journal of Eating Disorders, 40*, 95–101.

Mitchell, J. E., Devlin, M. J., de Zwaan, M., Crow, S. J., & Peterson, C. B. (2008). *Binge-eating disorder: Clinical foundations and treatment*. New York: Guilford Press.

Mitchell, J. E., & Peterson, C. B. (Eds.). (2005). *Assessment of eating disorders*. New York: Guilford Press.

Mitchell, J. E., Steffen, K. J., & Roerig, J. L. (2007). Management of bulimia nervosa. In J. Yager & P. S. Powers (Eds.), *Clinical manual of eating disorders* (pp. 171–193). Arlington, VA: American Psychiatric Publishing.

Moffatt, R. J. (1984). Dietary status of elite female high school gymnasts: Inadequacy of vitamin and mineral intake. *Journal of the American Dietetic Association, 84*, 1361–1363.

Mond, J. M., & Calogero, R. M. (2009). Excessive exercise in eating patients and in healthy women. *Australian and New Zealand Journal of Psychiatry, 43*, 227–234.

Mond, J., Myers, T. C., Crosby, R., Hay, P., & Mitchell J. (2008). 'Excessive exercise' and eating-disordered behaviour in young adult women: Further evidence from a primary care sample. *European Eating Disorders Review, 16*, 215–221.

Morse, B. (2008). Female distance runners and disordered eating. *Mind Matters: The Wesleyan Journal of Psychology, 3*, 29–38.

Mudd, L. M., Fornetti, W., & Pivarnik, J. M. (2007). Bone mineral density in collegiate female athletes: Comparisons among sports. *Journal of Athletic Training, 42*, 403–408.

Muller, S. M., Dennis, D. L., Schneider, S. R., & Joyner, R. L. (2004). Muscle dysmorphia among selected male college athletes: An examination of the Lantz, Rhea, and Mayhew model. *International Sports Journal, 8*, 119–125.

Müller, W. (2009). Determinants of ski-jump performance and implications for health, safety and fairness. *Sports Medicine, 39*, 85–106.

Müller, W., Platzer, D., & Schmolzer, B. (1995). Scientific approach to ski safety. *Nature, 375*, 455.

Nagel, D. L., Black, D. R., Leverenz, L. J., & Coster, D. C. (2000). Evaluation of a screening tool for female college athletes with eating disorders and disordered eating. *Journal of Athletic Training, 35*, 431–440.

National Collegiate Athletic Association. (2005). *NCAA coaches handbook: Managing the female athlete triad.* Indianapolis, IN: Author.

National Collegiate Athletic Association. (2007). *Managing student-athletes' mental health issues.* Indianapolis, IN: Author.

National Institute for Health and Clinical Excellence. (2004). *Eating disorders: Core interventions in the treatment and management of anorexia nervosa, bulimia nervosa and related eating disorders.* London: Author.

National Osteoporosis Foundation (NOF). *Disease statistics: "Fast facts."* Retrieved December 7, 2003, from http://www.nof.org/osteoporosis/stats.htm

Neumark-Sztainer, D., Story, M., Resnick, M. D., & Blum, R. W. (1997). Adolescent vegetarians. A behavioral profile of a school-based population in Minnesota. *Archives of Pediatrics & Adolescent Medicine, 151*, 833–838.

Nichols, J. F., Palmer, J. E., & Levy, S. S. (2003). Low bone mineral density in highly trained male master cyclists. *Osteoporosis International, 14*, 644–649.

Nichols, J. F., Rauh, M. J., Lawson, M. J., Ji, M., & Barkai, H. S. (2006). Prevalence of the female athlete triad syndrome among high school athletes. *Archives of Pediatric and Adolescent Medicine, 160*, 137–142.

Nieman, D. C. (2003). Current perspective on exercise immunology. *Current Sports Medicine Reports, 2*, 239–242.

Noakes, T. (2003). *The lore of running* (4th ed.). Champaign, IL: Human Kinetics.

O'Connor, P. J., Lewis, R. D., & Kirchner, E. M. (1995). Eating disorder symptoms in female college gymnasts. *Medicine & Science in Sports & Exercise, 27*, 550–555.

O'Connor, P. J., Lewis, R. D., Kirchner, E. M., & Cook, D. B. (1996). Eating disorder symptoms in former female college gymnasts: Relations with body composition. *American Journal of Clinical Nutrition, 64*, 840–843.

Ohwada, R., Hotta, M., Oikawa, S., & Takano, K. (2006). Etiology of hypercholesterolemia in patients with anorexia nervosa. *International Journal of Eating Disorders, 39*, 598–601.

Okano, G., Holmes, R. A., Mu, Z., Yang, P., Lin, Z., & Nakai, Y. (2005). Disordered eating in Japanese and Chinese female runners, rhythmic gymnasts and gymnasts. *International Journal of Sports Medicine, 26*, 486–491.

Oliosi, M., Dalle Grave, R., & Burlini, S. (1999). Eating attitudes in noncompetitive male body builders. *Eating Disorders: The Journal of Treatment and Prevention, 7*, 227–233.

243

Olivardia, R., Pope, H. G., & Hudson, J. I. (2000). Muscle dysmorphia in male weightlifters: A case-control study. *American Journal of Psychiatry, 157,* 1291–1296.

Olmsted, M. P. (2002). Day hospital treatment of anorexia nervosa and bulimia nervosa. In C. G. Fairburn & K. D. Brownell (Eds.), *Eating disorders and obesity: A comprehensive handbook* (2nd ed., pp. 330–334). New York: Guilford Press.

Olmsted, M. P., McFarlane, T., Carter, J., & Trottier, K. (2007). Assessment of eating disorders. In S. Wonderlich, J. E. Mitchell, M. de Zwaan, & H. Steiger (Eds.), *Annual review of eating disorders 2007* (Part 1, pp. 81–100). Oxon, England: Radcliffe.

Ongphiphadhanakul, B., Rajatanavin, R., Chanprasertyothin, S., Piaseu, N., & Chailurkit, L. (1998). Serum oestradiol and oestrogen-receptor gene polymorphism are associated with bone mineral density independently of serum testosterone in normal males. *Clinical Endocrinology, 49,* 803–809.

Oppliger, R. A., Landry, G. L., Foster, S. W., & Lambrecht, A. C. (1993). Bulimic behaviors among interscholastic wrestlers: A statewide survey. *Pediatrics, 91,* 826–831.

Oppliger, R. A., Nelson-Steen, S. A., & Scott, J. R. (2003). Weight loss practices of college wrestlers. *International Journal of Sport Nutrition and Exercise Metabolism, 13,* 29–46.

Oppliger, R. A., Utter, A. C., Scott, J. R., Dick, R. W., & Klossner, D. (2006). NCAA rule change improves weight loss among national championship wrestlers. *Medicine & Science in Sports & Exercise, 38,* 963–970.

Orlick, T. (2008). *In pursuit of excellence* (4th ed.). Champaign, IL: Human Kinetics.

Otis, C. L., & Goldingay, R. (2000). *The athletic woman's survival guide.* Champaign, IL: Human Kinetics.

Ousley, L., Cordero, E. D., & White, S. (2008). Fat talk among college students: How undergraduates communicate regarding food and body weight, shape, and appearance. *Eating Disorders: The Journal of Treatment and Prevention, 16,* 73–84.

Parks, P. S., & Read, M. H. (1997). Adolescent male athletes: Body image, diet and exercise. *Adolescence, 32,* 593–602.

Pasman, L., & Thompson, J. K. (1988). Body image and eating disturbance in obligatory runners, obligatory weightlifters, and sedentary individuals. *International Journal of Eating Disorders, 7,* 759–769.

Pate, R. R., Barnes, C., & Miller, W. (1985). A physiological comparison of performance-matched female and male distance runners. *Research Quarterly for Exercise and Sport, 56,* 245–250.

Pearlstein, T. (2002). Eating disorders and comorbidity. *Archives of Women's Mental Health, 4,* 67–78.

Pearsall, A.W., Kovaleski, J. E., & Madanagopal, S. G. (2005). Medicolegal issues affecting sports medicine practitioners. *Clinical Orthopaedics and Related Research, 433,* 50–57.

Perkins, S., & Schmidt, U. (2005). Self-help for eating disorders. In S. Wonderlich, J. E. Mitchell, M. de Zwaan, & H. Steiger (Eds.), *Annual review of eating disorders* (Part 1, pp. 87–104). Oxford: Radcliffe Publishing.

Peterson, C. B., & Miller, K. B. (2005). Assessment of eating disorders. In S. Wonderlich, J. E., Mitchell, M. de Zwaan, & H. Steiger (Eds.), *Annual review of eating disorders* (Part 1, pp. 105–126). Oxford, Radcliffe Publishing.

Petrie, T. A. (1996). Differences between male and female college lean sport athletes, nonlean sport athletes, and nonathletes on behavioral and psychological indices of eating disorders. *Journal of Applied Sport Psychology, 8,* 218–230.

Petrie, T. A., & Greenleaf, C. (2007). Eating disorders in sport: From theory to research to intervention. In G. Tenenbaum & R. Eklund (Eds.), *Handbook of sport psychology* (3rd ed., pp. 352–378). Hoboken, NJ: J. Wiley & Sons.

Petrie, T. A., Greenleaf, C., Carter, J. E., & Reel, J. J. (2007). Psychosocial correlates of disordered eating among male collegiate athletes. *Journal of Clinical Sport Psychology, 1,* 340–357.

Petrie, T. A., & Sherman, R. T. (1999). Recognizing and assisting athletes with eating disorders. In R. Ray & D. M. Wiese-Bjornstal (Eds.), *Counseling in sports medicine* (pp. 205–226). Champaign, IL: Human Kinetics.

Petrie, T. A., & Stoever, S. (1993). The incidence of bulimia nervosa and pathogenic weight control behaviors in female collegiate gymnasts. *Research Quarterly of Exercise and Sport, 64,* 238–241.

Picard, C. L. (1999). The level of competition as a factor for the development of eating disorders in female collegiate athletes. *Journal of Youth and Adolescence, 28,* 583–594.

Pickett, T. C., Lewis, R. J., & Cash, T. F. (2005). Men, muscles, and body image: Comparisons of competitive bodybuilders, weight trainers, and athletically active controls. *British Journal of Sports Medicine, 39,* 217–222.

Pietrowsky, R., & Straub, K. (2008). Body dissatisfaction and restrained eating in male juvenile and adult athletes. *Eating and Weight Disorders, 13,* 14–21.

Pike, K., Attia, E., & Brown, A. J. (2008). Treatment for anorexia nervosa. In S. Wonderlich, J. E. Mitchell, M. de Zwaan, & H. Steiger (Eds.), *Annual review of eating disorders* (Part 2, pp. 137–148). Oxford: Radcliffe Publishing.

Piran, N. (2002). Prevention of eating disorders. In C. Fairburn & K. Brownell (Eds.), *Eating disorders and obesity* (2nd ed., pp. 367–371). New York: Guilford Press.

Pomeroy, C., & Mitchell, J. E. (2002). Medical complications of anorexia nervosa and bulimia nervosa. In C. G. Fairburn & K. D. Brownell (Eds.), *Eating disorders and obesity: A comprehensive handbook* (2nd ed., pp. 278–285). New York: Guilford Press.

Pope, H. G., Gruber, A. J., Choi, P., Olivardia, R., & Phillips, K. A. (1997). "Muscle dysmorphia": An underrecognized form of body dysmorphic disorder? *Psychosomatics, 38,* 548–557.

Pope, H. G., & Katz, D. L. (1994). Psychiatric and medical effects of anabolic-androgenic steroid use: A controlled study of 160 athletes. *Archives of General Psychiatry, 51,* 375–382.

Pope, H. G., Katz, D. L., & Hudson, J. I. (1993). Anorexia nervosa and "reverse anorexia" among 108 male bodybuilders. *Comparative Psychiatry, 34,* 406–409.

Pope, H. G., Phillips, K. A., & Olivardia, R. (2000). *The Adonis complex: The secret crisis of male body obsession.* New York: Free Press.

Powers, P. S. (1999). Eating disorders: Cardiovascular risks and management. In P. S. Mehler & A. E. Andersen (Eds.), *Eating disorders: A guide to medical care and complications* (pp. 100–117). Baltimore: Johns Hopkins University Press.

Powers, P. S., & Cloak, N. L. (2007). Medication-related weight changes. In J. Yager & P. S. Powers (Eds.), *Clinical manual of eating disorders* (pp. 255–285). Arlington, VA: American Psychiatric Publishing.

Powers, P. S., & Johnson, C. (1996). Small victories: Prevention of eating disorders among athletes. *Eating disorders: The Journal of Treatment and Prevention, 4,* 364–377.

Powers, P. S., Schocken, D. D., & Boyd, F. R. (1998). Comparison of habitual runners and anorexia nervosa patients. *International Journal of Eating Disorders, 23,* 133–143.

Powers, P. S., & Thompson, R. A. (2007). Athletes and eating disorders. In J. Yager and P. Powers (Eds.), *The clinical manual of eating disorders* (pp. 357–385). Arlington, VA: American Psychiatric Press.

Powers, P. S., & Thompson, R. A. (2008). *The exercise balance.* Carlsbad, CA: Gurze Books.

Pugliese, M. T., Lifshitz, F., Grad, G., Fort, P., & Marks-Katz, M. (1983). Fear of obesity: A cause of short stature and delayed puberty. *New England Journal of Medicine, 309,* 513–518.

Pull, C. B. (2004). Binge eating disorder. *Current Opinion in Psychiatry, 17,* 43–48.

Quatromoni, P. A. (2008). Clinical observations from nutrition services in college athletics. *Journal of the American Dietetic Association, 108,* 689–694.

Raevuori, A., Hoek, H. W., Susser, E., Kaprio, J., Rissanen, A., & Keski-Rahkonen, A. (2009). Epidemiology of anorexia nervosa in men: A nationwide study of Finnish twins. *PloS One, 4,* e4402. Epub 2009 Feb 10.

Raglin, J. S., & Moger, L. (1999). Adverse consequences of physical activity: When more is too much. In J. M. Rippe (Ed.), *Lifestyle medicine* (pp. 998–1004). Malden, MA: Blackwell Science.

Raglin, J., Sawamura, S., Alexiou, S., Hassmen, P., & Kentta, G. (2000). Training practices and staleness in 13–18-year-old swimmers: A cross-cultural study. *Pediatric Exercise Science, 12,* 61–70.

Raglin, J. S., & Wilson, G. S. (2000). Overtraining in athletes. In Y. L. Hanin (Ed.), *Emotions in sport* (pp. 191–207). Champaign, IL: Human Kinetics.

Raudenbush, B., & Meyer, B. (2003). Muscular dissatisfaction and supplement use among male intercollegiate athletes. *Journal of Sport & Exercise Psychology, 25,* 161–170.

Raudenbush, B., & Zellner, D. A. (1997). Nobody's satisfied: Effects of abnormal eating behaviors and actual and perceived weight status on body image satisfaction in males and females. *Journal of Social and Clinical Psychology, 16,* 95–110.

Ravaldi, C., Vannacci, A., Zucchi, T., Mannucci, E., Cabras, P. L., Boldrini, M., et al. (2003). Eating disorders and body-image disturbances among ballet dancers, gymnasium users, and body builders. *Psychopathology, 36,* 247–254.

Reel, J. J. (1998). A thin line: Weight pressures, social physique anxiety, and weight loss strategies among college female dancers. *Journal of Applied Sport Psychology, 10* (Suppl. 78).

Reel, J. J., & Gill, D. L. (1996). Psychosocial factors related to eating disorders among high school and college female cheerleaders. *The Sport Psychologist, 10,* 195–206.

Reel, J. J., & Gill, D. L. (1998). Weight concerns and disordered eating attitudes among male and female college cheerleaders. *Women in Sport and Physical Activity Journal, 7,* 79–94.

Reel, J. J., & Gill, D. L. (2001). Slim enough to swim? Weight pressures for competitive swimmers and coaching implications. *The Sport Journal, 4,* 1–5.

Reel, J. J., SooHoo, S., Doetsch, H., Carter, J. E., & Petrie, T. A. (2007). The female athlete triad: Is the triad a problem among Division I female athletes? *Journal of Clinical Sport Psychology, 1,* 358–370.

Reel, J. J., SooHoo, S., & Estes, H. (2005). Weigh-ins and uniforms: Creating a prevention platform for disordered eating in sport. In L. Ransdell & L. Petlichkoff (Eds.), *Ensuring the health of active and athletic girls and women* (pp. 147–158). Reston, VA: NAGWS.

Reel, J. J., SooHoo, S., Jamieson, K. M., & Gill, D. L. (2005). Femininity to the extreme: Body image concerns among college female dancers. *Women in Sport and Physical Activity Journal, 14,* 39–51.

Reinking, M. F., & Alexander, L. E. (2005). Prevalence of disordered-eating behaviors in undergraduate female collegiate athletes and nonathletes. *Journal of Athletic Training, 40,* 47–51.

Resch, M., & Haasz, P. (2009). The first epidemiologic survey among Hungarian elite athletes: Eating disorders, depression and risk factors. *Orvosi Hetilap, 150,* 35–40.

Ringham, R., Klump, K., Kaye, W., Stone, D., Libman, S., Stowe, S., et al. (2006). Eating disorder symptomatology among ballet dancers. *International Journal of Eating Disorders, 39,* 503–508.

Robson, B. (2001). Disordered eating in high school dance students: Some practical considerations. *Journal of Dance Medicine & Science, 6,* 7–13.

247

Rohman, L. (2009). The relationship between anabolic androgenic steroids and muscle dysmorphia: A review. *Eating Disorders: The Journal of Treatment and Prevention, 17,* 187–199.

Rosen, L. W., & Hough, D. O. (1988). Pathogenic weight-control behaviors of female college gymnasts. *Physician and Sportsmedicine, 16,* 141–144.

Rosen, L. W., McKeag, D. B., Hough, D. O., & Curley, V. (1986). Pathogenic weight-control behavior in female athletes. *Physician and Sportsmedicine, 14,* 79–86.

Rosendahl, J., Bormann, B., Aschenbrenner, K., Aschenbrenner, F., & Strauss, B. (2009). Dieting and disordered eating in German high school athletes and non-athletes. *Scandinavian Journal of Medicine & Science in Sports, 19,* 731–739.

Rouveix, M., Bouget, M., Pannafieux, C., Champely, S., & Filaire, E. (2007). Eating attitudes, body esteem, perfectionism and anxiety of judo athletes and non-athletes. *International Journal of Sports Medicine, 28,* 340–345.

Rucinski, A. (1989). Relationship of body image and dietary intake of competitive ice skaters. *Journal of the American Dietetic Association, 89,* 98–100.

Russell, K. M. (2004). On vs. off the pitch: The transiency of body satisfaction among female rugby players, cricketers, and netballers. *Sex Roles, 51,* 561–574.

Ryan, J. (2000). *Little girls in pretty boxes: The making and breaking of elite gymnasts and figure skaters.* New York: Warner Books.

Sabo, D., Bernd, L., Pfeil, J., & Reiter, A. (1996). Bone quality in the lumbar spine in high-performance athletes. *European Spine Journal, 5,* 258–263.

Safer, D. L., Telch, C. F., & Agras, W. S. (2001). Dialectical behavior therapy for bulimia nervosa. *American Journal of Psychiatry, 158,* 632–634.

Safer, D. L., Telch, C. F., & Chen, E. Y. (2009). *Dialectical behavior therapy for binge eating and bulimia.* New York: Guilford.

Salbach, H., Klinkowski, N., Pfeiffer, E., Lehmkuhl, U., & Korte, A. (2007). Body image and attitudinal aspects of eating disorders in rhythmic gymnasts. *Psychopathology, 40,* 388–393.

Sandager, N., Peterson, C. B., Allen, S., Henderson, K. E., Crow, S., & Thuras, P. (2008). Tobacco use and comorbidity in bulimia nervosa. *International Journal of Eating Disorders, 41,* 734–738.

Sandoval, W. M., Heyward, V. H., & Lyons, T. M. (1989). Comparison of body composition, exercise, and nutritional profiles of female and male body builders at competition. *Journal of Sports Medicine and Physical Fitness, 29,* 63–70.

Sanford-Martens, T. C., Davidson, M. M., Yakushko, O. F., Martens, M. P., Hinton, P., & Beck, N. (2005). Clinical and subclinical eating disorders: An examination of collegiate athletes. *Journal of Applied Sport Psychology, 17,* 79–86.

Sansone, R. A., & Sansone, L. A. (2007). Eating disorders and psychiatric comorbidity: Prevalence and treatment modifications. In J. Yager & P. S. Powers (Eds.), *Clinical manual of eating disorders* (pp. 79–111). Arlington, VA: American Psychiatric Press.

Schlechte, J. A. (1999). General endocrinology. In P. S. Mehler & A. E. Andersen (Eds.), *Eating disorders: A guide to medical care and complications* (pp. 132–143). Baltimore: Johns Hopkins University Press.

Schnitt, J. M., Schnitt, D., & Del A'Une, W. (1986). Anorexia nervosa or thinness in modern dance students: Comparison with ballerinas. *Annals of Sports Medicine, 3*, 9–13.

Schtscherbyna, A., Soares, E. A., Oliveira, F. P., & Ribeiro, B. G. (2009). Female athlete triad in elite swimmers of the city of Rio de Janeiro, Brazil. *Nutrition, 25*, 634–639.

Schwarz, H. C., Gairrett, R. L., Aruguete, M. S., & Gold, E. S. (2005). Eating attitudes, body dissatisfaction, and perfectionism in female college athletes. *North American Journal of Psychology, 7*, 345–352.

Science and Environmental Health Network. (1998). Wingspread consensus statement on the precautionary principle. Retrieved July 8, 2009 from http://www.sehn.org/wing.html

Seigel, K., & Hetta, J. (2001). Exercise and eating disorder symptoms among young females. *Eating and Weight Disorders, 6*, 32–39.

Selby, R., Weinstein, H. M., & Bird, T. S. (1990). The health of university athletes: Attitudes, behaviors, and stressors. *Journal of American College Health, 39*, 11–18.

Shapiro, J. R., Berkman, N. D., Brownley, K. A., Sedway, J. A., Lohr, K. N., & Bulik, C. M. (2007). Bulimia nervosa: A systematic review of randomized controlled trials. *International Journal of Eating Disorders, 40*, 321–336.

Sherman, R. T. (2007, November). *Protecting the health of athletes: Possible rules changes.* Paper presented at the meeting of the International Olympic Committee Medical Commission, Monte Carlo, Monaco.

Sherman, R. T., DeHass, D., Thompson, R. A., & Wilfert, M. (2005). NCAA coaches survey: The role of the coach in identifying and managing athletes with disordered eating. *Eating Disorders: The Journal of Treatment and Prevention, 13*, 447–466.

Sherman, R. T., & Thompson, R. A. (2001). Athletes and disordered eating: Four major issues for the professional psychologist. *Professional Psychology: Research and Practice, 32*, 27–33.

Sherman, R. T., & Thompson, R. A. (2004). The female athlete triad. *Journal of School Nursing, 20*, 197–202.

Sherman, R. T., & Thompson, R. A. (2009). Body image and eating disturbance in athletes: Competing to win or to be thin? In J. Reel & K. Beals (Eds.), *The hidden faces of eating disorders and body image* (pp. 9–38). Reston, VA: NAGWS Publications.

Sherman, R. T., Thompson, R. A., & Rose, J. (1996). Body mass index and athletic performance in elite female gymnasts. *Journal of Sport Behavior, 19*, 338–346.

Sherwood, N. E., Neumark-Stzainer, D., Story, M., Beuhring, T., & Resnick, M. L. (2002). Weight-related sports involvement in girls: Who is at risk for disordered eating? *American Journal of Health Promotion, 16*, 341–344.

Shroff, H., Reba, L., Thornton, L. M., Tozzi, F., Klump, K. L., Berrettini, M. D., et al. (2006). Features associated with excessive exercise in women with eating disorders. *International Journal of Eating Disorders, 39*, 454–461.

249

Shry, E. A., Leding, C. J., Rubal, B. J., & Eisenhauer, M. D. (2002). The role of limited echocardiography and electrocardiography in screening physicals for amateur athletes. *Military Medicine, 167*, 831–834.

Silber, T. J. (2005). Ipecac syrup abuse, morbidity, and mortality: Isn't it time to repeal its over-the-counter status? *Journal of Adolescent Health, 37*, 256–260.

Silberstein, L. R., Striegel-Moore, R. H., Timko, C., & Rodin, J. (1988). Behavioral and psychological implications of body dissatisfaction: Do men and women differ? *Sex Roles, 19*, 219–231.

Slater, G. J., Rice, A. J., Sharpe, K., Mujika, I., Jenkins, D., & Hahn, A. G. (2005). Body-mass management of Australian lightweight rowers prior to and during competition. *Medicine & Science in Sports & Exercise, 37*, 860–866.

Smathers, A. M., Bemben, M. G., & Bemben, D. A. (2009). Bone density comparisons in male competitive road cyclists and untrained controls. *Medicine & Science in Sports & Exercise, 41*, 290–296.

Smith, A., & Petrie, T. (2008). Reducing the risk of disordered eating among female athletes: A test of alternative interventions. *Journal of Applied Sport Psychology, 20*, 392–407.

Smith, A. C., & Stewart, B. (2008). Drug policy in sport: Hidden assumptions and inherent contradictions. *Drug and Alcohol Review, 27*, 123–129.

Smolak, L., Murnen, S. K., & Ruble, A. E. (2000). Female athletes and eating problems: A meta-analysis. *International Journal of Eating Disorders, 27*, 371–380.

Solenberger, S. E. (2001). Exercise and eating disorders: A 3-year inpatient hospital record analysis. *Eating Behaviors, 2*, 151–168.

Spence, L., Brown, W. J., Pyne, D. B., Nissen, M. D., Sloots, T. P., McCormack, J. G., et al. (2007). Incidence, etiology, and symptomatology of upper respiratory illness in elite athletes. *Medicine & Science in Sports & Exercise, 39*, 577–586.

Spillane, N. S., Boerner, L. M., Anderson, K. G., & Smith, G. T. (2004). Comparability of the Eating Disorder Inventory-2 between men and women. *Assessment, 11*, 85–93.

Spitler, D.L., Diaz, F. J., Horvath, S. M., & Wright, J. E. (1980). Body composition and maximal aerobic capacity of body-builders. *Journal of Sports Medicine and Physical Fitness, 20*, 181–188.

Steen, S. N., & Brownell, K. D. (1990). Patterns of weight loss and regain in wrestlers. Has the tradition changed? *Medicine & Science in Sports & Exercise, 22*, 762–768.

Steen, S. N., & McKinney, S. (1986). Nutrition assessment of college wrestlers. *Physician and Sportsmedicine, 14*, 100–116.

Steffen, J., & Brehm, B. (1999). The dimensions of obligatory exercise. *Eating Disorders: The Journal of Treatment and Prevention, 7*, 219–226.

Steinhausen, H. C. (2002). The outcome of anorexia nervosa in the 20th century. *American Journal of Psychiatry, 159*, 1284–1293.

Stewart, A. D., Benson, P. J., Michanikou, E. G., Tsiota, D. G., & Narli, M. K. (2003). Body image perception, satisfaction and somatotype in male and female athletes and non-athletes: Results using a novel morphing technique. *Journal of Sports Sciences, 21,* 815–823.

Stewart, A. D., & Hannan, J. (2000). Total and regional bone density in male runners, cyclists, controls. *Medicine & Science in Sports & Exercise, 32,* 373–377.

Stice, E. (2002). Sociocultural influences on body image and eating disturbance. In C. G. Fairburn & K. D. Brownell (Eds.), *Eating disorders and obesity: A comprehensive handbook* (pp. 103–107). New York: Guilford Press.

Stice, E., Maxfield, J., & Wells, T. (2003). Adverse effects of social pressure to be thin on young women: An experimental investigation of the effects of "fat talk." *International Journal of Eating Disorders, 34,* 108–117.

Stice, E., & Shaw, H. (2003). Prospective relations of body image, eating and affective disturbances to smoking onset in adolescent girls: How Virginia slims. *Journal of Consulting and Clinical Psychology, 71,* 129–135.

Stice, E., Trost, A., & Chase, A. (2003). Healthy weight control and dissonance-based eating disorder prevention programs: Results from a controlled trial. *International Journal of Eating Disorders, 33,* 10–21.

Stoutjesdyk, D., & Jevne, R. (1993). Eating disorders among high performance athletes. *Journal of Youth and Adolescence, 22,* 271–282.

Striegel-Moore, R. H., & Bulik, C. M. (2007). Risk factors for eating disorders. *American Psychologist, 62,* 181–198.

Striegel-Moore, R. H., & Franko, D. L. (2008). Should binge eating disorder be included in the DSM-V? A critical review of the state of the evidence. *Annual Review of Clinical Psychology, 4,* 305–324.

Striegel-Moore, R. H., Franko, D. L., Thompson, D., Affenito, S., May, A., & Kraemer, H. C. (2008). Exploring the typology of night eating syndrome. *International Journal of Eating Disorders, 41,* 411–418.

Striegel-Moore, R. H., Franko, D. L., Thompson, D., Barton, B., Schreiber, G. B., & Daniels, S. R. (2006). Caffeine intake in eating disorders. *International Journal of Eating Disorders, 39,* 162–165.

Striegel-Moore, R., McAvay, G., & Rodin, J. (1986). Psychological and behavioral correlates of feeling fat in women. *International Journal of Eating Disorders, 5,* 935–947.

Striegel-Moore, R. H., & Wonderlich, S. (Eds.). (2007). Special issue on diagnosis and classification. *International Journal of Eating Disorders, 40* (Suppl.).

Strober, M. (1986). Anorexia nervosa: History and psychological concepts. In K. D. Brownell & J. P. Foreyt (Eds.), *Handbook of eating disorders: Physiology, psychology, and treatment of obesity, anorexia, and bulimia* (pp. 231–146). New York: Basic Books.

Strober, M., Freeman, R., & Morrell, W. (1997). The long-term course of severe anorexia nervosa in adolescents: Survival analysis of recovery, relapse, and outcome predictors over 10–15 years in a prospective study. *International Journal of Eating Disorders, 22,* 339–360.

251

Stunkard, A., Allison, K., & Lundgren, J. (2008). Issues for DSM-V: Night eating syndrome. *American Journal of Psychiatry, 165,* 424.

Stunkard, A. J., Grace, W. J., & Wolff, H. G. (1955). The night-eating syndrome: A pattern of food intake among certain obese patients. *American Journal of Medicine, 19,* 78–86.

Sundgot-Borgen, J. (1993). Prevalence of eating disorders in elite female athletes. *International Journal of Sport Nutrition, 3,* 29–40.

Sundgot-Borgen, J. (1994a). Risk and trigger factors for the development of eating disorders in female athletes. *Medicine & Science in Sports & Exercise, 26,* 414–419.

Sundgot-Borgen, J. (1994b). Eating disorders in female athletes. *Sports Medicine, 17,* 176–188.

Sundgot-Borgen, J. (1996). Eating disorders, energy intake, training volume, and menstrual function in high-level modern rhythmic gymnasts. *International Journal of Sport Nutrition, 6,* 100–109.

Sundgot-Borgen, J., Fasting, K., Brackenridge, C., Torstveit, M. K., & Berglund, B. (2003). Sexual harassment and eating disorders in female elite athletes— A controlled study. *Scandinavian Journal of Medicine & Science in Sports, 13,* 330–335.

Sundgot-Borgen, J., & Klungland, M. (1998). The female athlete triad and the effect of preventive work. *Medicine & Science in Sports & Exercise, 30* (Suppl. 5), S181.

Sundgot-Borgen, J., & Larsen, S. (1993). Pathogenic weight-control methods and self-reported eating disorders in female elite athletes and controls. *Scandinavian Journal of Medicine & Science in Sports, 3,* 150–155.

Sundgot-Borgen, J., Rosenvinge, J. H., Bahr, R., & Schneider, L. S. (2002). The effect of exercise, cognitive therapy, and nutritional counseling in treating bulimia nervosa. *Medicine & Science in Sports & Exercise, 34,* 190–195.

Sundgot-Borgen, J., & Torstveit, M. K. (2004). Prevalence of eating disorders in elite athletes is higher than in the general population. *Clinical Journal of Sport Medicine, 14,* 25–32.

Sundgot-Borgen, J., & Torstveit, M. K. (2007). The female football player, disordered eating, menstrual function and bone health. *British Journal of Sports Medicine, 41* (Suppl. 1), i68–i72.

Sutandar-Pinnock, K., Blake, W. D., Carter, J. C., Olmsted, M. P., & Kaplan, A. S. (2003). Perfectionism in anorexia nervosa: A 6–24-month follow-up study. *International Journal of Eating Disorders, 33,* 225–229.

Swanson, D. R. (2008). Running, esophageal acid reflux, and atrial fibrillation: A chain of events linked by evidence from separate medical literatures. *Medical Hypotheses, 71,* 178–185.

Swinburn, B. A., Walter, L. G., Arroll, B., Tilyard, M. N., & Russell, D. G. (1997). Green prescriptions: Attitudes and perceptions of general practitioners towards prescribing exercise. *British Journal of General Practice, 37,* 567–569.

Sykora, C., Grilo, C. M., Wilfley, D. E., & Brownell, K. D. (1993). Eating, weight, and dieting disturbances in male and female lightweight and heavyweight rowers. *International Journal of Eating Disorders, 14,* 203–211.

Takimoto, Y., Yoshiuchi, K., & Akabayashi, A. (2008). Effect of mood states on QT interval and QT dispersion in eating disorder patients. *Psychiatry and Clinical Neurosciences, 62,* 185–189.

Taub, D. E., & Blinde, E. M. (1992). Eating disorders among adolescent female athletes: Influence of athletic participation and sport team membership. *Adolescence, 27,* 833–848.

Taylor, G. M., & Ste-Marie, D. M. (2001). Eating disorders symptoms in Canadian female pair and dance figure skaters. *International Journal of Sport Psychology, 32,* 21–28.

Telch, C. F., Agras, W. S., & Linehan, M. M. (2001). Dialectical behavior therapy for binge eating disorder. *Journal of Consulting and Clinical Psychology, 69,* 1061–1065.

Terry, P. C., Lane, A. M., & Warren, L. (1999). Eating attitudes, body shape perceptions, and mood of elite rowers. *Journal of Science and Medicine in Sport, 2,* 67–77.

Thiel, A., Gottfried, H., & Hesse, F. W. (1993). Subclinical eating disorders in male athletes. A study of the low weight category in rowers and wrestlers. *Acta Psychiatrica Scandinavia, 88,* 259–265.

Thiels, C., & de Zwaan, M. (2007). Self-help treatment for eating disorders. In S. Wonderlich, J. E. Mitchell, M. de Zwaan, & H. Steiger (Eds.), *Annual review of eating disorders 2007* (Part 1, pp. 63–79). Oxon, England: Radcliffe.

Thomas, J. J., Keel, P. K., & Heatherton, T. F. (2005). Disordered eating attitudes and behaviors in ballet students: Examination of environmental and individual risk factors. *International Journal of Eating Disorders, 38,* 263–268.

Thomas, J. J., Roberto, C. A., & Brownell, K. D. (2009). Eighty-five percent of what? Discrepancies in the weight cut-off for anorexia nervosa substantially affect the prevalence of underweight. *Psychological Medicine, 39,* 833–843.

Thompson, R. A. (1987). Management of the athlete with an eating disorder: Implications for the sport management team. *The Sport Psychologist, 1,* 114–126.

Thompson, R. A. (1998). The last word: Wrestling with death. *Eating Disorders: The Journal of Treatment and Prevention, 6,* 207–210.

Thompson, R. A. (2003). The last word: Cheerleader weight standards. *Eating Disorders: The Journal of Treatment and Prevention, 11,* 87–90.

Thompson, R. A., & Sherman, R. T. (1989). Therapist errors in treating eating disorders: Relationship and process. *Psychotherapy, 26,* 62–68.

Thompson, R. A., & Sherman, R. T. (1993a). *Helping athletes with eating disorders.* Champaign, IL: Human Kinetics.

Thompson, R. A., & Sherman, R. T. (1993b). Reducing the risk of eating disorders in athletics. *Eating Disorders: The Journal of Treatment and Prevention, 1,* 65–78.

Thompson, R. A., & Sherman, R. T. (1999a). Athletes, athletic performance, and eating disorders: Healthier alternatives. *Journal of Social Issues, 55,* 317–337.

Thompson, R. A., & Sherman, R. T. (1999b). "Good athlete" traits and character-istics of anorexia nervosa: Are they similar? *Eating Disorders: The Journal of Treatment and Prevention, 7,* 181–190.

Thompson, R. A., & Sherman, R. T. (2009). The last word on the 29th Olympiad: Redundant, revealing, remarkable, and redundant. *Eating Disorders: The Journal of Treatment and Prevention, 17,* 97–102.

Thompson, S. H. (2007). Characteristics of the female athlete triad in collegiate cross-country runners. *Journal of American College Health, 56,* 129–136.

Thompson, S. H., Smith, P., & DeBate, R. D. (2004). Performance-related injuries and exercise orientation of National Collegiate Athletic Association Division I, II, and III female collegiate cross country runners. *Women in Sport and Physical Activity Journal, 13,* 17–26.

Toftegaard, J. (2001). The forbidden zone—About intimacy, sexual relations and misconduct in the relationships between coaches and athletes. *International Review for the Sociology of Sport, 36,* 165–183.

Toro, J., Galilea, B., Martinez-Mallen, E., Salamero, M., Capdevila, L., Mari, J., et al. (2005). Eating disorders in Spanish female athletes. *International Journal of Sports Medicine, 26,* 693–700.

Toro, J., Guerrero, M., Sentis, J., Castro, J., & Puertolas, C. (2009). Eating disor-ders in ballet dancing students: Problems and risk factors. *European Eating Disorders Review, 17,* 40–49.

Torstveit, M. K., Rosenvinge, J. H., & Sundgot-Borgen, J. (2008). Prevalence of eat-ing disorders and the predictive power of risk models in female elite athletes: A controlled study. *Scandinavian Journal of Medicine & Science in Sports, 18,* 108–118.

Torstveit, M. K., & Sundgot-Borgen, J. (2005a). The female athlete triad: Are elite athletes at increased risk? *Medicine & Science in Sports & Exercise, 37,* 184–193.

Torstveit, M. K., & Sundgot-Borgen, J. (2005b). The female athlete triad exists in both elite athletes and controls. *Medicine & Science in Sports & Exercise, 37,* 1449–1459.

Tozzi, F., Thornton, L., Klump, K., Fichter, M., Halmi, K., Kaplan, A., et al. (2005). Symptom fluctuation in eating disorders: Correlates of diagnostic crossover. *American Journal of Psychiatry, 162,* 732–740.

Troop, N. A., Allan, S., Treasure, J. L., & Katzman, M. (2003). Social comparison and submissive behavior in eating disorder patients. *Psychology and Psychotherapy: Theory, Research, and Practice, 76,* 237–249.

USA Equestrian. (2002). *Hunter seat equitation manual.* Lexington, KY: Author.

van Son, G. E., van Hoeken, D., Bartelds, A. I. M., van Furth, E. F., & Hoek, H. W. (2006). Time trends in the incidence of eating disorders: A primary care study in the Netherlands. *International Journal of Eating Disorders, 7,* 565–569.

Walberg, J. L., & Johnston, C. S. (1991). Menstrual function and eating behavior in female recreational weight lifters and competitive body builders. *Medicine & Science in Sport & Exercise, 23,* 30–36.

254

Walsh, B. T. (2002). Pharmacological treatment of anorexia nervosa and bulimia nervosa. In C. G. Fairburn & K. D. Brownell (Eds.), *Eating disorders and obesity: A comprehensive handbook* (2nd ed., pp. 325–329). New York: Guilford Press.

Walsh, B. T. (2007). DSM-V from the perspective of DSM-IV experience. *International Journal of Eating Disorders, 40,* S3–S7.

Wasilenko, K. A., Kulik, J. A., & Wanic, R. A. (2007). Effects of social comparisons with peers on women's body satisfaction and exercise behavior. *International Journal of Eating Disorders, 40,* 740–745.

Weidenbener, E. J., Krauss M. D., Waller, B. F., & Taliercio, C. P. (1995). Incorporation of screening echocardiography in the preparticipation exam. *Clinical Journal of Sport Medicine, 5,* 86–89.

Weight, L. M., & Noakes, T. D. (1987). Is running an analog of anorexia? A survey of the incidence of eating disorders in female distance runners. *Medicine & Science in Sports & Exercise, 19,* 213–217.

Welch, S. L., & Fairburn, C. G. (1998). Smoking and bulimia nervosa. *International Journal of Eating Disorders, 23,* 433–437.

Wethington, H., Flowers, C., Turner, M., & DeBate, R. D. (2002). Eating attitudes, body image, and nutrient intake in female triathletes. *Women in Sport and Physical Activity Journal, 11,* 115–139.

Wheeler, G. D., Wall, S. R., Belcastro, A. N., Conger, P., & Cumming, D. C. (1986). Are anorexic tendencies prevalent in the habitual runner? *British Journal of Sports Medicine, 20,* 77–81.

Whisenhunt, B. L., Williamson, D. A., Drab-Hudson, D. L., & Walden, H. (2008). Intervening with coaches to promote awareness and prevention of weight pressures in cheerleaders. *Eating and Weight Disorders, 13,* 102–110.

Wiita, B. G., & Strombaugh, I. A. (1996). Nutrition knowledge, eating practices, and health of adolescent female runners: A 3-year longitudinal study. *International Journal of Sports Nutrition, 6,* 414–425.

Wilkins, J. A., Boland, F. J., & Albinson, J. (1991). A comparison of male and female university athletes and nonathletes on eating disorder indices: Are athletes protected? *Journal of Sport Behavior, 14,* 129–143.

Williams, C. (2003). New technologies in self-help: Another effective way to get better? *European Eating Disorders Review, 11,* 170–182.

Wilmore, J. H. (1992a). Body weight and body composition. In K. D. Brownell, J. Rodin, & J. H. Wilmore (Eds.), *Eating, body weight and performance in athletes: Disorders of modern society* (pp. 77–93). Philadelphia: Lea & Febiger.

Wilmore, J. H. (1992b). Body weight standards and athletic performance. In K. D. Brownell, J. Rodin, & J. H. Wilmore (Eds.), *Eating, body weight and performance in athletes: Disorders of modern society* (pp. 315–329). Philadelphia: Lea & Febiger.

Wilson, G. T. (2002). The controversy over dieting. In C. G. Fairburn & K. D. Brownell (Eds.), *Eating disorders and obesity: A comprehensive handbook* (2nd ed., pp. 93–97). New York: Guilford Press.

Wilson, G. T., & Bannon, K. (2008). Treatment of bulimia nervosa. In S. Wonderlich, J. E. Mitchell, M. de Zwaan, & H. Steiger (Eds.), *Annual review of eating disorders 2008* (Part 2, pp. 125–136). Oxon, England: Radcliffe.

Winters, S. J. (1999). Current status of testosterone replacement therapy in men. *Archives of Family Medicine, 8*, 257–263.

Wiseman, C. V., Turco, R. M., Sunday, S. R., & Halmi, K. A. (1998). Smoking and body image concerns in adolescent girls. *International Journal of Eating Disorders, 24*, 429–433.

Wonderlich, S. A., Brewerton, T. D., Jocic, Z., Dansky B. S., & Abbott, D. W. (1997). The relationship of childhood sexual abuse and eating disorders: A review. *Journal of the American Academy of Child and Adolescent Psychiatry, 36*, 1107–1115.

Wonderlich, S. A., Engel, S. C., Peterson, C. B., Robinson, M. D., Crosby, R. D., Mitchell, J. E. et al. (2008). Examining the conceptual model of integrative cognitive-affective therapy for BN: Two assessment studies. *International Journal of Eating Disorders, 41*, 748–754.

Wonderlich, S. A., Joiner, T. E., Keel, P. K., Williamson, D. A., & Crosby, R. D. (2007). Eating disorder diagnoses: Empirical approaches to classification. *American Psychologist, 62*, 167–180.

Woodside, D. B., Walfish, P., Kaplan, A. S., & Kennedy, S. H. (1991). Graves' disease in a woman with thyroid hormone abuse, bulimia nervosa, and a history of anorexia nervosa. *International Journal of Eating Disorders, 10*, 111–115.

World Health Organization. (1994). Assessment of fracture risk and its application to screening for postmenopausal osteoporosis. Report of a WHO Study Group. *World Health Organization Technical Report Series, 843*, 1–129.

Yager, J. (2007a). Assessment and determination of initial treatment approaches for patients with eating disorders. In J. Yager & P. S. Powers (Eds.), *Clinical manual of eating disorders* (pp. 31–77). Arlington, VA: American Psychiatric Publishing.

Yager, J. (2007b). Cognitive-behavioral therapy for eating disorders. In J. Yager & P. S. Powers (Eds.), *Clinical manual of eating disorders* (pp. 287–305). Arlington, VA: American Psychiatric Publishing.

Yager, J., & Powers, P. S. (Eds.). (2007). *Clinical manual of eating disorders.* Arlington, VA: American Psychiatric Publishing.

Yates, W. R. (1999). Medical problems of the athlete with an eating disorder. In P. S. Mehler & A. E. Andersen (Eds.), *Eating disorders: A guide to medical care and complications* (pp. 153–166). Baltimore: Johns Hopkins University Press.

Yeager, K. K., Agostini, R., Nattiv, A., & Drinkwater, B. (1993). The female athlete triad: Disordered eating, amenorrhea, and osteoporosis. *Medicine & Science in Sports & Exercise, 25*, 775–777.

Yesalis, C. E., Barsukiewicz, C. K., Kopstein, A. N., & Bahrke, M. S. (1997). Trends in anabolic-androgenic steroid use among adolescents. *Archives of Pediatrics and Adolescent Medicine, 151*, 1197–1206.

Young, E. A., Clopton, J. R., & Bleckley, M. K. (2004). Perfectionism, low self-esteem, and family factors as predictors of bulimic behavior. *Eating Behaviors, 5,* 273–283.

Yumamiya, Y., Cash, T. F., Melnyk, S. E., Posavac, H. D., & Posavac, S. S. (2005). Women's exposure to thin-and-beautiful media images: Body image effects of media-ideal internalization and impact-reduction interventions. *Body Image, 2,* 74–80.

Zapf, J., Fichtl, B., Wielgoss, S., & Schmidt, W. (2001). Macronutrient intake and eating habits in elite rock climbers. *Medicine & Science in Sports & Exercise, 33,* S72.

Ziegler, P. J., Kannan, S., Jonnalagadda, S. S., Krishnakumar, A., Taksali, S. E., & Nelson, J. A. (2005). Dietary intake, body image perceptions, and weight concerns of female US international synchronized skating teams. *International Journal of Sport Nutrition and Exercise Metabolism, 15,* 550–566.

Ziegler, P., Hensley, S., Roepke, J. B., Whitaker, S. H., Craig, B. W., & Drewnowski, A. (1998). Eating attitudes and energy intakes of female skaters. *Medicine & Science in Sports & Exercise, 30,* 583–586.

Zimmerman, T. S. (1999). Using family systems theory to counsel the injured athlete. In R. Ray & D. M. Wiese-Bjornstal (Eds.), *Counseling in sports medicine* (pp. 111–126). Champaign, IL: Human Kinetics.

Zucker, N. L., Womble, L. G., Williamson, D. A., & Perrin, L. A. (1999). Protective factors for eating disorders in female college athletes. *Eating Disorders: The Journal of Treatment and Prevention, 7,* 207–218.

INDEX

for promoting weight gain, 137
sedation as side effect. *See*
    Lamotrigine (Lamictal)
weight effects, 177, 178
Anxiety disorders
    in anorexia nervosa, 12
    and anorexia nervosa, 175
    definition, 215
Aortic coarctation, 162
Apgar score
    definition, 216
    of newborns of those with eating
        disorders, 170
Appearance sports, 46, 135. *See also*
    Aesthetic sports; Revealing
    sport attire
Appetite suppression by smoking, 99
Approaching the sport participant,
    114ff
Aripiprazole (Abilify), 178
    effect on weight, 177
Arrhythmias
    anorexia nervosa symptom, 10
    as cardiac complication, 165
    definition, 216–217
    and esophageal acid reflux, 174
    in family history, 162
    in personal history, 163
    and QT interval, 166
Asceticism *vs.* mental toughness, 66
Assertiveness, 186
Assessment measures, 102ff
    for sport environment, 104
Asthma, 163; *see also* Exercise-induced
    asthma
    handled by medical professionals,
        155–156
    treatment, 176
        therapeutic use exemptions for,
            180
ATHENA, 186
Athletes@Risk, 184ff

Athletes Targeting Healthy Exercise
    and Nutrition Alternatives
    (ATHENA), 186
Athlete term use varies by country, 3
Athletic attributes *vs.* anorexic
    behaviors, 66
Athletic trainers
    approaching the at-risk participant,
        115
    certified, 112–113
    involvement in treatment, 136–137
    sport management team member,
        112–113
    statement on disordered eating, 157
Atrial fibrillation
    definition, 216
    and esophageal acid reflux, 174
At-risk populations, 184
Attention deficit/hyperactivity
    disorder medications
    as body-shaping drugs, 98
    weight effects, 178
Attention-getting mechanisms, 129
Attitude toward problem and
    treatment, 208
Atypical disorders, 175

B

Ballet dancers, 47
    competition level and eating
        disorders, 51
    eating disorders in participants, 50
Ball game sports, 49
    definition, 4
Basketball
    body image in, 48
    body type stereotype, 81–82
BC, *see* Body comparisons (BC)
Beach volleyball, 73
    revealing attire in, 72
BED, *see* Binge eating disorder (BED)
Behavioral presentation
    anorexia nervosa, 11–12